ANGLICAN WORSHIP TODAY

ANGLICAN WORSHIP TODAY

Collins Illustrated Guide to the
Alternative Service Book 1980

**Edited by Colin Buchanan, Trevor Lloyd
and Harold Miller**

Foreword by the Archbishop of Canterbury

COLLINS

Collins Liturgical Publications
187 Piccadilly, London W1V 9DA

© 1980 Grove Books, Bramcote, Notts
First published 1980

ISBN 0 00 5996661 9

Design by Colin Reed
Diagrams by Nuprint, Harpenden
Typeset by Morton Word Processing Ltd, Scarborough
Printed by Wm Collins Sons & Co Ltd, Glasgow

Contents

Foreword

When seeking lively and informed contemporary
reflection on matters liturgical, I, like many others,
have developed a habit of reaching for a Grove booklet.

Now from the same stable we have a comprehensive
family resource book, intended as a companion to the
new Church of England Alternative Service Book. I can
commend it unreservedly, particularly coming as it
does with the authority and from the hand of a team
which has played such a creative role in the recent
movement for liturgical renewal.

Robert Cantuar:

Introduction

The *Alternative Service Book 1980*, billed as the greatest publishing event in the Church of England for 300 years, marked a turning point in the Church's worship. Before 1980 the services, all in booklets, seemed always to be changing. From 1980, the services are fixed in a book which will shape Anglican worship for ten years or more. Now is the time for learning about the *ASB 1980* services, and learning to use them better.

Very many people are now involved in taking decisions about worship, and helping to lead it. The local church council, individuals leading intercessions or reading the scriptures, bride and groom preparing prayers for their wedding, and many more, have a responsible part to play in determining the direction our worship takes. This book is an aid not only to them, but to every ordinary worshipper. The information given here should be of value in every home in which worshipping Anglicans live.

It is produced through the planning of a group of youngish authors called the 'Group for the Renewal of Worship' (GROW). During the 1970s the Group was busy writing and commissioning Grove Booklets on Ministry and Worship, trying to give the right information and stimulus to the Church of England for its worship to be truly contemporary whilst true to New Testament principles.

The great bulk of contributors to these pages are members of that Group. However, they owe a special debt of thanks to others who have contributed, to Su Box who did the picture research, to Taffy Davies who drew the cartoons, and to members of the Liturgical Commission who gave advice when asked. In the last stages a debt of thanks is due also to Sue and Geoffrey Chapman who, on behalf of Collins Liturgical Publications, have provided invaluable resources, encouragement and expertise.

For ourselves, we greatly enjoy working together, and have gained greatly from the stimulus each is to the other. We offer this book in the hope that some of the joy and stimulus it has been to us will be passed on to others, and in the prayer that the worship of the Church of England in the 1980s will bring glory to God and blessing to his people.

Colin Buchanan
Trevor Lloyd
Harold Miller

30 May 1980

Contributors

Simon Barrington-Ward, General Secretary, Church Missionary Society. Honorary Canon of Derby.

Derek Billings, Rector of Houghton-with-Wyton, near Huntingdon: *Alternative Eucharistic Prayers*, Grove Booklet on Ministry and Worship 16 (1973).

Colin Buchanan, Principal, St John's College, Nottingham: editor *Modern Anglican Liturgies 1958-1968* (Oxford, 1968), and *Further Anglican Liturgies 1968-1975* (Grove Books, 1975). Contributor to J.G. Davies (ed.) *A Dictionary of Liturgy and Worship* (SCM, 1972); J.C. King (ed.) *Evangelicals Today* (Lutterworth, 1973); R.C.D. Jasper (ed.) *The Eucharist Today: Studies on Series 3* (SPCK, 1974). Editor of Grove Booklets on Ministry and Worship; of Grove Liturgical Studies; and of *News of Liturgy* (monthly). Member of the Church of England Liturgical Commission.

Ian D. Bunting, Rural Dean and Rector of Chester le Street: *Preaching at Funerals*, Grove Booklet on Ministry and Worship 62 (1978); *Preaching at Weddings*, Grove Booklet on Ministry and Worship 74 (1980).

David Frost, Professor of English at University of Newcastle, New South Wales. Member of the Church of England Liturgical Commission and of the Church of England in Australia Liturgical Commission. Contributor to R.C.D. Jasper (ed.) *The Eucharist Today: Studies on Series 3* (SPCK, 1974); joint translator of *The Psalms: A New Translation for Worship* (the liturgical psalter) (Collins, 1977); *The Language of Series 3*, Grove Booklet on Ministry and Worship 12 (1973). Writes on the drama of Shakespeare and his time.

Michael Harper, Chairman, Soma Trust; former director of the Fountain Trust: *Power for the Body of Christ* (1964); *As in the Beginning* (Hodder, 1965); *Walk in the Spirit* (1968); *Spiritual Warfare* (Hodder, 1970); *None Can Guess, Glory in the Church, A New Way of Living; Let My People Grow* (Hodder, 1977); *You Are My Sons* (1979); *This Is The Day* (1979).

Michael Hodge, Vicar of Cobham, Kent. Member of the General Synod of the Church of England and of its Legislative and Standing Order Committees and formerly on the panel of Chairmen of the General Synod.

Charles H. Hutchins, Principal of Wilson Carlile (Church Army) Training College, Blackheath, London: *Teaching in the Context of Worship*, Grove Booklet on Ministry and Worship 11 (1973); *Christian Education on Sunday Mornings*, Grove Booklet on Ministry and Worship 31 (1974); *Liturgy for Marriage*, Grove Booklet on Ministry and Worship 47 (1976).

Robin A. Leaver, Associate Librarian, Latimer House, Oxford, and priest-in-charge, St Mary's, Cogges, Oxon: *The Liturgy and Music*, Grove Liturgical Studies 6 (1975); *The Work of John Marbeck* (Sutton Courtenay Press, 1978); *Catherine Winkworth: The Influence of her Translations on English Hymnody* (Concordia Publishing House, St Louis, 1978); *A Hymn Book Survey 1962-1980*, Grove Booklet on Ministry and Worship 71 (1980).

Trevor Lloyd, Vicar of Holy Trinity, Wealdstone and Dean of Harrow: *Informal Liturgy*, Grove Booklet on Ministry and Worship (1972); *Institutions and Inductions*, Grove Booklet on Ministry and Worship 15 (1973); *Ministry and Death*, Grove Booklet on Ministry and Worship 27 (1974); *Liturgy and Death*, Grove Booklet on Ministry and Worship 28 (1974); *Evangelicals, Obedience and Change*, Grove Booklet on Ministry and Worship 50 (1977); contributor to *Obeying Christ in a Changing World 2, The People of God* (Collins, 1977).

Harold Miller, Chaplain and Director of Extension Studies, St John's College, Nottingham.

Nicholas Sagovsky, research student at St Edmund's House, Cambridge, currently working on Roman Catholic Modernism (George Tyrrell) and 19th century liberalism (Matthew Arnold): *Modern Roman Catholic Worship: The Mass*, Grove Booklet on Ministry and Worship 34 (1975); *Modern Roman Catholic Worship: Baptism and Penance*, Grove Booklet on Ministry and Worship 43 (1976); *Liturgy and Symbolism*, Grove Liturgical Studies 16 (1978).

Michael Sansom, Vice-Principal, Ridley Hall, Cambridge: *Liturgy for Ordination: The Series 3 Services*, Grove Booklet on Ministry and Worship 60 (1978); reviser of D.E.W. Harrison, *Common Prayer in the Church of England*.

John Tiller, Chief Secretary, Advisory Council for the Church's Ministry; Honorary Canon of St Albans: joint author *The Service of Holy Communion and its Revision* (Marcham Manor Press, 1972); *Justification by Faith and the Sacraments: the Great Acquittal* (Collins, 1980).

Michael R. Vasey, Tutor, St John's College, Durham: *Family Festivals*, Grove Booklet on Ministry and Worship 73 (1980).

Worship is . . .

HEAVENSGATE

Everyone suddenly burst out singing
And I was filled with such delight
As prisoned birds must find in freedom
Winging wildly across the white
Orchard and dark green fields; on; on; and out of
    sight.
Everyone's voice was suddenly lifted
And beauty came like the setting sun.
My heart was shaken with tears, and horror
Drifted away . . . O but everyone
Was a bird and the song was wordless
The singing will never be done.

Siegfried Sassoon's famous poem for Armistice Day 1918 celebrated the end of four years of war. He had described terrible glimpses of the nightmare of mind and wreckage and pointless pain in the trenches. Now, in one moment, the cloud parted. A long-dreamt-of breakthrough had come.

Can't you imagine the scene? The voices rising, blending, the overwhelming music surging up and singing its way through the singers.

In a less dramatic way, most of us have known moments like that: a sudden unexpected climax; a reunion of friends or a final gathering. The faces of some whom perhaps you love surround you in the crowd. A song begins. It is taken up. People begin to sway to the music. They put their arms round each other's shoulders perhaps. Then it happens. Your inner feeling and the world round you and the people with you all flow together into some greater unity. You are caught up into some kind of movement, some tide of the Spirit carrying you upward, forward, out of yourself into the possibility of some new world.

A moment like that seems to be a kind of harvest festival. We suddenly feel ready to put all we have got into it. We offer ourselves. The past is gathered in with the present. All that we have, all that we are, is taken up and laid open, ready to be changed, ready to be poured out: expended; wholly given. Our only thought is an inexpressible thankfulness and gladness.

Then was our mouth filled with laughter,
And our tongue with singing . . .

DOOR INTO HEAVEN

At such times a door seems to open in the surface of life and lead us deeper in; into the real heart of the world, into that greater wholeness which lies hidden beyond our so-called 'everyday' life. All of us sometimes have hints, little flashes of this underlying unity. All too often we dismiss it.

I often think we saw it more clearly when we were children. Perhaps it was clearest of all when we were on our mother's knee, before we could distinguish between her and everything else. She was our whole world, the source of good, and through her we knew something of that ultimate oneness. As we grew a little older we were still open to that feeling. Everything familiar round us still seemed to speak of it. The armchair, the pram, the shopping bag, were alive with this belonging. Children celebrate it in songs and dances and play. They can abandon themselves to it bodily.

They have an instinct too for the special rhythms and phases of this deeper reality. They like special occasions, special times, special actions, and words repeated in the right order. In other words they understand what we call 'symbols' and 'rituals': 'symbol' meaning a special object which gathers into one a whole range of linked feelings or thoughts, like a birthday cake or a Christmas tree, or you may have your own private ones; 'ritual' being a special action which helps to restore unity to life or to overcome separation.

I remember when a child's father was away at the time of her birthday and she was missing him. Some slides were shown at her party and a picture of her father came on to the screen. She walked up and kissed it solemnly and the other children spontaneously lined up behind her and unselfconsciously, one after the other, made as if to shake hands with the figure in the picture. So the absence was healed by a little ritual.

Children are ready to break through to this greater wholeness if they are given an opportunity. So in *The Trapp Family Singers* (the book of the 'Sound of Music' and an infinitely better story than the film version) Maria, the governess, brings life and love to the motherless children, and colour and warmth into their stiff military household, with an Advent Wreath, lighting a candle for each Sunday, and an Easter egg hunt, and numberless other little ceremonies which serve to enrich and unify their life.

The Brangwen family in D.H. Lawrence's *The Rainbow* find that the seasons and festivals of the village church, 'the epic of the Christian year' with its constantly spiralling cycle of birth, death and resurrection – even the mystery and radiance of Sunday as a special day – give the children

at least some rhythm of eternity
in a rugged inconsequential life.

As the poet Yeats puts it:

How but in custom and in ceremony
Are innocence and beauty born?

So in all societies, people grow up learning to discern the presence of these hidden doors.

When I was quite small I can remember going out from London to bluebell woods, somewhere in Kent. I had never seen anything like it before. As I lay down on the slopes, suddenly I felt as if I were melting into everything I was seeing; the dark trunks of the trees, the moist translucent leaves, the shafts of light, the receding waves of flowers. It was such a sharply poignant, overwhelmingly moving, feeling of oneness. I was shy of telling anyone. Years later, a great old man told me how as a child he put his hand on a warm

garden wall, casually, and, as he gazed around and listened to the birds singing, suddenly he had an instantaneous shock of sharing through that stone in some kind of a greater whole. Since then I have read of so many people, not only poets and artists, who have had similar experiences. They describe a sensation as definite and complete as stepping through a wardrobe into Narnia.

WHO CAN ENTER?

When such a disclosure comes, we want to respond to it with our whole being. This is the source – we recognise it – of all good. We have an urge to yield ourselves up to it. To this we must give supreme value, supreme *worth*-ship or, as we have come to call our self-offering, 'worship'. This is our immediate response. I never thought back to that bluebell woods experience without wanting to find something somewhere which had touched me at that moment, and to which I somehow wanted to give my life in return.

I believe everyone everywhere has, deep down within them, something of this sense. E.M. Forster, the agnostic humanist, expressed it when he said he often wanted to thank someone or something. All men in their different cultures or societies have some variant of this 'sense of worship' as you could call it. They have found their own very different ways of breaking through to this underlying reality, and their own infinitely varied forms of response; their differing symbols and rituals. Out of this recognition have flowed not only ways of trying to understand the world, to order it and cope with it, but also ways of celebrating its hidden unity in festivals which give scope for fantasy, humour, entertainment and sheer delight.

In this way everything that is distinctively human could be said to have its roots in worship: this deepest and fullest response to life as a whole, and to its hidden source. Here the arts, the sciences and philosophy have their origin. Like the priest and the oracle-man, so the singers and the dancers, the poets and painters, makers

and performers, have always sought to serve and celebrate this whole in the form in which they perceived it.

Still to this day the great discoverers of natural science and the arts often have a response akin to worship when they stumble on some great new intuitive vision. Kellin, the biochemist, once remarked to a friend, 'we scientists are all mystics at heart'. Michael Polanyi describes the great scientific explorers of the universe from Kepler to Einstein as people grasped by an overwhelming faith and wonder, even awe, and a longing to give their lives to what they have found awaiting them. I think of Boole, the admittedly eccentric founder of Boolian algebra who, after hitting on his key discovery, later heard voices in his head singing 'Thy word, O Lord, endures for ever in heaven'. It is no surprise that the really great artists and scientists (as contrasted with the merely clever) have about them, in their genuinely worshipful attitude, a kind of innocent wonder, a simplicity and directness not unlike that of a child.

And this itself is a kind of parable. For it seems that without this strange blend of humility and innocence,

though we may glimpse the door into the real secret of the whole universe, we cannot enter. We long to offer our whole life, but this seems to be a hard entry to make; too hard for you and me.

> Who shall ascend into the hill of the Lord,
> or who shall rise up in his holy place?
> Even he that has clean hands and a pure heart
> and that has not lifted up his mind to vanity
> nor sworn to deceive his neighbour.

Even if we come to the point where we want to worship, it seems it is not something that is easy for us to do.

MISTAKING THE DOOR

Alas, we have lost that true simplicity and become trapped in the complex net of man's age-long adolescence. We have lost sight of that greater unity in which we should have our part. We even lose touch with it altogether. We struggle with the fragments of a broken jigsaw of a world. We find ourselves caught in a tangle of faulty relationships; at odds with ourselves, with each other, with life, and stabbed through with yearnings and fears.

As Julian of Norwich put it 'for failing of love therefore is all our travail'. We just cannot find our way through. The door eludes us. And in its place we set some door or other of our own making, which never opens into that remembered place which is, all the

time, our true home. No wonder so many folk stories in the world's cultures and religions reflect some sense of lost innocence, of lost wholeness, and describe the way in which some original state of happiness was lost.

So we put our energies at the disposal of a mistaken door, a false object of worship, such as wealth or power or the state. We mistake the creation for the creator. We may even project all our longing for wholeness on to some wretched fellow being who can't really carry the weight of it. This tendency can take the form of the idealising of a friend, a teacher, a guru, a political leader, a hero, a pop star. At the height of the Beatles' fame, someone thrust a sick child at them, hoping some of their magic aura might brush off and bring healing. Raving fans yield themselves to the worship of some lonely singer who is forced to become the bearer of all their hopes.

Even genuine doors can be distorted by our self-seeking. Falling in love, which can be a means to a fuller grasp on the beauty and mystery of life, easily becomes an object of worship in itself. The physical side of sexual love detached from its other aspects has been made into a kind of cure for all ills. A romantic cult of feeling and emotion breeds many cruel illusions.

All over the world we see political rituals, great demonstrations, with chanted liturgies, and sacred pictures of political leaders paraded like images through the streets. Even football matches can take on something of the same atmosphere. The urge to worship abhors a vacuum. It must go somewhere. As Luther put it, 'man always has God or idols' (cf Romans 1).

FORCING AN ENTRY

Just as we deceive ourselves with false doors, so we attempt false means of passing through and securing our lost unity; that is false worship. The three most commonly found forms of these efforts to achieve our own fulfilment seek to evade the demands of a real offering up of our whole life and relationships. They are each of them mistaken ways of arriving at union with the source of unity and wholeness. You could call them false mysticism, manipulation and false moralism.

We know so many people in our own society in recent years who have followed a mystical byway. This can easily become a way of escape from one's self and from the rest of the world. Those who wander into this byway concentrate on an effort to detach themselves from everything and everyone else, looking at the rest of the world down the wrong end of a telescope. They may make use of techniques of breathing and posture, or of drugs. Essentially they are striving to attain union

with the One, to secure serenity for themselves at the cost very often of leaving out everyone and everything else. Again the subtle distortion at work here is the result of our innate tendency to self-seeking.

Manipulation is a form of symbolic or ritual action in which the would-be worshippers turn their self-offering into a kind of technique for securing their own satisfaction. Worship becomes separated from right relationships and a genuine effort at a different way of life, and ends up as a means of securing success or respectability for oneself. This is the kind of worship which the prophets of the Old Testament and Jesus in the Gospels denounce. Worship here has become a mode of self-enhancement, detached from right action, or the genuine offering up of our whole life. We in the affluent west have to look at our own way of worship critically from this point of view. How far is our worship still a true offering up of our whole shared life to God? This kind of worship can so easily become a means of trying to control reality rather than offering ourselves without reservation to the infinite source of all reality.

But the noblest self-deceit is a fervent moralism, a determination to make ourselves worthy of being offered up by conforming to some impossible, persecuting ideal. Some people who follow this approach are the most out-and-out traditionalists, sticking to every detail of the way things have always been done, finding their security in a comforting system. Others are extreme Utopian revolutionaries, unconsciously judging themselves, and most others too, very harshly for not having turned into perfect models of some newly perfected blueprint for humanity.

The coming of modern science and industrial and city life has brought with them secularism, the stripping away of all spirituality from our public world, which becomes grey and neutral so that religion and attempts at worship become the private hobby of those 'who like that kind of thing'.

This process only serves to bring home to people a stronger feeling of emptiness, a more frenzied quest for substitute doors or false methods of attaining wholeness. Their yearnings come out in the form of protest movements, violence and extremism, or some kind of Walter Mitty-like secret life.

Dennis Potter in plays like his skilful *Pennies from Heaven* has shown how spiritual longings pervade suburbs and housing estates through popular songs and news stories. Peter Berger points out that, for ordinary 'secular' people, life is still full of potential points of entry into the forgotten unity. He calls them 'signals of transcendence'. The climaxes of life, such as the birth of a baby, love and marriage, death and dying, and all the heights and depths of our human experience, keep pointing us to the 'beyond in the midst'.

JESUS THE DOOR

But all over the world today, whether in my own suburban street in London, in an Islamic state, in a train in India, among students in Japan, I keep meeting people who can no longer live in the broken religious frameworks of the past. They point out to me that even those who become caught in the so-called Islamic revival, or in the crowd surrounding some newly emerging popular Hindu guru or Buddhist monk, are essentially adrift in a way different from the past. There is no way back to the old conventional unities. Secularism has made clear the divide, the great gulf between earth and heaven. And growing numbers of sensitive people who realise this have found a new focus in One who seems to walk alongside them in this confusion. He bears the pain of our separation with us. He meets us as One who has himself come into our divided life and heart to bring us forgiveness and healing from within.

Jesus is releasing among his fellow beings today as much as ever a new love and an at-one-ment which reintegrates our broken worlds, and gathers all things into one. He opens up in the midst of our would-be humanised earth a 'new and living way' into a heaven where the truly human is shown to be at the heart of all – 'A Lamb slain . . .' He discloses in the midst of our world the possibility of true worship in union with him. Many are newly recognising the power of his claim 'I am the Way. I am the Door'.

THE SPIRIT AS THE MEANS OF ENTRY

In this new worship, people find themselves drawn into a new reconciliation with themselves and with each other. The love of a living and loving God is released in their hearts through the Spirit who flows from Jesus, as an energy from beyond themselves. They begin to be enabled to reach a genuine repentance, a true offering up of themselves, and of their first stumbling attempts to make amends to all whom they have wronged, to bring into being renewed friendships, renewed families, a renewed society.

So there arises in the midst of our times and history a great hymn of the universe, a new song among a renewed people. In David Fanshawe's amazing recording 'African Sanctus' you can hear a *kyrie*, the prayer 'Lord have mercy', soaring up behind and through and over the piercing cry of a mullah in the tower of a mosque, calling men to prayer. That 'Jesus have mercy' overarches all other attempts at worship. It brings us to that cross which grapples with the whole of our tragic separation and reunites us with heaven. It brings us to the one central eternal living symbol and rite, Jesus and his self-offering for us. It brings us in the Spirit, through Jesus the door, to the Father. And so we arrive already by faith at that final worship of the whole transformed creation, that final armistice and harvest festival where 'the song is wordless and the singing will never be done'.

If someone asks 'What is worship?' I hope those who use this book will be able to say 'Come with us and we will show you'.

Worship and the bible

Worship is a reflex action. It is not prompted by a vacuum, but is a response to a whole series of stimuli. Sometimes that response is carefully thought out, sometimes automatic, subconscious, unpremeditated. People do not just worship. They worship someone or something; they worship because of someone or something. With Christian worship, once we begin to take this response mechanism apart and examine it, we find something of the part played by the bible in our worship. It is not just a beautiful ceremonial volume carried in on a velvet cushion, but the vehicle which prompts and assists our response to God himself in Christian worship. Consider four areas of stimulation to worship: response to revelation, response to life, response to example, and response to precept.

RESPONSE TO REVELATION

When you worship a car, the degree of your response, or the 'worth' you give to the car, is determined by your appreciation of it. If you know it well and are familiar with what it is capable of, then the 'worth' you give it will be different from that of someone who is ignorant about cars in general and this one in particular. Christian worship is determined by the worshipper's appreciation of the worth of God. How does the Christian know how much God is worth? Simply because God has revealed himself – in nature, in history, in our experience, in his word. And important and essential as those other areas of revelation are, it is God's word which actually gives articulate meaning and context to them. So we can echo the words of Psalmist when he says, 'How clearly the sky reveals God's glory' (Psalm 19.1) only because God has spoken in his word to give some content to the concepts of God and of creation in our minds. So we find God acting in history, and also explaining in words to his people what he is doing. He acts to bring his people out of Egypt, gives them a set of actions in the passover, together with words to say which ensure that he is put at the centre of the action: 'When your children ask you, "What does this ritual mean?" you will reply, "It is the sacrifice of the passover to honour the Lord because he passed over the houses of the Israelites in Egypt" ' (Exodus 12.26, 27). Without words, both the historical act of God and the ritual remembrance of it would not have revealed the nature of God which prompts the worship of his people.

We find, then, in the Old Testament, that one strand of worship is a response to the saving action of God in history, a response in words and action which he provides. The keeping of the sabbath itself was a response to God's action. Keeping the passover took the worshippers vividly back into the situation of God's deliverance of his people from the land of Egypt in such a way as to bring into the present the benefits of remembering the power, love and faithfulness of the Lord. Similarly the Feast of Purim (Esther 9.20-22) was a response to the miraculous deliverance of the Jews in Persia during the reign of King Ahasuerus.

Again in the New Testament we find the revelation of God's saving action securely rooted in history, in the birth, death and resurrection of Jesus and in the birth of the Church. The Church identifies Jesus with the passover lamb, and ties its response in worship to the historic action of God – in the words from Revelation 5 which appear as the Friday evening canticle in Morning and Evening Prayer in *ASB 1980*:

'Glory and honour and power: are yours by right O Lamb who was slain:
for by your blood you ransomed men for God . . .'

And so a historical rhythm is established in the Church's worshipping year as we move from Christmas, through the events of Lent and Holy Week, to Good Friday and Easter Day, followed by the Church's birthday at Pentecost.

But this rhythmic response, worked out in the readings in the Lectionary and in special services, is only a partial response to the revelation of God. For he reveals himself in other ways than in history. In Old Testament times, the Feasts of Pentecost and of Tabernacles, and the Day of Atonement witnessed to aspects of God's character as creator, law-giver, and provider of the means of forgiveness. The worship of his people was a response, not to specific historical action, but to God's *theological* revelation of himself. So today you can see what people believe about God, and think of him, by their worship. From the response you can gauge the cause of the response. Our theology, our working out of the word of God, determines to a large extent what our worship is like.

So we have a second rhythm going through our worship. Sometimes it coincides with the first, annual, rhythm, as when we meditate on the theological themes of redemption and forgiveness on Good Friday, or the mystery of the Godhead on Trinity Sunday. But very often these major themes will tumble over one another Sunday by Sunday and day by day, as we move from the contemplation of the glory of God into the confession of sin and the assurance of forgiveness. It might be a good exercise to make a list of what we believe about God and then ask where and when we respond in our worship to those aspects of God's character. Our worship should be a total response – with all we have – to the totality of the revelation God has chosen to give to us. That way, we can be sure it will be God-centred and not man-centred.

RESPONSE TO LIFE

But there is a third rhythm running through our worship, in addition to the annual historic rhythm and the daily-hourly character or theological rhythm. This is the rhythm of ordinary life. We see God taking ordinary things and consecrating them, taking them over, investing them with a real meaning beyond what is obviously apparent. He does this with the human moments of birth, marriage and death. He does it with the wood of the cross and the bread of the eucharist. It is the principle of the incarnation, of God penetrating our ordinary life in order to open the gates of heaven to us. We see it in the Old Testament in all the varied materials, with their meanings, for the passover, in the first fruits of the harvest, in the three thousand lambs, bulls and rams sacrificed after David's words in 1 Chronicles 29.14:

'for everything in heaven and on earth is yours. All things come from you
and of your own do we give you.'

We can use these words in Rite A to express our giving of money to God. But the principle, that all life is his and that he gives to his created order and our actions those meanings which please him, runs much wider than our gifts of money. For example, the breaking of bread has God's given meaning:

> 'We break this bread
>   to share in the body of Christ.
> Though we are many, we are one body,
>   because we all share in one bread.'

And, just as the parables of Jesus operate by reminding us of his teaching when we see or use the ordinary things he speaks about, so God's taking over the ordinary things for worship reminds us to worship him. When we see a sheep, we praise God for the lamb of God; when we break a piece of bread at teatime, we might praise him for our fellow-Christians. So our Christian worship contributes to the sanctification of the whole of life.

RESPONSE TO EXAMPLE

Because of the way in which God uses his revelation of himself in words and actions, and his invasion of the whole of ordinary life, to stimulate us to worship him, it is ridiculous to expect him to give us a detailed set of instructions about how to do it. That would suggest that the worship of God is something which could be manipulated, a set of things and words which, if done, would ensure that worship had taken place. But worship is not a performance which guarantees access to God. It is more like an existential encounter with the transcendent, unapproachably holy God, on his own terms, the terms of his revelation of himself and his demands rather than the terms of a particular form of words to use in order to get to him. The Old Testament prophets denounce the idea that if you use the right words and actions, you get through to God: 'With what shall I come before the Lord ...? Will the Lord be pleased with thousands of rams ...? what does the Lord require, but to do justly ...?' (Micah 6.6). And in the New Testament the writer to the Hebrews tells us what

we do need to come before the Lord with: 'Let us come near to God with a sincere heart and a sure faith, with hearts sprinkled clean from a guilty conscience' (10.22).

And it is examples of this sort of encounter in the lives of the worshippers that we find in the bible, given to stimulate our own response to God rather than to be slavishly re-enacted as a process to ensure contact between us and God.

So in the Old Testament we find some examples of individual worship and prayer, like those of Nehemiah (1.5f: 'Lord God of heaven, great and terrible God ...'), Daniel (9.4f: 'Lord, great and dreadful God ...') or Abraham's servant (Genesis 24.26f: 'then the man knelt down and worshipped God ...'). But mostly the examples are of the worship of the people of God. Even when Isaiah has his vision calling him to be a prophet (Isaiah 6) it happens in the temple, and therefore presumably Isaiah is not separated from everyone else physically, even though God speaks directly to him alone. And it is the fullness of the revelation of God which overwhelms him – 'his train filled the temple'. To this his ultimate response is a total offering of himself (and not of some other object v.8). But this response is only possible after the earlier response of confession ('woe is me') of his own and society's sin, and the personal application of God's cleansing and forgiveness to him. Here we see man's response to God's revelation followed by further action by God, and further response from man, in a way that is echoed in

our present services of Morning and Evening Prayer, and in the Holy Communion.

The song Isaiah hears the winged creatures around God's throne singing is taken up again in a New Testament example of worship, in Revelation 4, and repeated in *ASB 1980* Communion Rite A:

'Holy, holy, holy Lord,
God of power and might,
heaven and earth are full of your glory.'

The Revelation picture is of worship in heaven, but the poetic bits are likely to reflect the things being sung in the worship of the Church. In Revelation 4 the seating/ standing arrangements for worship seem to be a circle, or a series of concentric circles, all centred on God and the Lamb. Such seating arrangements in churches today are often said to emphasise the horizontal in worship at the expense of the vertical, the relationship between Christians at the expense of the relationship to God. But the scriptural pattern here is to use the visual 'feel' to emphasise the absolute centrality of God as the focal point of our worship. This we acknowledge Sunday by Sunday when we are carried, like Isaiah and St John, to join in that heavenly chorus, 'with angels and archangels, and with all the company of heaven'.

So one set of bible examples places us with individuals who are sure of God's character and promises, asking him for specific things, thanking him for being the sort of God he is. Another set of bible examples places us in heaven, with a variety of new songs (e.g.

Revelation 5, and 7.10-12), actions and a question-and-answer liturgy. And yet another set of bible examples places us with crowds of worshippers here on earth, in the psalms for instance:

'These things I remember . . .
when I went with the crowds to the house of God,
leading them in singing and shouting praise to God
. . .' (Psalm 42.4).

1 Chronicles 29 is another of these examples, where we see one person, David, leading and giving expression to the people's worship, praising God because people had so willingly given gifts for the building of the temple. Like most of these examples it is centred on the character of God: 'great, powerful, glorious, . . . ruler of all . . . king . . . owner of all riches', etc. And David gives them instructions: 'Praise the Lord your God!' – and they do so. The same pattern of expectant corporate prayer can be seen in the New Testament in Acts 4.23-30, where the believers all join together in prayer to God as Lord and creator and speak of his actions in scripture and in recent history as a reason why he should answer prayer now.

The most obvious example of the way in which this biblical pattern of dwelling on God's character and actions ruled the worship of the early Church (and so ours today) is in the description we have in 1 Corinthians 11 of the communion. Here we have by implication a rare bit of description of how the early Church worshipped, remembering the death of Jesus during a 'bring your own grub' sort of love-feast, which in Corinth at least was getting out of hand. The words Paul uses to recall the Church to the actions of Jesus in the last supper are the basis of that narrative, now standardised in each of the eucharistic prayers in Rite A in *ASB 1980*:

'Who in the same night that he was betrayed,
took bread and gave you thanks . . .'

The Church today follows these biblical patterns and examples. More than that, it lifts whole chunks of them to use in its worship. Thus, the hymnbook of temple and synagogue is the hymnbook of the Church. The history of God's dealings with his people, his character, holiness, power, love, the experience of believers down the centuries, are brought home to us in the regular reading of the bible in worship. We sing and say other chunks of scripture in the Lord's Prayer, the sentences which start most of the *ASB 1980* services, and the canticles in all their new and rich variety. The way in which we do it in our worship acts as a sort of kaleidoscope in which new light is thrown on readings, psalms and canticles by their conjunction.

RESPONSE TO PRECEPT

The Church today does not only follow biblical examples and fill its worship with bible quotations. It also obeys some of the precepts, rules, commands, suggestions laid down in the bible. Sometimes we might think, 'How good it would be to have a clear example of exactly what the Church's worship was like in the Acts of the Apostles, or a set of clear instructions so that we knew exactly what we should be doing in worship.' God has not done this for us, because he wants us to concentrate our attention on him, and to work out our response to him, rather than following a set of instructions. Nevertheless, we do have some straight teaching about worship, scattered through the bible. So in the Old Testament we have virtually the whole book of Leviticus, and parts of Exodus and Deuteronomy, teaching about how to approach a holy God through sacrifice – sacrifices largely summed up in the death of Christ. The eighth century prophets attack the unthinking nature of Israel's worship in their day and stress the moral requirements of worship: 'I hate, I despise your feasts, and I will take no delight in your solemn assemblies . . . I will not accept your burnt offerings . . . Did you bring me sacrifices in the wilderness for forty years?' (Amos 5.21-25).

When we come to the New Testament we face some straight instructions which can give us principles for our worship. The God-centredness of our worship is underlined for example in 1 Peter 4.11: 'Whoever speaks, as one who utters the oracles of God . . . in order that in everything God may be glorified through Jesus Christ.' Ephesians 5.18-20 says this as well: 'always and for everything giving thanks in the name of our Lord Jesus Christ to God the Father' but precedes this with both an agenda ('addressing one another in psalms and hymns and spiritual songs, singing and making melody

to the Lord with all your heart') and a command: 'Be filled with the Spirit.' Obedience to the command seems a necessary prerequisite to the worship of a God of whom Jesus says, 'God is spirit, and those who worship him must worship in spirit and in truth' (John 4.24). But there are two other things there in Ephesians. Worship is not the same old thing again and again, but a rich variety of different ingredients; and these ingredients come not from one person 'up front', but from the worshippers, 'addressing one another'. Colossians 3.16 brings this out and adds more ingredients: 'Let the word of God dwell richly in you as you teach and warn one another in all wisdom, and as you sing psalms and hymns and spiritual songs with thankfulness in your hearts to God.' Again the centrality of God is there, with the addition of mutual teaching and encouragement as the word of God rules over them in their worship. 1 Corinthians 14.26 gives a further example of the variety: 'When you come together, each of you has a hymn, a lesson, a revelation, a tongue, or an interpretation.' The Church of England has not yet got this far in its implementation of biblical precepts, though there are churches which evidence a Spirit-given freedom in which people can contribute items to the worship. But the Church does, in *ASB 1980*, follow these basic principles of God-centredness, variety and the congregational nature of worship. There is plenty of scope in the new services both for varied contributions and for a large number of different people to contribute to the worship.

The New Testament also gives us instructions about the intercessions (e.g. in 1 Timothy 2.1-3: 'I urge that supplications, prayers, thanksgivings be made for all men, for kings and all who are in high positions . . .') and about the intelligibility of our worship (in the argument of 1 Corinthians 14 about the use of tongues: 'how can anyone . . . say "Amen" to your thanksgiving when he does not know what you are saying?').

Two further principles which affect the whole pattern of the Church's agenda for Sundays are brought out in Acts 2.42, the description of how the infant Church spent its time right after the day of Pentecost: '. . . and they devoted themselves to the teaching of the apostles, the fellowship, the breaking of bread and the prayers.' This four-part view of what happened when the Church came together underlines the need to make time not only for eucharist and praying but for learning (which should be *apostolic* doctrine and, if we follow Colossians 3.16 above, involve some mutual teaching element) and for fellowship. The writer of the letter to the Hebrews (10.24,25) stresses the positive nature of meeting together for fellowship.

THE RESPONSES WORKED OUT DOWN THE YEARS

The history of the Church's worship is the history of the working out of these responses, to revelation, to life, to the example and the precept of scripture. At times the Church has overlaid the principles with other, non-biblical ones, or got into some sort of deadening rut; at other times the Church has gone through times of reformation and renewal, recovering some parts of the biblical pattern again. The rhythms of the year, of life, of thinking about God, became reflected for the Church (as for the Jewish people before it) in lectionaries, psalm-lists, liturgical prayer and congregational responses which gave a familiar 'feel', clear expectations for those attending, and a sense of security in worship. No doubt we can look back today and see that as the Church moved into the dark ages and the middle ages it suffered a slow decline in intelligent participation by the worshippers, until only a clerical 'stage drama' remained, and worshippers became 'those who stand around'. But the principles were clear enough for a real recovery to be sought by the reformers as they reshaped the medieval worship in the sixteenth century.

When Cranmer wrote his English-language Prayer Books in 1549 and 1552 he clearly devoted himself to the ordered round of biblical content, worked out in worship on biblical principles. His books provided the base from which liturgical worship in this country has proceeded in the centuries since. But the value of his books lies not only in their particular wording and form, but in his aspiration for scriptural worship at its best – instructing, building up, sanctifying the people of God. This was the unselfconscious character of New Testament worship, put into consciously ordered form by Cranmer, and retained almost unchanged by the Restoration churchmen of 1662. The changing rhythms of the Church's year, the daily rhythm of prayer in the offices, the rhythm of life worked out in the provisions for birth, marriage and death – none of these may be today exactly as Cranmer gave it to the Church (for then there would be no new Book at all), but all reflect that recovered concern for biblical words and patterns which was his legacy to us.

Anglican worship across the world

Everywhere in the world, at least until the last two decades, where there have been Anglican Christians, there has also been a Prayer Book. And everywhere there has been a Prayer Book it has descended from the two first Church of England Prayer Books, of 1549 and 1552, written largely by Cranmer and imposed on the parishes by Acts of Uniformity. Cranmer's conservative temperament, coupled with his reformed theology, his superb gift of writing liturgical English, and the happy accident of being in power at the right time, all conspired to set his stamp distinctively upon Anglican worship thereafter. The Preface to 1662 Book of Common Prayer, (a Book very largely identical with Cranmer's 1552 Book) gave a first hint that there were Anglicans overseas – probably African slaves and native Red Indians in America!

And so, as colonies and chaplaincies were formed overseas the Prayer Book passed into use everywhere, almost without exception. Even when the Protestant Episcopal Church in the United States of America drew on the 1764 Episcopal Church of Scotland rite for part of the eucharistic prayer, in its 1790 revised Prayer Book, it scarcely disrupted the general principle of using the Church of England's Prayer Book.

In the nineteenth century, the spread of the Prayer Book continued in almost every part of the world. In a few places – as e.g. in the Pacific and Central America – it was American Episcopal missionary enterprise which established new Churches, and in those places the American liturgical tradition was followed. But elsewhere the Church of England's Prayer Book went with Anglican missionaries, translated into some hundreds of vernacular tongues. Often it was the first book after the bible to be so translated, thus acquiring some of the same sense of 'givenness' that the bible itself had.

The first new Prayer Book of the nineteenth century originated much nearer home. When the English and Irish parliaments were fused in 1802 the two established (Anglican) Churches were also fused and became the United Church of England and Ireland. But in 1870 the Church of Ireland was separated and disestablished, and immediately undertook a very cautious revision of the 1662 Book, which was authorised in 1878. However, a more far-reaching series of events was shaking the Prayer Book worship of the Church of England itself. The Oxford Movement, beginning in 1833, led to a 'catholicising' of Anglican worship, bringing into parish use ceremonies and practices which had not been seen for three hundred years in the Church of England. In particular the new thinking looked to the Church of Rome for its liturgical ideas, and many mildly 'catholic' features of Anglican worship – such as the use of candles, wafers, and vestments – date from this period, and were not necessarily impossible to graft onto the texts of 1662. But the new liturgical thinking of the second half of the nineteenth century also created a desire for texts which were catholicised. Usually the heart of such desire was for a 'long canon' – i.e. a eucharistic prayer which went on from the Narrative of Institution with an anamnesis and a prayer of oblation and ended with a doxology (instead of the 'Amen' straight after the narrative, which is what 1662 has). Scotland and America already provided examples of Anglican texts which did something like this. The position of the Lord's Prayer following on from the canon was also important.

Mission church in South West Africa

Archbishops and presiding bishops process to the opening of the 1948 Lambeth conference at Canterbury

Such texts could not easily be authorised in England, where there was not only the apparatus of parliamentary control of worship to be braved, but also a tremendous division of opinion as to the propriety of tampering with the 1662 material. But overseas, where whole provinces of the rapidly growing Anglican Communion might be monochrome anglo-catholic, there was much more scope for such change. Between 1900 and 1950 new, and sometimes exotic, texts for the eucharist appeared in parts of East and Central Africa, in South Africa, in India and Ceylon, in Korea, and elsewhere. Although these did not automatically lead to whole new prayer books (which are lengthy and expensive productions), yet they set in train a liturgical diversity between provinces which made it hard to insist that liturgical uniformity is a hallmark of Anglican Christianity.

1928 AND AFTER

Even so, there were many common features still in Anglican worship. Partly, there were many areas of the world where the 1662 Prayer Book remained the norm until the 1960s. Partly, even where new prayer books came in, they often exhibited much in common with 1662 along with their differences. And so, whether on

pioneering shipboard, or in trading stations built up over the world, or in newly-claimed colonies or in newly-evangelised territories not part of the Empire, the eighteenth and nineteenth centuries give a clear picture of sober Anglican Prayer Book worship flung like a net around the globe, and offered equally to expatriate and native alike – a religious equivalent of the building up of the British Empire itself.

Meanwhile very modest changes were made in Canada (1918) and Ireland (1926) to 1662-type prayer books, the Scottish Episcopal Church incorporated its Scottish Liturgy into its own provincial Prayer Book (1912, revised in 1929), and the American Episcopal Church mildly updated its own book with versions in 1892 and 1928. The Church of England finally went to parliament with a revised book (including the 'long canon' and other mildly 'catholic' features as options) in December 1927 and June 1928 – and was defeated in the Commons on each of these occasions. This meant that for many years thereafter the Church of England was committed rather to seeking changes in the procedural rules for authorising liturgy (so as to bypass parliament) than to seeking to authorise actual new texts.

In 1948 the Lambeth Conference was still able to affirm that a mark of a common understanding of authority in the Anglican Communion was 'our adherence to ... the Book of Common Prayer as the standard of our worship'. But the bishops were also aware of the centrifugal tendencies being shown in many parts, and ten years later the next Lambeth Conference found itself considering ways in which Prayer Book revision could be conducted without complete loss of a common style and culture for worship. By this time the trends of the previous seventy or eighty years were finding clearer expression in new prayer books – such as the South African Book (1954) (itself adopted by the Province of Central Africa soon after), the next Canadian Book (1959), and the Book of the Church of India Pakistan Burma and Ceylon (1960). However, although these all involved some remodelling of the eucharistic rites, they were in virtually all other respects still wholly recognisable as traditional Anglican productions.

Centenary church in Tonga

In the 1960s and 1970s, two underlying principles of all the previous prayer books have been fundamentally challenged. The first principle to come under question was the concept of each Province having a single prayer book in use. Instead there grew up in most Provinces of the Anglican Communion a period of liturgical experimentation, the main feature of which has been the little booklets which could be purchased in quantity quite cheaply and then be discarded in favour of a further round of experimentation only a few years later. The Church of England's own period of experimentation from 1966 to 1980 has been very closely matched by similar periods in other Provinces.

The second principle to be challenged was the style of English language which had sprung from Cranmer and had still been used in all twentieth century liturgical writing in English until the 1960s. But very cautiously, starting with New Zealand and Australia in 1966, Anglicans began in their little booklets to address God as 'you' (and thus to lose the famous 'dost' 'wouldst' and 'wert'). From 1970 onwards there became available texts for the Lord's Prayer, creeds, canticles, and other liturgical materials shared by all Christian churches, produced by an international ecumenical committee and all in this more modern style of address to God. Although the Lord's Prayer has been the scene of some confusion, yet in general these texts have become part of the backbone of the experimental services produced since 1970, and have indeed so matched the desires of worshippers that virtually no 'thou' form texts have been put out for experimental use in the 1970s.

BOOKLETS INTO BOOKS

As the period of experimentation has gone on, it has become clear that in many places it was leading back towards a more solid (though greatly revised) 'Book of Common Prayer'. In country after country the booklets have started to give way to more definitive books.

The first modern English prayer book in the Anglican Communion seems to have come in the diocese of Melanesia (it is now a Province) in 1972 – the first independent set of services the diocese had ever produced. The second was *Liturgy 1975*, a solid (though paper-backed) collection of modern services in the Church of the Province of South Africa. In the United States two semi-definitive collections were produced for the General Conventions of 1970 and 1973, and the use of these books led into the production of a definitive new Book of Common Prayer which was provisionally authorised by the General Convention of 1976, and then became *the* Book of Common Prayer at the General

Convention of 1979. Because it is the one definitive book of the Episcopal Church in USA it contains 'thou' form services alongside the 'you' form ones. In Australia the General Synod of 1977 authorised a collection which was published in 1978 as *An Australian Prayer Book*. This, as its title shows, is more akin to the Church of England's new *Alternative Service Book*, as 1662 remains legal (and, indeed, in some sense normative), and the new book does not in any way supersede it.

The Church of England is next in line, and at the time of writing it is unclear who will come next. In third world countries economics tend to forbid producing more books than the minimum needed, and 1662 does not seem so dated when it is in a vernacular tongue. In Canada and one or two other places revision has been inhibited by the existence of a recent book of an old-fashioned style, making it difficult to produce another whole new book. In Ireland there exists a half-collection called *Revised Services*, and in New Zealand there are distant plans to turn the booklets into a book around 1984.

However, it may be that variations between Anglicans depend less upon which book they use than upon other factors. There are arising great differences in the manner of initiation – so that, for instance, in America and New Zealand young children are communicants long before reaching an age for confirmation. In these

same countries (and in Canada and Hong Kong) women are ordained to the presbyterate, and therefore preside at holy communion. In many places a charismatic renewal has altered the style of celebration, and in many more the gentler influence of the liturgical movement has led to a reordering of furnishings and fabric, a larger employment of lay persons for various liturgical

functions, and a simplification of ceremonial. Yet, when all these points are noted, Anglican worship still has an indefinable common quality throughout the world (with at least a hint of English religious culture thrown in). Many parts of the Anglican Communion consciously look towards England for their texts, and will presumably therefore draw heavily upon *ASB 1980*. And many more unconsciously reveal English ways, even when they are unaware of it.

The Rev Carol Anderson, rector of All Angels Episcopal Church, West Side, New York

Service books in the Church of England – authors and influences

The Alternative Service Book is fresh and new, and relevant to the latter part of the twentieth century. But it is also the product of many hundreds of years. It has not been written from scratch, but contains elements which go right back to the New Testament (and, indeed, even the Old Testament – e.g. the Sanctus, which is based on Isaiah 6). So, you have a book which has taken more than two thousand years to write! Naturally, as a Church of England service book, it draws a good deal from the genius of Archbishop Thomas Cranmer, who was such a powerful influence on the prayer books written at the time of the Reformation; but it also draws from various individuals, groups, denominations and nations down through the centuries. This chapter will guide you through the development of the Alternative Service Book; and it will give you some insights into some of the people who were involved in writing both it, and the 1662 Book of Common Prayer (to which it is an 'alternative'). These are only some of the major 'authors'; there are many, many others.

INFLUENCES ON THE 1662 PRAYER BOOK

The chart alongside shows how various influences came to bear on the prayer books written between 1549 and 1662.

On the next pages you will find portraits of some of the people who were influential in the different groups mentioned. These are *Cranmer*, who almost single-handedly wrote the 1549 and 1552 Books; *Bucer*, who was a reformed critic of the 1549 Prayer Book; *Elizabeth I*, at the beginning of whose reign the 1559 Book was imposed; *Laud*, the founder of 'Laudianism', and *Baxter*, one of the leading Puritans who campaigned for changes in 1662.

The chart below shows how one small piece of the 1662 Litany has within it phrases which come from

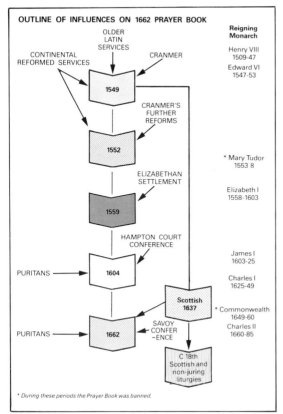

OUTLINE OF INFLUENCES ON 1662 PRAYER BOOK

* During these periods the Prayer Book was banned.

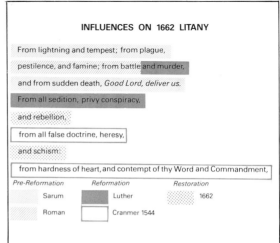

INFLUENCES ON 1662 LITANY

From lightning and tempest; from plague, pestilence, and famine; from battle and murder, and from sudden death, *Good Lord, deliver us.*
From all sedition, privy conspiracy, and rebellion,
from all false doctrine, heresy,
and schism,
from hardness of heart, and contempt of thy Word and Commandment,

Pre-Reformation	Reformation	Restoration
Sarum	Luther	1662
Roman	Cranmer 1544	

various different stages of the history of the church. From pre-Reformation days, we have the influence of the English 'Sarum' rite (the most widely used of the various services available in England at the time) and also the Roman rite. Then Cranmer, in his first fully English service (the 1544 Litany) adds something of the stamp of his own personality, and makes use of Lutheran sources as well. It is interesting to note that Cranmer also added the words 'from the tyranny of the bishop of Rome and all his detestable enormities ...', but this was later felt to be rather strong, and was omitted from the 1559 Book onwards.

Thomas Cranmer   1489-1556

Cranmer was Archbishop of Canterbury from 1533. He was the great reformer of the Anglican liturgy. He apparently wanted to reform the Anglican liturgy under Henry VIII, but had little opportunity till Henry's death in 1547. Before that he had brought the bible into English, and a Litany in 1544. But when Edward VI inherited the throne, Cranmer came into his own. His greatest achievement was his work on the communion service. His first English eucharist was ready in 1548, and was incorporated into the First Prayer Book of Edward VI in 1549. This was, however, only the first stage of his liturgical reform. The second was three years later (1552) when he introduced a Prayer Book which more openly embraced protestant doctrine. Cranmer, like the writers of the Alternative Service Book, did not start from square one in his liturgical writings: he brought scripture (primarily), the work of the early Fathers, and what he considered to be good in the old Latin orders, to bear on them. The 1549 and 1552 Prayer Books were to be the basis of the 1662 Book of Common Prayer. During the reign of Mary, on 21 March 1556, Cranmer was burnt at the stake as a heretic.

Martin Bucer   1491-1551

Martin Bucer was one of the chief reformed critics of Cranmer's 1549 Prayer Book. He had lived in Strasbourg until things began to 'hot up' in Europe, and he was exiled in England. Bucer became regius professor in Cambridge, and his most famous work is his *Censura* in which he noted all the problems he had with Cranmer's First Prayer Book. The kind of changes he was asking for included the abolition of vestments, gestures, wafers, and other more catholic elements. Bucer found two supporters in Peter Martyr (who had also come over from the continent) and Hooper, one of the English reformers. No one knows exactly how much influence he had on Cranmer in his 1552 revision, but certainly many of his ideas were incorporated into it whilst many were not.

Queen Elizabeth I   1533-1603

Elizabeth's predecessor, Mary, was very anti-protestant, and had restored the Roman Catholic faith in England. This had led to a deep division in the country. So Elizabeth, being slightly intolerant of religious bigotry, sought to find a 'middle way', which would satisfy as many people as possible. In her heart, however, she was basically protestant, and so she restored the 1552 Prayer Book in a slightly amended form. This book was enforced by the 1559 Act of Uniformity.

William Laud   1573-1645

Laud became Archbishop of Canterbury in 1633 (exactly one hundred years after Cranmer). His name came to be given to the church party which, in the first half of the seventeenth century was trying to reintroduce pre-Reformation practices into the Church of England. The Laudians became very keen on the 1637 Scottish Prayer Book, which was quite 'high church' in its ethos, and hoped for something like that to be introduced in England. The kind of things the Laudians wanted were: stained glass windows, railed-off altars against the east wall, and crosses. Laud was executed for treason during the period of the Commonwealth when the puritans held sway, but the party which followed him returned as a force in liturgical revision, and we can see some Laudian influence on the 1662 Book of Common Prayer.

Richard Baxter   1615-91

The group which opposed Laudianism, and sought to make the Church of England more reformed were called 'puritans', and Baxter was one of their chief liturgical leaders. Although he did not support the Commonwealth, as most of the puritans did, he had very definite puritan ideas in the area of prayer book revision. The puritan party had generally supported the introduction of the Westminster *Directory* in 1645, which was an outline of how worship should be conducted rather than a full blown liturgy, though Baxter would have been prepared to accept a revision of the Prayer Book. When the monarchy was restored,

Charles II tried to give both sides (puritans and Laudians) an opportunity to air their views at the Savoy Conference. Baxter brought together all his ideas in the Savoy Conference, hoping that it might meet his demands. However, neither the Laudians nor the puritans got their way in 1662, and, although there were certain small concessions to each side, the book remained much as it had been in 1552.

INFLUENCES ON *ASB 1980*

The chart opposite follows on from 1662 (where the one on p.24 finished). Several points need to be kept in mind when reading it. First of all, the 1928 Prayer Book was not passed by parliament, and therefore was never legal; however, it was very widely used throughout the country and many bishops gave permission for its use within their diocese. Secondly, Series 1, Series 2, Series 3, and Series 1 and 2 were only issued as series of booklets, so do not represent books as such. Thirdly, Series 1 and 2 Holy Communion, and most of the Series 3 services have been incorporated into the Alternative Service Book without any further alteration, so the arrows do not necessarily imply that change has taken place.

The people mentioned on the following pages are all involved in areas which have been particularly influential on Series 2 and Series 3, and therefore on the Alternative Service Book. You will also find a chart laying out the process by which a new service is authorised.

Gregory Dix   1901-52

A Benedictine prior, whose most significant study of Christian worship, *The Shape of the Liturgy*, was published in 1945. This work drew out the four-fold structure of the eucharistic action (the taking of the bread and wine; the thanksgiving; the breaking of bread, and the giving). This shape can be seen (with some refinements) in the Alternative Service Book rites. Dix also translated the *Apostolic Tradition* of Hippolytus (dated c.215), which contains the earliest surviving standard text of a eucharistic prayer. This particular prayer has influenced all the eucharistic prayers in *ASB 1980*, and particularly the third, which is very closely modelled on it.

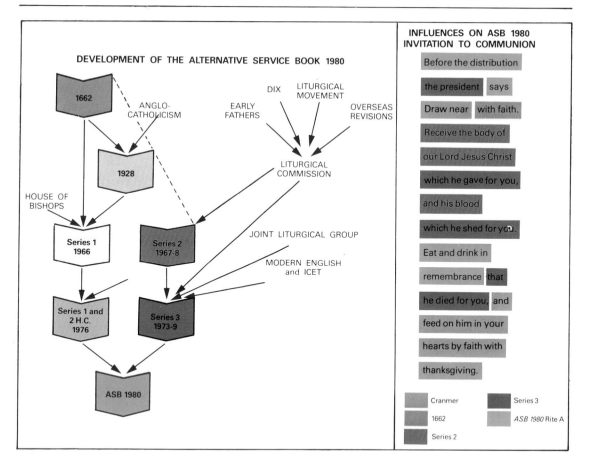

DEVELOPMENT OF THE ALTERNATIVE SERVICE BOOK 1980

1662

ANGLO-CATHOLICISM

DIX

LITURGICAL MOVEMENT

EARLY FATHERS

OVERSEAS REVISIONS

1928

LITURGICAL COMMISSION

HOUSE OF BISHOPS

Series 1 1966

Series 2 1967-8

JOINT LITURGICAL GROUP

MODERN ENGLISH and ICET

Series 1 and 2 H.C. 1976

Series 3 1973-9

ASB 1980

INFLUENCES ON ASB 1980
INVITATION TO COMMUNION

Before the distribution

the president says

Draw near with faith.

Receive the body of

our Lord Jesus Christ

which he gave for you,

and his blood

which he shed for you.

Eat and drink in

remembrance that

he died for you, and

feed on him in your

hearts by faith with

thanksgiving.

Cranmer | Series 3

1662 | ASB 1980 Rite A

Series 2

Leslie Brown b.1912

Leslie Brown was, until the end of the seventies, bishop of St Edmundsbury and Ipswich. He is one of the significant people in terms of the worldwide influences which came to bear on the new services. He was involved first of all in constructing a liturgy for the new Church of South India (a union of three churches – Anglican, Methodist and Congregational/Presbyterian – which took place in 1947). This was drawn up in the post-war years, when liturgical revision was just beginning to come to the forefront of people's minds again, and it was the first eucharistic liturgy to incorporate Dix's four-fold shape. Then, in the 1960s he was a leading light in writing a new 'Liturgy for Africa'. This was specifically Anglican – the bishops had asked for a rite which could be used throughout the continent – and so it drew a lot from the 1662 Book of Common Prayer, while restructuring the service in a way which we have now become quite used to.

The Liturgical Movement

Liturgical revision in the Church of England has been influenced very strongly by the liturgical movement. This started in the Roman Catholic Church at the end of the nineteenth century, but only filtered into the Church of England in the 1930s. Its main emphases have had an impact on the Alternative Service Book. These are:

intelligibility (services which could easily be understood);

participation (of the congregation in worship in every possible way);

simplicity (rubrics were cut down to a minimum so that services could be followed easily);

and the need for *experimentation*.

The International Consultation on English Texts (ICET)

Several of the best-known and most important parts of our new services have been written by this group. It was drawn together from various English-speaking nations, from both protestant and Roman Catholic Churches, and given the task of drawing up translations of the most universally used parts of our services. In 1970 and again in 1971 and 1975, it produced successive proposals in books called *Prayers we have in common*. The versions used for the creeds, the Lord's Prayer, Te Deum, Sanctus, Gloria, in the Alternative Service Books are those proposed by ICET, slightly altered in the case of the Lord's Prayer and the Nicene Creed.

The Liturgical Commission

The archbishops set up a Liturgical Commission in 1955, though it was not possible for new services to be authorised until ten years after that. It was chaired first by Bishop Colin Dunlop, the Dean of Lincoln; then from 1960-4 by Dr Donald Coggan, who went from being Bishop of Bradford to become Archbishop of York in 1961; and from 1964-80 by Dr Ronald Jasper, who has been Dean of York since 1975. The Commission ceased to be an Archbishops' Commission in 1972, and became a Commission of General Synod. Its proposals, even when adopted, have usually been altered or

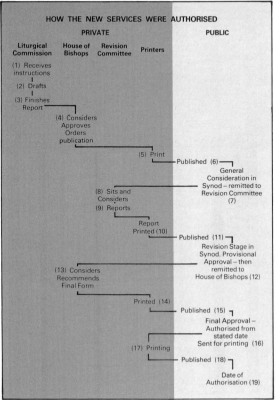

HOW THE NEW SERVICES WERE AUTHORISED

PRIVATE | PUBLIC

Liturgical Commission | House of Bishops | Revision Committee | Printers

(1) Receives instructions
(2) Drafts
(3) Finishes Report
(4) Considers Approves Orders publication
(5) Print
Published (6)
General Consideration in Synod – remitted to Revision Committee (7)
(8) Sits and Considers
(9) Reports
Report Printed (10)
Published (11)
Revision Stage in Synod. Provisional Approval – then remitted to House of Bishops (12)
(13) Considers Recommends Final Form
Printed (14)
Published (15)
Final Approval – Authorised from stated date
Sent for printing (16)
(17) Printing
Published (18)
Date of Authorisation (19)

amended by the Church Assembly (in the years before 1970) or the General Synod (in the years since). The authorised services are thus the products of General Synod, even if they were originally drafted by the Commission.

The Commission had no part in preparing Series 1 services. The Series 2 services were its first venture – and these were similar to those in *ASB 1980*, but still addressed God as 'thou'. They were authorised in the years 1967 and 1968. The Commission then went to work to prepare texts which addressed God as 'you', which were published as Series 3 services and steered through Synod in the 1970s. In the later 1970s the Commission prepared material specifically for *ASB 1980*; their work included choosing the version of the Bible to be used for the readings set out in *ASB 1980*, and preparing the 'adaptations' which Synod had to authorise in order to present all the services in a fairly standard way. The Commission also produced its own theological and historical commentary on *ASB 1980*, which was published on the same day as the new Book. The Liturgical Commission of the 1970s finished its work on services to be used with the sick in May 1980, had a celebration dinner in September 1980, and then disbanded as the new Synod was elected.

The General Synod of the Church of England in session

A history of St Agatha's

We live in an age of great change in our words and patterns of worship. At times like this some imagine the Church has always been the same, and can never imagine it going through similar times of upheaval in the past. In this section we look at a 'typical' parish church, St Agatha's, to catch something of the flavour of these changes in worship.

Ernest, vicar of St Agatha's in 1980, is dreaming in his armchair after a particularly stormy Church Council meeting. Some of the more recent arrivals in the Church were pushing for changes in the worship, but met stiff opposition from the traditionalists who felt the tradition of the Church was being ignored. 'But what,' thought Ernest, 'if we go a bit further back?'

1080

His imaginary time machine carries him far away in time from the streets, shops and factories of the town-centre church, back to the year 1080. Here, where the vicarage was later to be, are small fields divided by low banks, with a grassy track leading to the village. Rising high and impressive over the village shacks is a new building – St Agatha's. But it is tiny by comparison to the church of 1980: a two-room building, nave and round-ended chancel. Ernest goes in through the west end doorway.

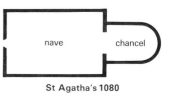

nave   chancel

St Agatha's 1080

It is dark and draughty: small windows with no glass in them, closed with shutters. The walls are painted with all sorts of pictures; there are saints, bible stories and other legends. There are no seats, only a low stone bench along one wall. 'That's the origin of the saying about the weakest going to the wall,' thinks Ernest. In the chancel, standing free from the wall, is a low stone altar, covered with a cloth, but with no other ornaments. As Ernest watches, a man appears, carrying lights which are placed on the altar and around the centre of the church. A congregation gathers, and the service is conducted by a priest dressed in quite colourful vestments. It is all in Latin, as Ernest expected, but most of it is said out loud, and all who can join in the creed. Parts of the service are sung by a choir on a platform in the middle of the church. People stand or kneel on the bare earth floor, some saying their own prayers, some listening to the priest. At the 'ministry of the sacrament' part of the service, the centre of action moves from the central platform to the altar in the chancel. The priest can be seen facing the people through the smoky atmosphere caused by the candles and incense. Many of the congregation receive wafers and wine, going into the chancel for communion.

1480

Ernest's imaginary time machine whisks him forward four centuries to 1480 and he finds himself outside the church again. The village looks very different. There are now three very large fields, divided into long strips marked out by pegs and stones. The forest has been pushed further back and cattle graze down by the river. There are now a few notable stone houses in the village, a new water mill and moated manor house.

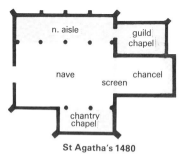

St Agatha's 1480

The church too has grown. Two centuries earlier a lofty, square-ended Early English chancel had replaced the small, heavy Norman one. The round arch between chancel and nave is now high and pointed, filled with a large wooden screen in the bottom half and a lath and plaster screen at the top. This (the tympanum) is painted with a lurid scene of the last judgement, the separation of the sheep and the goats and the sufferings and tortures of the damned. In contrast to this stand out the life-size figures in painted wood, set on a platform on top of the wooden screen: Jesus on the cross, with Mary and John on either side.

The whole feel of the building is lighter, more airy, larger. The roof is higher, with light streaming in through a clerestory of Decorated windows. There is a new north aisle with a chapel at the end, parallel to the chancel, dedicated to St Mary, with the brilliant colours of the stained glass giving it a warm glow. This guild chapel was paid for by a local guild, a sort of medieval trades union, and the guild priest says a daily mass for the guild, and its members, past and present. On the other side of the church another extension houses an enclosed chantry chapel where a chantry priest is saying mass on his own for the repose of the soul of the late lord of the manor (who had left the money to build the chapel and to pay the priest).

The high altar, right up against the east wall of the chancel, with curtains on three sides of it, is richly decorated with a frontal in warm silk bearing an embroidered picture of a lamb with a sword through it, surrounded by colourful cherubim singing their eternal song. Above all this swings the tabernacle in mid-air, containing the Blessed Sacrament in an ornately gilded pyx in the shape of a dove. At the high altar the service is just beginning. Candles are lit on the altar and a crucifix placed between them. The priest and his two

assistants face east (with their backs to the people), wearing colourful vestments decorated more lavishly on their backs than on their fronts. Ernest can hear little of the Latin words, but catches the sound of something very like the Collect for Purity before the introit and psalm. These are sung by the choir, up in the rood loft, the platform over the screen – where there is also a group of musicians. The next words Ernest recognises are the Kyrie eleison (Lord have mercy) and Paternoster (Lord's Prayer). After an action which looks very much like the kiss of peace which his 1980 congregation finds so difficult – but here it is restricted to the three ministers – Ernest recognises the familiar words Gloria in Excelsis. The ministers sit on stone seats in the chancel for the reading of the epistle from a large book carried from the altar. There are no seats in the nave so the congregation stay standing. Another large book (the fourth so far) is used for the gradual (or grail), sung before the gospel. The Gospel Book is taken from the altar, attended by assistants with candles, and the priest sings the gospel so badly that Ernest has no idea what it is. The congregation do not seem too worried. There is plenty of action to watch ('A bit different from us,' thinks Ernest) and enough visual aids, in the stories from the bible and the lives of the saints in the stained glass and wall paintings, for the congregation to learn something. Some are using a rosary to say their own private prayers, and one or two wealthy ones have little primers or prayer books of their own.

By now the priest has washed his hands and said

some prayers even more inaudibly than the rest, and the choir is singing 'Sanctus ... (Holy, holy ...)'. There is a sense of expectation as the priest begins the very long prayer of thanksgiving, intercession, commemoration and consecration (the 'Canon'). There is a deep reverence and bowing in the congregation when the bell is rung, indicating that Christ has come down to be in the bread on the altar, for his sacrifice to be re-presented to God. As the prayer goes on, Ernest hears the name of Agatha spoken loudly, between Perpetua and Lucy in the list of saints the priest mentions.

What happens after this is a solemn blessing of the people, who do not receive communion (they do so only rarely, and then only bread and not wine). When the priest and his assistants have received communion and a final prayer is said, the deacon stands and says to the people 'Ite, missa est' (Go, the mass is over). Ernest joins the crowds leaving the medieval church of St Agatha, and is immediately taken on another hundred years.

1580

The church looks different now, though still much the same size. The great west tower has been completed, and a peal of bells rings out to let people know the service is about to begin (there is a fine if they fail to attend). And on the south side of the church there is a magnificent new porch, about forty years old, with a chamber above it. Inside, though, there are even

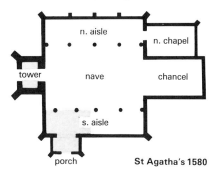

St Agatha's 1580

greater changes. The chancel screen is still there, but the rood loft and the figures of Christ, Mary and John are gone. The statues of the saints have been defaced and the wall paintings washed over. All the separate altars with their colourful frontals have disappeared, even the great stone high altar in the chancel.

'Yes, it went thirty years ago,' said a man Ernest found standing next to him. 'They ordered all the stone altars to be destroyed in 1550 because people thought you had to have a stone altar to make a sacrifice on – and our communion service is no longer a sacrifice of Jesus.'

'What has happened over there?' asked Ernest, pointing to where the chantry chapel used to be.

'That was all taken away when the chantries were abolished; someone made a lot of money out of that lot. You've no idea what we've been through. All these changes, and all in the last thirty years or so. I remember the day – it was Whitsunday in 1549 – when we used the new Prayer Book for the first time. Mind you, it was expensive, three shillings and eight pence (the price was fixed by the government), but a lovely volume all in red leather. Our old priest, who was always losing his way among all the books he used to need to take the service, said using the new one would save him hours of time swotting it all up. But I'm forgetting: the real change was that it was all in English. That took some getting used to. And three years later we had another Prayer Book, even simpler this time. Then the next year the young King died and we all went back to Latin with Queen Mary. Those were terrible times, so many people burnt for not being willing to become Catholics again – we had them even in our own town here. Fortunately she didn't last long and in 1558 Good Queen Elizabeth came to the throne and we went back almost completely to how things were in 1552. Four radical changes in ten years: I suppose you could say the Church is used to change now!'

It is about 9.30 in the morning and people are coming in and sitting on the benches now filling the church. 'Are you going to take communion?' Ernest's neighbour asks him. 'Usually the service stops half way through and we all go home, but today is a communion Sunday: the minister announced it last week and we have to go and give him our names if we are coming. He reads us a long exhortation about how to receive communion and really mean it.'

People are now singing a metrical psalm, led by the choir still over the chancel screen, but facing west towards the people. The minister, wearing a long white surplice nearly down to his ankles, a black scarf and a hood, stands at his reading desk in the nave. He reads through Morning Prayer, including two long lessons from the bible, and then when Ernest is just looking forward to hearing him preach, begins to read one of the long homilies from the book put out in 1547, to be used instead of sermons. 'There are more ways than one of getting people to know what they believe,' thinks Ernest, looking round the amazingly attentive congregation. An anthem, then the Litany, come before the

The alms box at Kedington church, dating from 1400, is a tree dug into the floor

beginning of the communion service. For this, the minister has moved into the chancel, where the moveable table is set lengthwise, at right angles to the east wall.

Bread and wine are placed on the white cloth on the table, and people not taking communion leave after the next prayer. Ernest hears the words of the long exhortation on the meaning of communion as if for the first time. He is impressed by the way the old Prayer Book order makes sense in its right setting, and gladly joins the congregation as they fill the chancel when the minister says, 'Draw near ...' Both bread and wine are distributed to the communicants as they kneel around the holy table.

'Is this the only service?' Ernest asks his neighbour before going.

'No: there is Evening Prayer. Everyone will be back here for that at 3.00 – yes, even after two and a half hours this morning. There are psalms and readings, and there might be a baptism after the second lesson. Then the minister teaches a part of the catechism (from the Prayer Book) to the children. And we sing some more metrical psalms.'

1680

Ernest finds himself another hundred years on, inside St Agatha's again after the time of Cromwell and the Commonwealth, twenty years after the Restoration of the monarchy under Charles II. The church seems much lighter and Ernest realises that all the stained glass has been smashed out and replaced by plain glass. There is now absolutely no trace of the old wall paintings, but up on the east wall at the end of the chancel is a brand new panel with the words of the creed, Lord's Prayer and ten commandments written up. The table, now draped with a velvet cloth, is right up against the east wall again, surrounded by lovely wooden communion rails.

Ernest glances through the lovely printed Prayer Book, dating of course from 1662. His eye is caught, too, by some new services. There is a Form of Prayer with Thanksgiving to Almighty God for having put an end to the Great Rebellion and restored the monarchy with Charles II; a Form of Prayer and Fasting on the anniversary of the martyrdom of King Charles I, and some pages headed 'Gunpowder Treason' commemorating the deliverance of James I and Parliament from their intended massacre by Guy Fawkes. 'Now, there's nothing much like that in our Service Book in 1980,' thinks Ernest.

Looking up in the nave, Ernest sees the royal coat of arms above the chancel arch, and takes time to look at the colourful dress of the people. The minister looks much the same as a hundred years before, and the service too is little changed, apart from the fact that now people go up to receive communion at the communion rail in an orderly fashion.

1780

Another hundred years on and the interior of the church has changed again, with a private pew for the

squire and his family now built over where the rood loft was, with comfortable chairs, a fireplace and chimney. The whole church is now packed with high box pews, with doors and locks on them. Ernest looks at the names painted on the doors and realises that the pews are only available to those who have paid the rent for them. Some obviously poor people who cannot afford a pew are sitting on a couple of benches right at the back of the church. Visibility is bad because the pews are so high, and people cannot relate to each other except

within their pews. Perhaps one advantage is that people can sleep unnoticed in their pews – but the churchwardens staves are for poking them awake again. At least the minister can be seen, in his high three-decker pulpit.

The service begins at 9.30 with Morning Prayer, read by the minister from the second stage of the three-decker pulpit. He is wearing a cassock under his full surplice, hood, and preaching bands at his neck. The parish clerk, on the bottom deck, wears a black gown. He makes the responses in the service on behalf of the people, apart from those responses now sung by the choir from their new gallery in the west end of the church. The orchestra up there with them looks like the local town band. Now that their parts are taken by the clerk and the choir, the congregation seem to have little to do but just be there, attending worship and listening to the sermon.

At the end of the Litany comes a break when the congregation stretch their legs. Then follows the communion service, again apparently happening very infrequently: the congregation do not seem to know it very well now. Large pewter flagons, cup and plates are used for communion. The words of the service have not changed.

As he leaves, Ernest notices a group of people rushing off, with bibles under their arms. 'Methodists!' he hears someone mutter, and realises that they must be members of the local Methodist class meeting, still coming regularly to the church for worship, but finding their spiritual nourishment elsewhere, in studying the bible together and in visiting teachers and open-air preachers. 'Clearly the church, with its sermons on

logic and right living like that one today, is nowhere near meeting the spiritual needs of ordinary folk,' thinks Ernest, as his time machine drops him forward another hundred years.

1880

How different everything looks in the town! Almost all the old fields have gone, replaced by streets and factories as farmer after farmer has found it more profitable to sell up and reinvest in industry. The church is now surrounded by streets on every side, and looks black with the smoke pouring from the chimneys.

Inside, everything is different. Most of the old high box pews have gone, and a notice in the porch proclaims that the seats in the church are now free. The squire's pew has gone from the chancel arch, which is now more empty than at any time for the last six hundred years. A low stone screen separates nave from chancel, which is now raised two steps above the newly tiled nave floor. There is a large robed choir in the two rows of choir stalls on each side of the chancel, and

music is coming from a new organ built out into the old side chapel. The altar, now made of stone again, is backed by an ornate reredos which blocks part of the east window. An ornate wrought-iron rail with a wooden top cuts off the sanctuary at the east end, and the altar is three steps up from the chancel floor.

As the opening hymn (from Hymns Ancient and Modern, by then nearly twenty years old) is ending, the sanctuary procession enters: two taperers with candles, priest, deacon and subdeacon, thurifer with censer full of incense, and clerk carrying the Gospel Book. They bow, and the priest goes to the altar, bows and kisses it.

The censer is made ready, handed from thurifer to deacon to priest, who swings it nine times towards the altar before returning it. 'Have I seen this all before?' Ernest begins to think, and is vaguely surprised to hear the familiar words of the Collect for Purity.

He notices various things now inserted into the service from medieval times: the Kyrie has reappeared, and so has a gradual anthem before the reading of the Gospel. The deacon is taken in procession, again with censing and candles, to the entrance to the chancel, where he reads the Gospel. There is a shuffle of annoyance from some in the congregation as

he makes the sign of the cross – as there is later when the priest does the same at the absolution. Full Victorian crinolines enable quite a rustle to be made and there is a bit of a murmur from those not yet used to the new customs.

At the offertory there seems to be quite an elaborate ritual with the plate and cup, involving all six ministers, at the end of which the priest washes his hands. The prayer for the church, confession and absolution follow, with not a whisper of the long exhortation on the meaning of holy communion. The priest sings 'The Lord be with you' and the preface and *sanctus* – joined by the deacon and subdeacon who then retreat to their respective steps below the priest. The one great difference, in this conscious recall of the medieval services, is that the congregation receive communion in both kinds – though some of them wrinkle their noses at the new wafers, embossed with a crucifix, and try to take the chalice into their hands as they have been used to doing until the arrival of their new vicar.

Ernest looks around. The new vicar seems to have reintroduced the hanging lamp in the sanctuary, lit before the reserved sacrament, this time locked in an aumbry in the east wall. The words of the service, with some addition and a bit of re-arrangement, are still the 1662 service, but done in a way the Church has not known for four hundred years. The people are still basically the same sort of people, perhaps more prosperous at this service than those at the newly-introduced 'early service' at 8.00 or the servants who come to Evensong in the gaslight at 6.30. The Church, like society around it, is becoming fragmented, different groups coming at different times, different activities laid on for various sections of society in the new church hall down the road. Ernest notices the warmth from the new hot water heating system, fed by a coke-fired boiler: another reflection within the church of the increasing comfort of the society in which it now stands.

The service draws to a close with the prayer of thanksgiving, the Gloria and blessing, followed by some elaborate ablutions (washing up of the vessels) in which most of the ministers seem to get involved. Ernest finds himself back in his chair in 1980, reflecting on the changes at St Agatha's down the centuries and the need to get both *ASB 1980* and the reactions of the ordinary worshipper into some sort of historical perspective.

The Church's role in worship

CHURCH AND WORSHIP

The Christian Church is an enigma. It is often dismissed as irrelevant, many confidently predict its gradual withering away, and yet the twentieth century has seen growth unparalleled in Christian history and everywhere the Church shows unexpected resilience and vitality. Neither communism nor materialism nor even Islam have been able to suppress its life. Jesus promised his disciples, 'Because I live you also will live' and the New Testament everywhere speaks of the Spirit of Jesus Christ as an unseen life-giving presence restoring man's relationship with God and binding up his broken humanity.

The worship of the Christian Church is an expression of that Spirit-given life. It is not merely a rationally constructed embodiment of Christian belief and commitment. Even less is it a public performance imposed by ecclesiastical authority. Reason, Christian doctrine and ecclesiastical authority all have their part to play but essentially Christian worship is the corporate expression of the Church's new life in Christ. It is a spontaneous growing thing that is shaped by many different factors, but which has its origin in the Holy Spirit. This can be seen clearly in the life of the New Testament Church where developing patterns and traditions of worship are everywhere present. Examples of these are fixed exclamations (Amen, Abba, Maranatha), doxologies (1 Timothy 1.17), hymns (Ephesians 5.14; 1 Timothy 3.16), creeds (Romans 10.9; 1 Corinthians 15.3-5; 1 Corinthians 8.6), gestures (1 Timothy 2.8; 1 Corinthians 16.20; Acts 21.5), annual festivals (1 Corinthians 16.8). In Ephesians 1.3ff and 1 Peter 1.3ff the two apostles freely adapt accepted styles of Jewish prayer. These forms were not imposed by authority but freely developed as the first Christian communities sought ways of expressing their new life. Those who regard extempore spontaneous prayer as the only valid form of prayer may be surprised at the early evolution of such forms. But any common group life requires the development of recognised patterns of speech and action so that this life can express itself. This can be seen in families, in the life of any business or factory as well as in the world of sport; each has its own rituals and liturgical forms. Imagine trying to invent a new way to wish your son goodnight each evening!

Many traditional English churchgoers may find it hard to see the worship with which they are familiar as the community's expression of its Spirit-given life. It is perhaps most obvious when you consider the place of hymns in Church of England worship. The use of hymns has never been regulated by authority in the Church of England, indeed the Book of Common Prayer makes no provision for the singing of hymns in Sunday worship. English hymnody has been a major outlet for expressing English Christian life for the last three hundred years. Obviously each hymn has been the composition of one or two individuals but many hymns have become community property. Think of the place in English worshipping life of hymns like Hark, the herald angels sing, There is a green hill far away, Jesus Christ is risen today, or Patrick Appleford's Living Lord.

The words and actions of Christian worship are the expression of the Church's Spirit-given life. However they should not be thought of purely as man's response to God's initiative. All worship has within it a subtle interplay of hearing and responding to God. In the songs, words and gestures of Christian worship Christians find God speaking to them.

FORM AND WORSHIP

The Church is an international community which is as culturally diverse as the world community of which it is a part. However behind this variety there is also a fixed shape to Christian worship which comes from God himself. The four elements of this God-given skeleton for the Church's life and worship are the two rites of baptism and the Lord's supper, the weekly gathering of the Christian community on the Lord's Day with its remembrance of Jesus' resurrection, and the sacred writings of the Old and New Testament which are read to the gathered Church (1 Timothy 4.13, Colossians 4.16). The Church receives these four as from Christ himself and they imprint a Gospel shape on church communities as different as Greek Orthodox and South

American Pentecostals. Between them these four enable, or maybe even compel, the Church to approximate to Jesus' will for it.

Modern disciplines such as social anthropology provide some clue to the bewildering variety of ways in which different church communities express their life within this framework. In stable and structured societies the Church will tend to express itself in structured and formal ways. In more mobile and changing societies the Church will find a more open and informal style appropriate. Where the Church is accepted by the surrounding society it will tend to adopt that society's style of corporate life; where it is rejected the Church is compelled to find its own style. The style of a Church's life and worship in turn influences the way God is understood. A more formal style brings home to the worshipper God's majesty and leads to sin being seen in terms of breaking commands; a less formal style points to a more intimate and personal view of God and leads to sin being seen in terms of a spoiled relationship. Although the community in which a Church exists exercises a strong influence on the style of its life, the source of that life is the liberating power of Jesus Christ. This will give the common life of any living Church qualities of joy and freedom that must affect its worship.

A man alone is nothing. God has made us social beings. This means expressing ourselves through the agreed language, customs and gestures of the community. These things become part of our identity as human beings. A baby needs a family and a society to become an adult. In the same way we realise our potential as Christians by sharing in the life of a Christian community. The words and actions of that community's worship become part of our identity as Christians. This has some very important results. It explains why it may be difficult for Christians to accept other Christians of a different tradition of worship. It also explains why Christian communities find it so agonising to adapt their style of worship in a time of social change. They feel their very identity is threatened and therefore make the mistake of clinging more tightly to the old forms. The strain of such a transition is eased where Christians are working out how to express their faith within the changing society itself, and where new Christians are joining the church community without being forced to learn the old forms.

In seeking to express its new life in Christ a Christian Church draws its forms of expression from two main sources: the Christian past and the culture of the surrounding community. Forms from the past are taken over and adapted; examples of this are prayers, hymns, service outlines, actions such as the Peace. The culture of the surrounding community through such things as its music, architecture, poetry, styles of expression or greeting provides ways of expressing joy, reconciliation and common life. The use of forms from both sources brings home the fact that the Church is both a community in history and a community created by the Spirit in the present. The Roman Catholic Church since the Second Vatican Council has made a priority of adapting worship to the temperament, traditions and cultures of individual peoples; the result has been new discovery of Christian life and community all over the world.

The worship of a Christian community is often strongly influenced by one or two factors in the surrounding culture. The invention of printing in the fifteenth century has meant that for the past four hundred years each worshipper in the west has expected to have his own service book. This means that people have found their way into the drama of worship not by watching the other players and being welcomed

by them but by following their own copy of the text and stage directions. This has helped people's understanding but has made change difficult and has led to many worshippers remaining hesitant semi-spectators all their lives. The invention of television will have its own influence on worship in the late twentieth century. Colour and variety have become more important. People find it harder to concentrate on words. The style of ordinary language has become simpler. The danger that worshippers will find it hard to enter into the worship and not just remain spectators has probably increased.

ANGLICAN WORSHIP

The central core of Anglican worship for the past four hundred years has been the Book of Common Prayer. The liturgical principles of its main author, Archbishop Cranmer, can be summarised as follows.

First, worship should be biblical in the doctrine it expresses, should familiarise worshippers with the content of scripture and should draw on the imagery and ideas of the bible.

Second, worship should be adapted to the language, customs and circumstances of the worshippers.

Third, where it is possible and helpful, worship should continue the customs and traditions of the ancient Church.

Fourth, worship should be the ordered, reverent, corporate activity of the whole Church of Christ, clergy and people together.

These principles have remained central to the Church of England's tradition of worship and find renewed expression in the Alternative Service Book.

In the last twenty years the Church of England has found itself in a time of rapid social change and has responded in a variety of ways. Some hope to salvage traditional English Christian culture, others feel the Church has no choice but to go its own way. Where a country has made Christianity part of its national life, Christian and human identity become confused. Pagan Englishmen have no rites to mark their birth, marriage and death except the rites of a Church they otherwise avoid. Traditional Christians do not know how to respond to the rapid social change; they often cling to the traditional symbols of their Christian identity and need help in re-expressing their Christian identity in new ways. The charismatic movement has not only marked a new encounter with Christ for many, it has also been one means by which many traditional Christians have found a more appropriate contemporary expression for their Christian life. *ASB 1980* is obviously part of the Church's response to this change.

At three particular points social anthropology throws light on the situation of the Church of England today.

First of all, most Englishmen have experience of only two types of community; the nuclear family and the national industrial network which treats them as a faceless unit to be deployed as convenient. Already in 1942 William Temple deplored the decline of intermediate social groupings in English life. A result of this decline is that most English people don't have the skills necessary to share unselfconsciously in the life of a community like the Church. This obviously contributes to people's embarrassment with worship.

Second, the Church of England is not one single Christian culture but consists of a number of inter-penetrating Christian communities. In each of these Christ is at work but they express their life in different ways. This variety can be bewildering and it makes the Church of England a strange and complex body to those who first meet it. However it imparts a richness to its worship which usually comes to mean a great deal to those who are not put off by the shock of their first encounter. A new Christian needs to go at his own pace if he is to gain from the richness and diversity of Anglican worship. Peter speaks of 'God's varied grace' (1 Peter 4.10) and Christians need to learn to enjoy the rich variety of ways in which Christ's life is seen in the Church while keeping their roots firmly in Christ and in the Christian community and secular situation in which God has put them.

Third, during the Industrial Revolution the buildings, rites and customs of Church of England worship came to have different associations for the middle class and for the new urban working class. For example, in nineteenth century Liverpool St George's Church, Everton, was surrounded by 60,000 poor immigrants from Ireland and Lancashire. They did not attend worship because they did not have Sunday clothes to match the frockcoats of the middle class commuters who ran the Church! A similar pattern in many great cities has led to the activities and buildings of the Church of England expressing not only the reality and love of Christ but also the community's long-standing and hurtful rejection by the Church. In this community the Christian rite of baptism finds itself pointing simul-taneously towards and away from membership of the Christian community. 'You don't have to go to church to be a Christian.' This will only change as groups in this community find new life in Christ and as the Church of England as a whole begins to renounce its past insistence that Christian life be expressed only through middle class culture.

AUTHORITY AND WORSHIP

Christian worship is an expression of the Spirit-given life of the Christian community. Like any other corpo-rate activity it needs to be directed and regulated if the full intention of the common action is to be achieved. This is the function of authority in the life and worship of the Church. Authority cannot create life; it exists to enable life to find its full and proper expression. God alone gives life and all authority in the Church is delegated authority from God. This does not mean that whatever is is right. Authority in the Church can be

usurped, can be wrongly delegated and can be misused even when it is rightly delegated. The bible has serious warnings against the misuse of authority in the people of God.

Authority in the worshipping life of the Church of England is exercised in many different ways. A vicar and Parochial Church Council decide together what services and robes are used in a congregation's public worship and are urged in canon law to work together in fostering the whole life of the parish. Worship is led and planned by the clergy and other authorised leaders. In many parishes this is now being done by a group, appointed by the Parochial Church Council, that includes laity as well as clergy and other full-time church workers. Some features of worship are decided locally, others are regulated at a national level. Forms of service and rules about worship are determined nationally, and here again authority has been exercised in a variety of different ways.

The Prayer Books of 1549, 1552 and 1662 were imposed on the whole Church by Acts of Parliament (the Acts of Uniformity). Parliament saw itself as

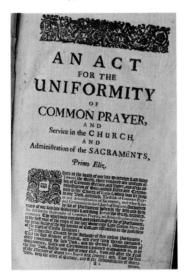

regulating the life of the Christian Church of a Christian nation. Its efforts were not always welcomed; for example, the 1662 Act of Uniformity resulted in above a thousand ministers leaving the Church of England. The acceptance of the Prayer Book in English church life really comes from the quality of Cranmer's work and from the renewal of Christian life that flowed from the rediscovery of the bible in the sixteenth century, a renewal of which Cranmer himself was a part. In this century the Church of England has gained the right to regulate its own life through elected councils of clergy

and laity. A national Church Assembly was set up in 1920 and was replaced by the General Synod in 1970. In 1974 the Worship and Doctrine Measure was passed by Synod and parliament; this gave the Church of England the right to regulate its own worship through General Synod and to introduce permanent alternative forms of service to the Book of Common Prayer. The services of the Alternative Service Book are the result of a long process of discussion and consultation. The Revision Committee of General Synod that examined the proposed changes to the Series 3 Communion considered 1,030 recommendations from different people before Synod authorised the changed text as Rite A. Certainly the new services result from wide study and discussion within the Church.

What principles underly the way in which Church of England worship is regulated at the national level? The first is expressed in Article 20 of the 39 Articles: 'The Church hath authority to decree Rites or Ceremonies, and authority in Controversies of Faith; and yet it is not lawful for the Church to ordain anything that is contrary to God's Word written . . .' All forms of worship are to be tested against scripture and nothing is to be included that contradicts or distorts the teaching of scripture. This principle greatly influenced Cranmer's revision of English worship in the sixteenth century. It has clearly operated in the new services, not only in their preference for biblical phrases and imagery but particularly in their refusal to go unambiguously beyond the language of scripture in some disputed areas of doctrine.

A second principle is that of unity. One factor in the introduction of the Book of Common Prayer was a desire to unite all English Christians in a common form of worship. In the formation of the new services there has been a recognition that there is a tension between encouraging unity and allowing for adaptability to local circumstances and the expression of the distinctive life and concerns of the local Christian community. The result has been services which allow much greater flexibility and local colour than did the Book of Common Prayer and the hope is that this will lead to new unity and a return to common patterns of worship in the Church of England. The principle of unity has operated in other ways in the preparation of the new services. The new services in a number of respects go back to the customs and structures of worship in the Church in the first four centuries. A similar tendency can be seen in the new services of the Roman Catholic Church. One reason behind these moves has been the desire to build on those things that unite Christians of different denominations and traditions.

DOCTRINE AND WORSHIP

Christian worship is an activity of the Church and of the Holy Spirit. The words and actions used in worship not only express the beliefs of Christian people but also embody the God-given truths which have brought them life. This means the language of worship looks two ways. It provides evidence as to what truths have proved in experience to bring Christian life. At the same time great care needs to be taken that it represents faithfully what God has said and done in Jesus Christ.

Some scholars have criticised the new services for preserving traditional beliefs about God, the bible and the person of Jesus Christ which they regard as irrelevant or untenable for modern men. It is perhaps true that the services do not go far enough in using ways of expressing the Christian faith that find an immediate echo with modern people. However when it comes to the substance of Christian belief the worshipping experience of the Christian Church is against them; it seems that it is precisely the beliefs that these scholars question that result in living, worshipping Christian communities. Perhaps the way forward is for such scholars to express their convictions in songs and prayers so that what is good in them can be taken up into the worshipping life of the Church.

Many members of the Church of England would like to have seen the new services include ways of speaking about the eucharist, the ministry of priests and other matters which have a long history in Christian tradition but which are not present in scripture and which were deliberately excluded from the Book of Common Prayer. Many others regard these as distortions of the biblical witness and alien to Anglican tradition. The 1974 Worship and Doctrine Measure lays on the General Synod the responsibility for ensuring that new services are 'neither contrary to, nor indicative of any departure from, the doctrine of the Church of England in any essential matter'. The 1974 Measure, like the canon law, describes the doctrine of the Church of England as follows: 'The doctrine of the Church of England is grounded in the holy scriptures, and in such teachings of the ancient Fathers and Councils of the Church as are agreeable to the said scriptures. In particular such doctrine is to be found in the Thirty-nine Articles of Religion, the Book of Common Prayer, and the Ordinal.'

Wherever possible, forms of expression have been found which satisfy all views; this has often been done by returning to the language of scripture or by a re-examination of tradition. In cases where agreement has not been possible the matter has been left or forms of words which allow of different interpretations have been used.

The Church of England does not require that each member, minister or office holder in the Church assent to every article of belief contained in its formularies and services. However clergy and laity licensed to lead public worship rightly have to agree to use the authorised forms of service. Some of those who have taken exception to the presence of traditional beliefs in the new services may find themselves unable to use the new services with a good conscience. The Church must not weaken in its witness to the fullness of the Christian faith and they will perhaps have to draw their own conclusions from the extent of the divergence from the living Christian community both past and present. However, for all Christians worship is not only an expression of their experience of reconciliation and life in Christ but is also an opportunity to learn more with all God's people of the unsearchable riches of Christ.

The language of worship

Language is never still. It lives and grows, develops and decays like an organism in the natural world, and all these processes are taking place simultaneously. Poets and creative writers develop a language by new coinages and combinations of words. The decay comes when words are used in a slipshod or unadventurous fashion so that the range of expression shrinks.

We live in a time when much of our language seems to be decaying. Although our vocabulary has been vastly increased by new words from many parts of the world, and especially by new coinages from the world of science, so that we can indicate an immense range of things and speak with great logical precision, there has been a corresponding decline in our ability to express

feeling. We read endless newspapers, but very little poetry. We seem to be less adept than previous generations at the creative use of symbol and metaphor.

By no means was this the situation when Cranmer devised a new English Prayer Book. English as a poetic and scholarly language was developing rapidly. The energies that we put into scientific research were then put into other forms of exploration, including the exploration of language. Words were borrowed from Latin and Greek, Italian and French. English grammar was far more flexible than it later became. No major English dictionary had ever been written. The feel of English was nearer to our experience of Joyce or Beckett than to a Times editorial. At the time when

England was dividing itself from the Latin Church, Cranmer was able to draw upon a lively tradition of popular English devotion and widespread enthusiasm for the national language. He had the most wonderfully musical ear for the cadences and rhythms of English. All this has not made the job of his successors an easy one.

One could almost say that Cranmer did his work too well. Had the Book of Common Prayer been less the work of genius it would long ago have been buried under a welter of additions, modifications, and improvements. In fact this did not begin to happen until the twentieth century. *If Cranmer had been able to foresee the immense social and linguistic changes that have taken place between his own century and ours, he would have been horrified to think that we were still using his Prayer Book, for his aim was to write in language clearly 'understood of the people'.* In his time the debate was between Latin and English; in a debate between Tudor and contemporary English he would have maintained that we should worship God in the language of our own time. He would certainly have expected us to use dignified and attractive English, but he would not have expected the language that we use to give any impression of being old-fashioned.

More and more we have needed a new idiom for worship. The Book of Common Prayer and the Authorised Version of the Bible inspired a whole range of magnificent musical settings to be sung in the ancient parish churches and cathedrals of England. Again, people have been understandably reluctant to give these up, but if these are all that we use, if we refuse to use contemporary music and language in worship, the impression is reinforced that the Church has never quite caught up with the Industrial Revolution. It exists in a world of 'thees' and 'thous', where people say 'lo' in surprise and 'beget' or 'bring forth' children. It is amiable, eccentric, quintessentially English. When the horrors of the trenches in the First World War made clear how far the troops were from living contact with the Church, the movement for reform began to gain momentum.

The writers of the Alternative Service Book have assumed that the language of worship should be as

Victorian family devotions: 'thee' and 'thou' were appropriate in worship then

immediately accessible as God himself. In the bible God is shown to be as much the God of the future as of the past; the Son of God is more at home with prostitutes and tax-collectors and fishermen than with the wealthy and educated; the Church is radical and dynamic and expectant, offering a new vision of society and working in the power of the Spirit to bring that vision about. There is no time for literary refinement; the important thing is to know Christ, live the life and pass on the message before the End.

The writers of the Alternative Service Book have caught something of the same urgency. They have attempted to maintain continuity with the language of Cranmer, to respect the rhythms of English and to provide for an age when it is easier to write a report than a poem, and when the Church represents only a fragment of society at large. The new services have to satisfy those who use them daily or weekly, and yet not to mystify those who come with little or no religious background. For these reasons they are plain-spoken, direct and clear. Let us look at some examples from the Order for Holy Communion (Rite A).

Cranmer wrote with extreme simplicity at times, and some of his best-known prayers have been kept with minimal changes. The Collect for Purity is set out in *ASB 1980* in lines down the middle of the page, which makes it easier to read, 'thee' becomes 'you' and 'hid' becomes 'hidden', but 'magnify' in the old sense is retained. As with the Absolution and the Prayer of Humble Access, it is possible to recognise the old words in a more modern form.

This is not always possible with the prayers in *ASB 1980* because some are completely new, although they are included after a period of experimental use. A comparison of confessions will show what has happened. Cranmer has two confessions, one for Communion and one for Morning and Evening Prayer. *ASB 1980* has just one, which is simpler than Cranmer's and easier to learn. Doublets such as 'acknowledge and bewail', 'wrath and indignation' are gone; repetition such as 'have mercy upon us most merciful' is avoided; adjectives are toned down: 'we do earnestly repent and are heartily sorry' becomes 'we are truly sorry and repent'; 'Almighty God, Father of our Lord Jesus

CRANMER	ASB 1980
Almighty God,	Almighty God,
father of our Lord Jesus Christ,	our heavenly Father,
maker of all things, judge of all men,	
we acknowlege and bewail our manifold sins	we have sinned against you
and wickedness,	and against our fellow men,
which we from time to time most grievously	
have committed,	
by thought, word, and deed,	in thought and word and deed,
against thy divine majesty:	through negligence, through weakness,
provoking most justly thy wrath and	through our own deliberate fault.
indignation against us:	
we do earnestly repent, and are heartily	We are truly sorry,
sorry for these our misdoings:	and repent of all our sins.
the remembrance of them is grievous unto us,	
the burden of them is intolerable:	
have mercy upon us,	
have mercy upon us, most merciful father,	
for thy son our Lord Jesus Christ's sake:	For the sake of your Son,
	Jesus Christ, who died for us,
forgive us all that is past,	forgive us all that is past
and grant that we may ever hereafter	and grant that we may serve you
serve and please thee in newness of life	in newness of life
to the honour and glory of thy name:	to the glory of your name.
through Jesus Christ our Lord, Amen.	Amen.

Christ, Maker of all things, Judge of all men' becomes 'Almighty God, our heavenly Father'. It is interesting to see the words that have gone: 'acknowledge', 'bewail', 'wickedness', 'grievously', 'provoking', 'wrath', 'indignation', 'burden', 'intolerable' – none of them in themselves hard to understand, but taken together, somewhat overpowering for many people today. It is the plainest words of Cranmer that remain: 'thought (and) word and deed'. When we add 'through negligence, through weakness, through our own deliberate fault' we see plainly that language which expressed the *feeling* of the guilt and burden of sin has been replaced by a more detached report upon sins committed. The same has happened with the second prayer after Communion.

If the language of the Alternative Service Book seems in places to concentrate on the plain facts, two things should be noted. The congregation has more opportunities to join in, with frequent acclamations and dialogue, and there are many places where silence is suggested. If these are used well this is one way in which the communion service improves on Cranmer. Besides, the words given to the president are not so spare. The best example of this is the first prayer after communion. Here we have doublets: 'thanks and praise'; repetition: 'live his risen life'; the echoing of 'life' and 'light', the inversion of 'dying and living'. A sentence like 'dying and living, he declared your love, gave us grace, and opened the gate of glory' with its alliterative d-l, d-l, g-g, g-gl, is excellent, and the same marks of style can be found elsewhere in less concentrated form. It is not true to say that *ASB 1980* has no fine writing.

The question to ask about the language of the 1980 Book is not 'Is it as good as Cranmer?' In many ways it is language for an age whose first question is 'Does it work?' So the Christian asks, 'Does it enable us to express our love of God, our longing for him, our penitence and praise and hope, in a way that is unforced and natural?' If the answer is 'Yes', we have the Service Book that we need.

Worship and books

It is clearly obvious that the early Christians were not in the habit of carrying their prayer books with them to worship – printing hadn't been invented! They did, of course, have scrolls in the churches with different parts of scripture contained in them, and these would have had a liturgical purpose in the sense that they would have been regularly (and presumably systematically) read in public worship. The first believers did not rely on the written word to the same extent as we do in the twentieth century. They would have been used to memorising psalms, hymns and parts of scripture. Many of the elements to be found in our worship books today are already very clearly present in the early Church – for example psalms, hymns, responses (e.g. 'Amen' 'Maranatha'), acts of praise (Ephesians 5.19; Colossians 3.16), prayers (e.g. the Lord's Prayer), but these were passed on by oral tradition (word of mouth) rather than, as in our day, by printing.

Not all Christian denominations place as much emphasis on 'Service Books' as the Church of England does. It can be quite refreshing for those who are used to the 'library' of books which are found in many Anglican pews (bible, service book, psalter, hymn book, supplements etc., etc) to visit a nonconformist church, and find solely and simply a hymnary. However, the fact that most nonconformist churches do not use a service book does not mean that there is no order in their worship – very often they have a clear structure in the service, and a strong 'word-of-mouth' tradition which is assumed; and even a large number of recurring phrases in the extempore prayers.

Very few nonconformist churches nowadays *never* use a prayer book – most will use them at least for holy communion, baptisms, marriages and funerals, and many are rediscovering the value of fresh modern liturgy (see for example the modern Methodist Service Book, and the Church of Scotland Book of Common Order). There are nevertheless some strands within nonconformity which would assert very strongly that worship should be under the immediate and direct guidance of the Holy Spirit and that set orders are therefore a hindrance rather than a help. Examples of these would be the Society of Friends (Quakers),

classical Pentecostalism and the Christian Brethren.

So prayer books are not, in any absolute sense, *necessary* to worship, but, for most of us, they are helpful. We praise God for the discovery of printing, and use it to God's honour and glory in worship.

It is interesting to note at this point that it is not very long after the New Testament that we can clearly discern patterns of worship emerging. The *Didache*, which was probably written in the second century, but possibly as early as the second half of the first century, lays down a simple outline for certain parts of the eucharistic worship, while retaining freedom for those who are 'prophets' to 'give thanks as much as they wish'. Justin Martyr in his *First Apology* (c.150) describes the eucharist in outline, but again allows a certain amount of freedom: 'the president likewise offers prayers and thanksgiving to the best of his ability' – so a balance is kept between the formal and informal, the set and the extempore.

Look now at some ways in which the use of books can influence worship today – first some negative areas, and then positive ones.

Negative

- The use of worship books can make us appear to be rather intellectualist in our approach – especially to the larger section of the community who rarely read, and the great number of people who are illiterate. It can be argued, of course, that if the responses, prayers etc are simple enough and the book easily followed, the danger of this criticism is reduced.

- If we are overkeen on the use of printed forms for all our worship, it is very easy for our services to become stereotyped, and divorced from the real-life situation in which we find ourselves. How many of us have experienced continual generalised prayers for 'the whole world' or 'all men', when we need to be praying more specifically and relatedly about particular needs? Of course *ASB 1980* discourages our being so bound to books that we never utter an unrehearsed word!

- Following on from the last point, there need to be times when we as individuals are allowed to express our worship in terms of our own experience of God – and that is important, too, for a church community.

- There is the danger of having 'heard it all before' – often we know more or less what will be said from the beginning of the service to the end – we may well feel that we could say it in our sleep, and thus our worship can become dull and routine. (Of course this can happen without books as well.)

Positive

- There is the value of having 'heard it all before' – that is, we have a structure in which we feel at home – the words become part of us, and can be a real help in time of need.

- A balanced liturgical worship – one in which there is space for the individual extempore contribution, and the shared ministry of 'the Body of Christ' gives us both objectivity and subjectivity in our services. There is the sense that this offering to God goes on week by week, day by day, no matter whether we personally feel up or down; and this can be a real anchor for people. On the other hand, there is room to stamp something of our own individual situation and needs on the services.

- Worship does not become over-dependent on the leader, and includes participation for every member of the congregation.

- Having worship books can make it easier to keep our services up to date. How do people, for example, go about learning the Lord's Prayer in the revised form, if they do not have it in print in front of them. For most non-liturgical churches, it simply is not worth the effort, and they stay with the old version.

- Worship books, if carefully and spiritually thought out, give us a balanced diet – made up of praise, thanks, prayer, confession, declaration of God's Word etc. They ensure that we do not go off at tangents and over-emphasise one or two aspects to the detriment of others; and also ensure that we do not leave out vital elements.

- What we say in worship affects our theology (what we believe about God). We do not glorify God by saying wrong or careless things about him – therefore we need to have a proper concern that worship should be tuned to the word of God.

Music in church today

'Sing to the Lord a new song' are words which recur in the bible, particularly in the psalms, like a refrain to the unfolding pattern of God's plan of salvation (see Psalms 33.3, 40.3, 96.1, 98.1, 144.9, 149.1; Isaiah 42.10; Revelation 5.9, 14.3). There are always new occasions for the people of God to sing new songs of praise and thanksgiving to the God who has redeemed them in Jesus Christ. With a new book of worship we have the opportunity to investigate what new approaches to music in worship we can make. (On the musical opportunities created by *ASB 1980*, see further *Music and the Alternative Service Book*, edited by Lionel Dakers, RSCM, Croydon, 1980.) But before we can look forward, we need to look back.

MUSIC IN WORSHIP

As the Church has progressed through the generations opinions (and practice) regarding the place of music in worship have swung backwards and forwards between two points of view. On the one hand, music has been regarded as a work of man and therefore of doubtful propriety in the worship of God. In the first few centuries of the Church there were many protests by church fathers against what they saw as musical abuses, particularly instrumental music, which at the time was a prominent feature of pagan worship. A thousand and more years later the Swiss reformer, Ulrich Zwingli, excluded *all* music, even the simplest unaccompanied singing, from the churches in Zurich. He argued that the essence of worship is the spiritual work of God in the heart of man and that the essence of music is the physical and external work of man. Therefore, for him, the two had nothing in common. The later puritans shared a similar suspicion of music in worship, although they did allow the simple singing of metrical psalms.

On the other hand, there have been those who have had a different point of view. They have seen music as the gift of God and therefore as highly appropriate for the worship of the people of God. Augustine, in his treatise on music, regarded it as a vehicle for bringing the truth of God to man and for man to convey his

Martin Luther
(1483-1546)

thoughts to God. The German reformer, Martin Luther, viewed music as the creation and gift of God which has the unique ability to touch the heart of man with the Gospel of Christ. Later Lutherans have developed Luther's understanding of the ministry of music in worship and today the musical tradition of the Lutheran Church stands unique in Christendom.

In the history and practice of the Church of England both points of view have developed simultaneously! The cathedral music tradition, with its elaborate choral music, has pursued high artistic ideals but often at the cost of making the Gospel serve the art. The parish music tradition, certainly until the mid-nineteenth century, with its simple congregational metrical psalm, has followed the ideal of simplicity at the expense of art. Neither tradition has adequately served the needs of the worship of the people of God.

MUSIC OF WORSHIP

Part of the problem is that music has been thought of as an optional extra rather than as an integral part of worship. There is the tendency to speak of 'music *at* worship' rather than the 'music *of* worship'. Music in

worship is often considered, as someone has said, in terms of an 'aural lubricant', something done to bridge the gap between one section of the liturgy and another, to fill up silences, to allow the clergy to move from A to B, to create an 'atmosphere', to 'beautify' the liturgy, and so on. But the purpose of church music is not to be prosaically functional, nor to be aesthetically or emotionally gratifying to the congregation. It may be so, but to make church music serve such ends is to keep it earth-bound, man-centred, and restricted to 'what we like'. When the composer Johann Sebastian Bach compiled his *Little Organ Book*, a collection of organ preludes on hymn tunes for church use, he wrote on the cover that the compositions were written 'to the glory of God and the edification of my neighbour'.

The music of worship, truly understood, is always God-centred and God-directed. But this vertical dimension explodes horizontally to draw all the worshippers together. The music of worship is not merely notes and sounds. It is essentially an expression of heart and mind as, filled with the Spirit, the people of God address one another in psalms and hymns and spiritual songs, singing and making melody to the Lord with all their hearts (Ephesians 5.19). Such music is an expression of our faith in God in Christ.

Congregational music

The music of worship is not the special preserve of a chosen few but the inheritance of all the people of God; it is the practical expression of the priesthood of all believers. The congregation does not sing in order to make music but in order to confess its faith, praise and thank its God, and proclaim God's word to its members.

ASB 1980 makes four main provisions for congregational music. First, there are *hymns*. Unlike the Book of Common Prayer *ASB 1980* gives specific indications where hymns may be appropriately sung, which is a move away from the old stereotyped pattern of singing hymns at the static points of the liturgy and an encouragement to make hymn singing a necessary part of the worship. With a new book of worship there is the opportunity to learn new hymns, and that includes 'old' hymns which have yet to be discovered by some congregations who will consider them 'new' when first introduced. But new hymns cannot be effectively introduced without some kind of congregational practice. There is also the need for careful planning and preparation. An annual hymn festival is a useful way of getting a congregation to learn new hymns which can then be used during the following months. In churches where musical talent is discovered, it should be fostered and encouraged to ensure that it is used to the full, not simply in singing and playing but also in writing appropriate music for the worship of their congregations.

Second, there are *psalms*. In the singing of the psalms the Church of the New Covenant shares in the praise of the Church of the Old Covenant. Undoubtedly, psalms will continue to be sung to Anglican chant where there is the right musical leadership and the necessary enthusiasm. But there are other ways of singing the psalms. There are metrical versions, such as those in *Psalm Praise* and *With One Voice*, which can be easily sung without the difficulties some small congregations find with a pointed psalter. Then there are responsive psalms, such as those of Joseph Gelineau, where the verses are sung by a cantor or choir with the congregation responding with a repeated refrain. (A full collection of responsive psalms will be found in *A Responsorial Psalm Book*, edited by Geoffrey Boulton Smith, Collins, London 1980.)

Third, there are *canticles*. In general these are the songs of the New Covenant, the counterparts of the psalms, the songs of the Old Covenant, which express the joy and fulfilment of salvation in the Lord Jesus Christ. Again, with the exception of *Hail, gladdening Light*, these will be sung to Anglican chant, but there is no need always to use traditional chants. There are modern chants which need exploring. (A good mixture of old and new chants can be found in *The RSCM Chant Book*, edited by Lionel Dakers, which is designed to complement *The Psalms, A New Translation for Worship*, the liturgical psalter used in *ASB 1980*. About twenty-five modern chants can be found in *Psalm Praise*.)

Fourth, there are *responses* and *acclamations*. These are the responsive prayers and praises of the congregation and there are many of them in *ASB 1980*. There

J.S. Bach (1685-1750) leading his family in morning prayers

are the versicles and responses in Morning and Evening Prayer, but the old settings associated with the Book of Common Prayer cannot effectively be used with the new words. Here, again, is the opportunity to learn to sing a 'new song' by using the settings specially written for *ASB 1980* responses.

Particularly important are the acclamations which punctuate the eucharistic prayers. Music is able to convey the deeper meaning of words and these acclamations cry out to be sung aloud by the whole congregation: *Christ has died: Christ is risen: Christ will come again.* Here the corporate expression of faith is given an extra dimension of unanimity and power through music.

Choir music
The choir is part of the congregation, part of the people of God, and not some special hybrid group set apart from both clergy and congregation. The choir is the servant of the larger congregation, leading and supporting the whole assembly. Depending on the size of the church, the choir may comprise twenty or thirty people, or just two or three. But whatever the size the function is the same: to lead and stimulate the singing

of the whole congregation. A common temptation for churches with choirs is to use them to entertain the congregation, usually about half-way through the worship proceedings. Although there is a place for choral pieces on the theme of the day or season, most choirs would be better occupied in using their gifts to encourage the singing of the congregation. This is best done by the so-called 'alternation practice', that is, in the singing of a hymn, the choir and the greater congregation take a verse in turn. The choir sings, perhaps in a special setting, one verse, and then the congregation sings the next verse on its own, and so on alternately through the hymn. Responsive psalms can be sung in the same antiphonal manner with the choir singing the verses and the people answering with the refrain.

Instrumental music
The psalms are full of references to the use of musical instruments in the worship of the people of God. The tabernacle and temple services were attended by a tremendous variety of instrumental sound. However, in the early Church instruments were generally forbidden and only the music of the human voice allowed. John Calvin, in sixteenth century Geneva, argued that in-

John Calvin (1509-1564)

strumental music was part of Jewish ceremonial and was therefore abrogated by the sacrifice of Christ. Thus for Calvin, instrumental music is a pre-Christian phenomenon which cannot form part of the worship of the Church of the New Covenant. But the Lutheran Church has argued that in Christ we are free to use the gifts of God's creation in his worship. Psalm 150, therefore, is equally applicable to the people of God under the New Covenant as it was to the people of God under the Old Covenant, that is, anything that is bangable or blowable can and should be used in the worship of God.

Every congregation has within it people who are musically gifted. The New Testament teaches that individual gifts are to be used to build up the whole body, yet we generally allow only one musically gifted person to have a leading role in our worship, and he or she sits at the organ console. We need to replace our overbearing organs with smaller ones (or at least learn to restrict the use of the ones we have to genuinely leading the congregation), to discover what instrumentalists we have – brass, woodwind, strings, recorders, whatever – and then to use them together to lead the congregation, which may well discover what a joy and a wonder it is to hear itself sing!

A question of perspective

We need to remember that the song we sing today follows in the wake of the song of the morning stars at creation (Job 38.7) and in anticipation of the song of the redeemed in the new creation (Revelation 14.1-3). The music of our worship, as each forgiven sinner sings and plays his praise to God in the company of other forgiven sinners, may not be technically perfect. But God's ears hear differently from ours and are attuned to the heart as well as the sound made by mouth and hand. What God requires from us is not musical perfection but that each may be faithful in using all the musical skills, gifts and accomplishments he has created to glorify him and to enrich and support the music of the worship of his redeemed people.

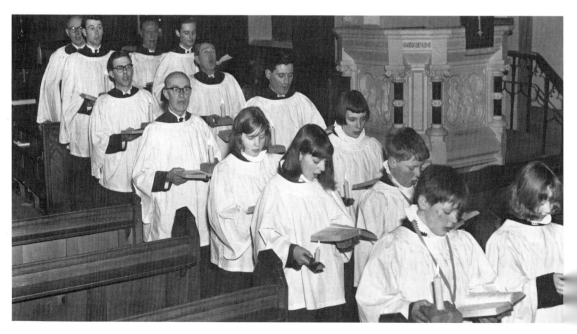

Souls and bodies

Augustine of Hippo once described a Christian as 'a halleluiah from head to foot and from top to toe'. At an Easter communion service one year a dramatic healing took place in his presence. 'Everyone', he wrote, 'burst into a prayer of thankfulness to God. The whole church soon rang with the clamour of rejoicing.' It was spontaneous and united and Augustine writes about it as something natural and not altogether unexpected and certainly not to be frowned on. In the words of Peter, we are to be 'a people set apart to tell out the praises of God' (1 Peter 2.9).

All Christian gatherings should be permeated with praise, not just the so-called worship services. In some churches even the holy communion can be devoid of any praise. It can be said or intoned in a dull monotonous voice and can be more reminiscent of the funeral than the marriage service. (Though, in passing, it should be said that the funeral of a Christian ought to be a worship service as much as anything else.) There should be praise in our homes, praise in our Parochial Church Council meetings, praise in the General Synod, praise in prison; in fact praise everywhere and at all times.

'Prepare to meet your God'

The text beloved of bill-board evangelists can only mean one thing. Amos, when he prophesied these words, had no doubt about the reception God's people were going to receive at that meeting. It was to be anything but warm and friendly. But the text does express the need for God's people to prepare themselves for the celebration of their God. What was to the prophet a word of impending doom can be for us a word of instruction.

We need to get to church in good time and be properly prepared for what is to follow. The practice of fasting on Sunday morning is recommended. We need to 'hang loose' during this time, open to the Lord and prepared to meet him. If we have a static view of worship – that it consists of sitting and listening to sermons, standing to sing hymns and kneeling to pray prayers – all of which is led by a few remote people, then preparation is rather less important. Even then we do need to prepare ourselves for *listening* as well as making our own contribution. But if we have a more dynamic concept of worship, which involves a whole lot of people in active participation, then it is all the more important that we *all* come prepared and ready.

A good rule for a minister is to be in church or vestry at least thirty minutes before every service and earlier still if he has a lot to do in preparation. The last half hour before the service should be spent quietly preparing himself for what is to take place. For others, ten minutes should be a minimum time for preparation in church before the service.

TAKING PART

The New Testament concept of worship implies the active involvement of those present. There is never the suggestion that some people (a priestly élite) should be doing it for everyone else. We need to be sensitive to those around us in a service or meeting. It is not the height of spirituality to ignore everyone and concentrate on the Lord; or to be so lost in God that we are not aware of our fellow worshippers. In a sense we need to be tuned in both to the Lord and to them at one and the same time so that we are really together in what we are doing. Our neighbours may well not be in the same position as we are in. They may be fearful, depressed, feeling trapped, inhibited or plain browned off. They may be strangers or pillars of the Church. They may be Christians, humanists or Zen Buddhists. The Holy Spirit will teach us sensitivity and give us awareness of human need around us. Obviously if we raise our hands in worship and sing lustily and show immense enthusiasm when we are standing next to a person in the pit of depression it will not exactly be helpful.

This brings us to an important point in our participation; how far should we be governed by our feelings when it comes to worship and how far should this affect our worship? If we don't 'feel like it', should we desist and will it be hypocritical to go on when we are feeling like death warmed up and wishing we were almost anywhere else? There is a simple answer to this – our feelings should never dictate to us or deflect us from that fundamental duty of man to worship God and enjoy him for ever. Only when we have sinned, particularly when it is against our brother Christians, are we prohibited from worshipping God. Jesus said, 'therefore, if you are offering your gift at the altar and there remember that your brother has something against you, leave your gift there in front of the altar. First go and be reconciled to your brother; then come and offer your gift' (Matthew 5.23-24). Private and, if necessary, public confession of sin is always (if sin has been committed) a necessary prelude to worship. Without it our worship is hypocritical. The prophet Amos had something to say about this. He brings this word from the Lord, 'I hate, I despise your religious feasts . . . away with the noise of your songs! I will not listen to the music of your harps. But let justice roll on like a river, righteousness like a never-failing stream' (5.21,23-24). The prophet castigates the people of God

TURNING EAST

Turning east for the saying of the creed began in the Church of England in the 17th century but makes less sense now that many churches are no longer east/west in their liturgical orientation. In the early Church, people used to turn east to confess their faith at baptism or to pray facing the paradise 'Eastward of Eden'; there is no sense in which one part of the church at the east end is more holy or contains more of God's presence. The new services have no instructions about which way to face. Often in a re-ordered church (for example, where the seating has been turned into a semi-circle) the ministers will be facing the people throughout.

STAND, KNEEL, SIT

At some points in the Alternative Service Book services a one word instruction is given to indicate where it is particularly appropriate to stand, kneel, sit. The notes to the services say 'for the rest of the service, local custom may be established and followed'.

The practice of kneeling for so much of the service spread gradually during the middle ages and was enshrined in the 1662 Prayer Book to such an extent the people need stand only for the Gospel and the creed and sit for the Epistle and the sermon, remaining kneeling during the rest of the service. Standing for prayer, was the custom of the early Church (and still is in the eastern Orthodox Church); in early basilicas and churches right up until the time of the reformation there were seats provided only for the bishop and ministers with the congregation remaining standing throughout the service, apart from the weak and the feeble who had benches along the walls (hence the saying about the weak going to the wall), but nowadays the minister tends to be on his feet doing things all the time with the congregation just sitting there watching, as in a theatre.

When you visit different churches, you will find that each is adopting its own particular customs about sitting and kneeling and standing. In general, there is much to be said for sitting to listen to the readings, sermons and for some meditation; for kneeling for the penitential parts of the service; for standing to praise God, to be ready to serve him and to be ready to walk about to exchange greetings with fellow worshippers as in the Peace in the communion service.

EXCHANGING THE KISS OF PEACE

Simply called 'The Peace', in Alternative Service Rite A, this is the point at which a number of different things might happen. The president says some words emphasising our unity in Christ and he then says 'The peace of the Lord be always with you' and everyone replies 'and also with you'. That might be all that happens, or he might go on to say 'Let us offer one another a sign of peace' or use some other words to indicate that people should greet one another in a way that is appropriate for them. Sometimes the Peace is exchanged between the ministers on the sanctuary and then brought down to the end of each row by one of them or by a server. Sometimes there is a spontaneous eruption in the congregation with people shaking hands or hugging one another, or moving around from one part of the church to another in order to greet people. Clearly the action needs to be related to the relationship between the two people doing it. For husband and wife solemnly to shake hands when they might give one another a hug or a kiss would seem a little incongruous, but it is as well to remember what is happening at this point, it is a demonstration of the Lord's peace existing between us and, if there is not that peace, this is perhaps a good point in the service to ask one another for forgiveness, to get straight with one another as we have just got straight with God.

THE SIGN OF THE CROSS

Making the sign of the cross is acceptable if it is a helpful reminder to us that we are saved by the cross of Christ and cleansed by his blood, and provided it is not just a lucky gesture or done, perhaps, half automatically.

for worshipping God and at the same time continuing to deal unjustly with one another. God would not, in these circumstances, accept their worship as authentic. Ritual can never replace righteousness.

But other than sin we are to worship and praise God in all circumstances. 'I will extol the Lord at all times; his praise will always be on our lips' wrote the Psalmist (34.1). 'Rejoice in the Lord always', says Paul; 'I will say it again: Rejoice' (Philippians 4.4.). In the Sermon on the Mount Jesus spoke of the blessedness of those who are insulted, persecuted, slandered and falsely accused, '*rejoice and be glad* because great is your reward in heaven' (Matthew 5.11-12). We are to worship and praise God regardless of our feelings, although we are to be sensitive to the feelings of others in the way we do it. We are not to wait until we 'feel like it'. Nor when we do worship God are we to be crippled with false guilt. Rather we shall find, when we obey God and worship him, that the feelings may soon catch up.

THE SHOUT OF PRAISE

The New International Version has translated Psalm 66.1 'shout with joy to God, all the earth'. This is a faithful rendering of the Hebrew. The RSV has softened the implications of this with 'make a joyful

noise to God'. The word *ruwa* means literally 'to split the ears with sound; that is, to *shout* (for alarm or joy); to make a joyful noise'. The noun (*teruwah*) means a battle cry. In Psalm 89.15 we are told 'blessed are the people who know the *battle cry*'. It is interesting, too, that Psalm 66 in some Greek manuscripts used by the early Christians is given the title 'a psalm of the resurrection'. We catch the significance of this in the Orthodox Church's declaration 'the Lord is risen' and the response which is shouted out 'He is risen indeed, alleluia'.

Of course not *all* praise should be noisy. But the distinct impression we get of praise in both Old and New Testaments is that it contains a healthy dose of *fortissimo* alongside the more lyrical *pianissimo* parts. In Nehemiah 12.43 we are told 'the sound of rejoicing in Jerusalem could be heard far away'. How far does the sound of our rejoicing carry? The reality of praise must never be registered in decibels. But there is an important place for the shout of praise in our worship, particularly in the versicles and responses of our services. Let the 'festal shout' as someone has called it (not the frenzied primal scream) go up – and reverberate in our worship.

HANDS UP

In the first line of the famous hymn of Martin Rinkart are the words, 'Now thank we all our God with hearts *and hands* and voices'. This seventeenth century author regards our hands as a part of our anatomy which should be active in worship and he wasn't thinking of our holding a prayer book or a hymn book! The lifting up of hands in worship is as old as the bible. In Psalm 63.4 we read, 'I will praise you as long as I live, and in your name *I will lift up my hands*'. In Psalm 134.2 the Psalmist writes '*lift up your hands* in the sanctuary and praise the Lord'. Paul says the same thing about prayer in 1 Timothy 2.8 'I want men everywhere *to lift up holy hands in prayer*'. There is evidence that this predominantly Jewish practice continued to be normal in the Christian Church for several centuries. St Augustine of Hippo wrote a short homily on Psalm 63.4 encouraging Christians to raise their hands in prayer because 'our Lord raised his hands for us on the cross'. To raise one's hands is universally to declare 'I surrender', and as such it is a meaningful gesture.

The practice can also be inferred from one of the most basic Hebrew words for 'worship' – *yadah*. This means 'to proclaim, to testify, to worship with extended hands'. There is an alternative but similar posture which symbolises silent adoration. The outstretched hands are lowered until they are parallel to the ground with our elbows tucked into our side. This has been called the *deisis* posture beloved of Russian icons. It is as if one is receiving a baby into one's arms.

But the open hands express something else. They are in marked contrast to the clenched fist sign of armed revolution. Christians in worship open themselves to the Lord. Open hands symbolise the readiness to receive anything – a new call to arduous service, the operating of charismatic gifts or crucifixion itself. Paul sums this up in Romans 12.1, 'I urge you, brothers, in view of God's mercy, to offer your bodies as living sacrifices, holy and pleasing to God, *which is your spiritual worship*'. True worship implies self-sacrifice, without which the outward postures and gestures are meaningless. It is such worshippers for whom Jesus said the Father was searching (John 4.23).

Anglican diversity

The proverbial diversity of the Church of England, catholic and protestant, ancient and modern, is nowhere better seen than in the variety of its worship. The *via media* beloved of historians writing about the days of the first Elizabeth is a myth. The Church has never had an established, uniform, 'middle of the road' line, but has successively swung backwards, forwards and

sideways and yet contained most of its swinging under the C of E umbrella. Even the Act of Uniformity, now replaced largely by the Worship and Doctrine Measure and the new Canons, seems to have allowed considerable scope for differences between churches in the way they worshipped.

But it is particularly at times of great creativity, change and experiment, such as we have seen in the last twenty years, that the diversity becomes even more apparent. To suppose that this is entirely due to the work of the Liturgical Commission would be an error. Spiritual and sociological forces have been at work in other areas than merely the words we use for worship. Theological thinking, architecture, sociological work on the nature of community, the new burst of creativity in song and hymn writing, renewal in all its various forms: these have hit different churches and congregations in different ways, and the result can be seen in the increasing variety in their worship. The immense scope for variety now allowed both by the Worship and Doctrine Measure and the Canons, and by *ASB 1980* has been yet another vehicle and stimulus to all this.

What follows is an attempt to give a kaleidoscopic impression of this variety – the sort of thing one might find as a casual dropper-in at a number of different churches up and down the country. It provides some indication of the things to look for: the words of the services being used; the relationship of the worship leader to the congregation; the number of different people involved in leading the service; the evidences of the Spirit's presence; the arrangement of seating and the worship area; the use of colour, music, movement, both ceremonial and dance or drama; the effect of all this on the congregation, as the needs of individuals are met, as they feel disturbed or threatened, and as they are drawn closer to God who is the centre of their worship.

A country parish

We worship in a setting that is traditional in setting and moderately catholic in emphasis. The service itself is a Series 3 Parish Communion, but the colour, the choir, the candles take away from it the pushing modernity that it might have in other settings and give it a timelessness that is enlarging rather than restricting. It is a service that tends sometimes to be rather weak in the ministry of the word, although we have one regular preacher who knows how to make a ten minute sermon telling and powerful. But the real emphasis and power of the service is in the ministry of the sacrament. It was the objectivity and spiritual quality of this that drew us to the church and that continues to feed us in it. We are drawn away from all the bustle of activist Christianity and given space to share real food and drink for the journey.

Outer-London urban parish

This church turned its furnishings sideways a few years ago. The communion table, covered with a simple white cloth, is now situated centrally on a low dais, and worship takes place in the semi-round. Structural adjustments inside the building have yet to be completed (the old chancel is to be screened off for example), but the lay-out has a pleasing simplicity about it and creates an immediate sense of full congregational involvement in what is going on. The main service is the weekly family communion. Here, as in the other services, members of the congregation are active in different parts of the worship and all the family come forward to the communion rail. Once a month there is the opportunity to remain at the rail for prayer and laying on of hands for healing. The service is followed by breakfast together before the congregation divides up into all-age Sunday school (including the adults), and this is where the main ministry of the word takes place.

A market town parish

Chaos! This was my first impression of the church. I was thrown headlong into the Family Service on Harvest Sunday.

A gaggle of children running up to the front to deposit baskets of flowers and fruit at the benevolent feet of the vicar; one tiny child needed help with a basket almost as big as himself; the vicar wore a suit to conduct the service; readings from a lady from the congregation; prayers led by primary school children; choruses by infants; a 'talk' lavishly illustrated by an overhead projector.

The service has no apprarent shape or direction; it lacked the beauty, formality and dignity of my own, more catholic tradition. I found the whole service rather disturbing.

In a Midland town

The service begins with a procession of the choir from the west door to the stalls in the chancel. Our church is very old – 12th century in fact – and very beautiful. It has that deep calm about it, and that strong sense of the presence of God, and the dignity of the robed choir and clergy fit in well with this.

We sing the service to one of the more highbrow settings (not many people join in but the choir sings well). Just recently, members of the congregation have started to get involved in reading lessons, and even in reading the prayers. Some people like it, but others don't, because they can't hear so clearly. The children go out before the Gospel, and stay out during the rest of the service, so that we can have a quiet and reverent atmosphere. We don't share the Peace together, as some people find that disruptive to their concentrating on worship. When we go up for communion, the choir sing quiet eucharistic hymns, and that really draws me close to God. I go away from the service sensing that I have been in a different world, and feeling refreshed to go out into the week ahead.

A student community

At first it was very strange to me – the whole idea of being gathered around the 'table' I had always been used to the communion table being at the sharp end of the church, closed in by rails, and here we were sitting around a simple wooden table, with no rails, just as if we had come together for a meal. The congregation was on six sides in a kind of 'rugby ball' shape. In some ways I liked it because you felt part of a big family; but in other ways, there was a lack of awesomeness and reverence. When we came to the prayers, everyone chipped in with their own, and no one seemed to be embarrassed to speak. At the Peace we all got up and walked around, greeting (sometimes even hugging!) our brothers and sisters in Christ. Then we stood for the Thanksgiving Prayer, and received the bread and wine standing in a circle around the table. That was very hard at first, because it meant looking into the eyes of the person who was administering – but then when he said my name, it struck me that Jesus had actually died for *me*! It was that strange mix of being a community together, and yet being important as an individual in the sight of God.

A North of England parish

Our church has changed over the past ten years – the new services have been welcomed, and the furniture has been moved around accordingly. The altar has been moved to the part of the chancel nearest to the congregation, and our robed choir has been disbanded. (We now have a music group with guitars, flute, drums, and other instruments instead.) The changes have livened up our worship, and drawn a lot of young people in. We even experiment from time to time with drama, presenting the Gospel in modern terms, and dance – sometimes planned, and sometimes a spontaneous expression of the joy of being in God's presence. The Lord has also blessed our church with charismatic gifts and so people from time to time speak in tongues or prophesy. Healing is experienced, too; and sometimes, at the end of the communion, some people remain kneeling at the rails for the laying-on-of-hands. I feel our church has changed for the better, but there are some people who left because they preferred the old ways.

In South London

Our parish church has been gently introducing the alternative communion service to its Sunday morning worship, and it now alternates week by week with the Prayer Book. Though the building itself is always full at festivals, it is much larger than the weekly requirements of the church and a very high ceiling creates a feeling of emptiness that is very difficult to fill. The church is uncommitted in terms of tradition. Led by a robed choir and clergy the services are dignified and reflective in character – the pace of the service being generally determined by the size of the building. There is certainly a stillness about the building that is valued by many who worship here. The new communion service still involves a feeling of slight awkwardness and the change for many of us has been painful and not always easy to understand. What is slowly growing in the services is a renewed awareness of the *corporate* nature of worship.

Law and choice

Like any other large institution in the land, the Church of England has to have rules and be subject to the law of the country. But its rules are more complex than those of most churches because of its particular history. In the middle ages the clergy, along with all the regulations governing the worship they led, were ultimately dependent upon Rome, and not on any English government at all. The whole Roman Catholic Church was, in our terms, a 'multi-national company'! At the Reformation, Henry VIII nationalised the English branch of this company, by a series of Acts of Parliament which detached the Church from its obedience to Rome, and made it in effect a department of state (with Henry himself as the 'Head'). Then in Edward VI's time (1547-53) parliament imposed successive forms of worship upon the Church of England by 'Acts of Uniformity'. Thus, from the time of the Reformation onwards, the law of the land *was* the law of the Church of England. Parliament made the law – bishops and clergy were supposed to enforce it and to keep it. In 1662 the Convocations of Canterbury and York (which are representative bodies of the bishops and clergy of the two Provinces) revised the Book of Common Prayer, but it was still Parliament which imposed it on the Church – and 'Uniformity' in the use of 'Common' Prayer was the law of the *land*. The Church of England was the English nation in its religious aspect, and therefore was governed by parliament.

Over the centuries this position has slowly changed. In 1920 a new arrangement came into force, whereby the 'National Assembly of the Church of England' (corresponding to the present General Synod) was allowed (by Act of Parliament, of course) to draft church legislation and to present it to parliament as 'Measures'. A 'Measure' cannot be amended by parliament, but is subject to a single vote in the Lords and in the Commons before gaining the Royal Assent. The new arrangement was quickly tested when, in 1927 and again in 1928, the National Assembly passed a com-

pletely new Prayer Book (though it contained the old services as well as the revised ones) and the Commons twice rejected the Measure which would have authorised it for use.

After this the policy of the Church of England for many years was not to revise the services till there was a change in the law. What was wanted was that parliament should give to the Assembly – or, now, the General Synod – powers over liturgy. So there came in the 'Prayer Book (Alternative and Other Services) Measure 1965', which allowed the Assembly to authorise services for short-term experiment 'off its own bat' without going to parliament. In 1970 the National Assembly was converted into the General Synod. Then there came the Church of England (Worship and Doctrine) Measure 1974, and this gave to the General Synod full powers in relation to liturgy, saving only that Synod cannot withdraw the authorisation of the 1662 Book of Common Prayer – parliament remains the guardian of that book.

The Church of England makes its own rules in General Synod, and these are called 'Canons'. Where the law of the land is changed by a Measure (as with the Worship and Doctrine Measure mentioned above), then Synod also passes Canons to give expression to those changes. But at many points nowadays parliament has already given power to Synod to make Canons, and thus no change in the law of the land is needed. A complete new code of Canons has been authorised in the years since 1964, and it is currently published in a loose-leaf binder. There is continuous change (usually of a minor sort) happening to the Canons, so that this is the best form in which to produce them. The law of the Church which is quoted in the questions and answers below is as it stood in the summer of 1980. After a lapse of time it will be important to check whether any changes have been made.

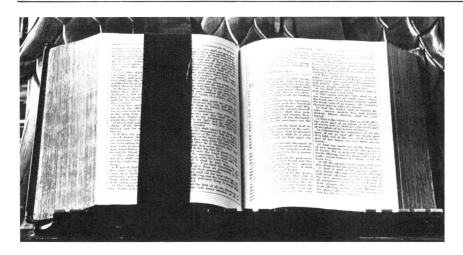

QUESTIONS

1 Who authorises different sorts of services?

a. The 1662 Book of Common Prayer	Parliament
b. All services 'alternative' to those in the Book of Common Prayer, including the Alternative Service Book	General Synod
c. Services for special diocesan use (as, for instance, the institution and induction of a new vicar)	The bishop of the diocese
d. Other parish services, which are not 'alternative' to those in the Book of Common Prayer (as, for instance, a family or evangelistic service)	The minister of the parish
e. Accession and other similar services	The monarch

2 What powers has the diocesan bishop?

a. He has no power to prohibit services authorised by monarch, parliament or Synod, or to authorise 'alternative' services *not* authorised by these bodies.

b. He *has* power to authorise services for special diocesan use (see under 1c above).

c. He *has* power to decide which form of authorised service shall be used at ordinations and confirmations.

d. He has the power (and the duty) to decide certain matters which may be referred to him when there are disagreements in a particular parish. But these are very rarely needed.

3 What powers has the minister?

a. He *has* power to produce services which are not 'alternative' to those in the Book of Common Prayer, and are not diocesan services authorised as under 2 above.

'Subject to any regulation made from time to time by the Convocation of the Province, the minister may on occasion for which no provision is made in the Book of Common Prayer or by the General Synod under Canon B2 or by the Convocation, archbishops or Ordinary under Canon B4 use forms of service considered suitable by him for those occasions' (Canon B5, 1 and 2).

b. He has no power to decide on his own *which* forms of authorised services shall be used for the regular public services in church (excluding the 'Occasional Offices'). He has to agree with his PCC (see under 4 below) about these.

c. He *has* power to decide which form shall be used of the 'Occasional Offices' (which are usually reckoned as the initiation services, marriage, and funeral services), except for the confirmation service (which is decided by the bishop, as under 2c above). However, his power is limited in that in the use of these 'Occasional Offices' he must inform the persons concerned, and they have the right to object (and, if they cannot persuade the minister, to appeal to the bishop, as under 2d above).

When holy communion is used at a marriage or at a funeral, it forms part of the latter service. Therefore, even if (for instance) the Parochial Church Council has decided to use only the Prayer Book Communion Service, they cannot prevent an alternative form of Communion being used at a Marriage or at a Funeral.

4 What powers has the Parochial Church Council?

a. The PCC has *no* power to authorise any service.

b. The PCC *has* the power to decide jointly with the minister (as under 3b above) on the form of services (whether, for instance, they should come from 1662 or from the *ASB 1980*) for regular public worship in church, i.e. for Morning and Evening Prayer and Holy Communion.

5. But can a PCC decide *which* options shall be used within a service which they agree should be used?

In law they have no powers to do this. If they objected to the use of some optional part by the minister, they *could* withdraw permission for the use of the service as a whole, until he agreed with them about this option. But, as with so many matters, this should be settled by frank and loving discussion with a view to finding agreement with each other without using legal powers as a threat.

6. What happens when minister and PCC cannot agree about which forms of authorised service to use?

Canon B.3 says that the general answer is that the 1662 forms shall be used. But where another authorised form has been used for at least two of the previous four years, then the PCC can order that that form shall be used during the period in which minister and PCC are trying to find agreement. (This means that a new minister cannot insist on taking a parish back to 1662 if they have already used another form which they prefer for that minimum period of two years). Once there is agreement, then the agreed services are used. There is no 'appeal' to the bishop mentioned in the Canons – the matter has to be 'sweated out' locally! And it *may* be that agreement will only come by the provision of a mixed pattern – perhaps some ancient and some modern services on different occasions in the month.

7. What about minor variations in conducting services?

Canon B.5.1 permits the minister to 'make and use variations which are not of substantial importance in any form of service authorised by Canon B.1.' The variations are to be 'reverent and seemly and neither contrary to nor indicative of any departure from the doctrines of the Church of England.' For this there *is* an appeal allowed to the bishop (see under 2d above).

8. What about hymns?

The Church of England has *no* authorised hymn books, and anything (yes, anything!) can be sung as a hymn. The minister has the right to choose hymns to go with authorised services (and the organist or musical director has the right to resign!). Usually a PCC (which spends the money) will decide which hymn book to have in the pews.

9. What powers has the 'ordinary worshipper'?

None, except to keep his mouth shut when he does not want to join in, or to stay away when he does not wish to attend. If he desires a 'say' in what goes on, he will have to be elected to his PCC at the Annual General Meeting. He should not write to his bishop with complaints unless he has clear evidence that the rules (as summarised above) are not being observed.

10. Who decides which version of the bible should be used?

When the version is used to replace a passage of scripture, including the psalms, printed in the Book of Common Prayer, both minister and Parochial Church Council must first agree. If they disagree, the printed passage is used.

On all other occasions, the minister decides which version to use.

The following versions are authorised for use:

The Authorised or King James Version (AV or KJV)

The Revised Version (RV)

The Revised Standard Version (RSV)

The New English Bible (NEB)

The Jerusalem Bible (JB)

The Good News Bible (GNB)

The Revised Psalter

The Liturgical Psalter (The Psalms: A new translation for worship)

As well as the versions authorised he may use any version found by the House of Bishops to be doctrinally sound (Report of Proceedings, November 1976 page 120).

11. Who can take services?

- *Holy Communion.* Note 2 in Rite A in *ASB 1980* indicates the parts of the service which must be taken by the President, who must be in priest's orders. It also says that if necessity dictates, a deacon or lay person may preside over the ministry of the word, presumably here meaning ante-communion.
- *Morning and Evening Prayer.* The whole service may be taken by a clergyman, deaconess, lay worker, reader, or (in an emergency) a churchwarden. A lay person should use 'us' instead of 'you' in the absolution. There is no need to use a blessing at the end of the service.
- *Initiation Services.* An ordained clergyman or a deaconess may baptise, as may a lay person in an emergency. Only a bishop may confirm.
- *Marriage Service.* Only an ordained clergyman (including a deacon) may perform a marriage.
- *Funeral Services.* A funeral may be taken by an ordained clergyman, or, with the authorisation of the bishop and the goodwill of the persons responsible, by a deaconess, accredited lay worker or reader.

The law runs on far beyond these points. It covers the vesture of ministers, the provision of the bread and wine for communion, the publication of banns of marriage, and a host of other matters. Many are mentioned elsewhere in this book. But for detailed knowledge, the first place to look is in the loose-leaf binder which holds the code of Canons.

Warning footnote: Christianity is about a law of love, and not about 'my rights'. The law of love demands that very special regard should be paid to the consciences of minorities, and that every attempt should be made to reach decisions by consensus without minorities feeling hurt. It is better to use the 'less than the best' service with unanimity, than the 'best' one with division.

Finding the service you want

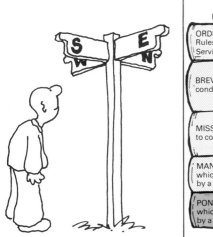

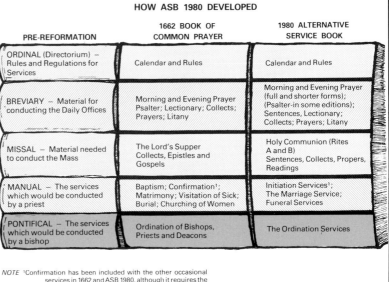

	HOW ASB 1980 DEVELOPED		
PRE-REFORMATION	1662 BOOK OF COMMON PRAYER	1980 ALTERNATIVE SERVICE BOOK
ORDINAL (Directorium) – Rules and Regulations for Services	Calendar and Rules	Calendar and Rules
BREVIARY – Material for conducting the Daily Offices	Morning and Evening Prayer Psalter; Lectionary; Collects; Prayers; Litany	Morning and Evening Prayer (full and shorter forms); (Psalter-in some editions); Sentences, Lectionary; Collects; Prayers; Litany
MISSAL – Material needed to conduct the Mass	The Lord's Supper Collects, Epistles and Gospels	Holy Communion (Rites A and B) Sentences, Collects, Propers, Readings
MANUAL – The services which would be conducted by a priest	Baptism; Confirmation[1]; Matrimony; Visitation of Sick; Burial; Churching of Women	Initiation Services[1]; The Marriage Service; Funeral Services
PONTIFICAL – The services which would be conducted by a bishop	Ordination of Bishops, Priests and Deacons	The Ordination Services

NOTE [1]Confirmation has been included with the other occasional services in 1662 and ASB 1980, although it requires the presence of a bishop.

HOW THE SHAPE AND BALANCE OF *ASB 1980* DEVELOPED

The chart above shows that the shape of *ASB 1980* and the kind of material included in it are not very different from the 1662 Book of Common Prayer; and it has its basis in services which went back even further than that. Cranmer's 1549 and 1552 Prayer Books drew together, under one cover, material for all the services of the Church. Previously, there had been various separate books, as the diagram shows. In pre-Reformation days, a priest would have had a Breviary, which would have been used for all his daily offices, a Missal which would have included all that was necessary for celebrating Mass, and a third book, called a Manual, which contained all the other specifically priestly services apart from the Mass. He might also have needed a book of rubrics, like the Consuetudinary or the Ordinal, as these were not included within the actual text of the services. It is worth noting that the Roman Catholic Church still makes available several worship books in this kind of way. Cranmer, however, simplified all this in his Prayer Books, drawing together into one volume all that he considered necessary for the worship of the Church, and the Alternative Service Book basically follows that tradition. Many other 'unauthorised' services which are available for occasions other than those mentioned in *ASB 1980*.

Some people, on seeing the Alternative Service Book for the first time, find it rather formidable, with its thousand and more pages, in comparison to the few hundred they may have been used to in the Book of Common Prayer, or the simplicity of the small booklets of the sixties and seventies, which were so easily followed. The reason for this is that the Alternative Service Book offers much more variety than the Book of Common Prayer. The chart on p.71 will guide you through the book. It follows the basic outline of the previous chart, with a note of all specific services included under each heading, and a list of variable material for use with the particular service in column three.

FINDING THE SERVICE YOU WANT

CALENDAR AND RULES	Seasons and Special Days 15 Rules to order the Service 26 General Notes 32	
TYPE OF SERVICE	**SERVICE**	**VARIABLE MATERIAL**
DAILY SERVICE	Morning Prayer (full form) 48 Morning Prayer (shorter form) 73 Evening Prayer (full form) 61 Evening Prayer (shorter form) 82 Morning or Evening Prayer with Holy Communion 71 (notes)	Sunday Themes 1092 Scripture Sentences 35,47 Psalter(1095) Table of Psalms 983 or 1047 (acc to BCP) Lectionary 983 Prayer Book Canticles* 88 Prayers for Various Occasions 97 Litany 99 Subject Index of Prayers 109
COMMUNION SERVICES	**Rite A 113** including Order following the pattern of the Book of Common Prayer 146 **Rite B* 175**	Sunday Themes 1092 Scripture Sentences 35,398 Alternative forms of Commandments 161 Alternative Confessions 165 Collects 398 Readings 398 Table of Psalms 1049 Lectionary 1049, 1071 Alternative forms of Intercessions 166 Alternative Prayer of Humble Access 170 Other Introductory Words to the Peace 170 Proper Prefaces 154 (Special rubrics 1049) Additional Words of Invitation to Communion 172 Alternative Final Prayer 173 Alternative Blessings 159 Eucharistic Prayer for use with the Sick 171 Commandments and Kyries* 207,208 Proper Prefaces* 201,203 Alternative Blessings* 205 Alternative Final Prayer* 209
INITIATION SERVICES	Thanksgiving for the Birth of a Child 213 Thanksgiving after Adoption 218 Baptism, Confirmation, and Holy Communion 223 Baptism and Confirmation without Holy Communion 236 (notes) Baptism and Confirmation at Morning or Evening Prayer 239 (notes) The Baptism of Children 241 The Baptism of Children at Holy Communion 250 (notes) The Baptism of Children at Morning or Evening Prayer 251 (notes) The Confirmation of those already baptised 252 (notes) Confirmation with Holy Communion 253 Confirmation without Holy Communion 258 Confirmation at Morning or Evening Prayer 260 (notes) Renewal of Baptismal Vows 275 Conditional Baptism 279 Emergency Baptism 280	Readings for occasions on which Thanksgiving Services are used on their own 217, 222 Prayers of Penitence 120 Readings 228, 262 Psalms 261 Renewal of Baptismal Vows 275 Communion Propers 235 Psalms for Baptism 261 Readings for Baptism 261 Communion Propers 250 Psalms for Confirmation 261 Readings for Confirmation 262 Communion Propers 257 Other Prayers 258
THE MARRIAGE SERVICE	The Marriage Service 283 The Marriage Service with Holy Communion 301 (notes)	Readings 302 Psalms 294 Additional Prayers 298 Communion Propers 304, 923
FUNERAL SERVICES	The Funeral Service 307 The Funeral of a Child 318 Prayers after the Birth of a still born Child, or the Death of a newly-born Child 322 A Form for the Interment of the Ashes 324 A Service which may be used before a Funeral 325 The Funeral Service with Holy Communion 328	Scripture Sentences 307, 318 Sentences for Committal 315, 321 Additional Prayers 334 Collects 329, 331, 334 Readings 329 Psalms 308 Communion Propers 333, 936
ORDINATION SERVICES	The Ordination of Deacons 339 The Ordination of Priests (also called Presbyters) 351 The Ordination of Deacons and Priests 365 The Ordination or Consecration of a Bishop 382	

* *'Thou' 'thee' form material*   *References are to page numbers in ASB 1980*

WHERE TO FIND WHAT IS NOT IN THE ALTERNATIVE SERVICE BOOK

1 There are services and material authorised in the 1662 Prayer Book which are not to be found in the Alternative Service Book. These are the Quicunque Vult or Athanasian Creed; the service for the churching of women; the Catechism; the commination service; the form of prayer to be used at sea; the accession services. There are also other traditional services such as the coronation service which is authorised by Royal Warrant, but not in the Prayer Book.

2 Various Series 1, 2 and 3 services are authorised until 1985 as follows:
Series 1: Marriage and Burial – this is the set of services similar to the 1928 Prayer Book.
Series 2 revised; Morning and *Evening Prayer* – to be found in the yellowy-green booklet.
Series 2: Baptism and Confirmation – to be found in the dull pink booklet.
Series 2: Holy Communion – to be found in the blue booklet.
Series 3: Holy Communion – to be found in the green booklet.

3 The annual working out of lectionary material is to be found in the SPCK/Mowbrays lectionary.

4 The services to be used with the sick, published as a liturgical commission report in summer 1980, will be a separate booklet if authorised by the General Synod. These include the communion of sick, the ministry of healing with the laying-on of hands and anointing.

5 The Revised Catechism, commended by the Synod for use until 1985. Published by SPCK.

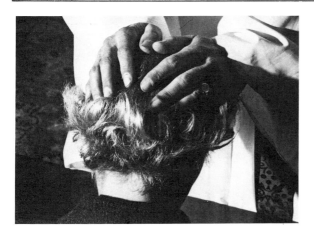

6 Other services not authorised (hence not alternative to the Prayer Book):

Anointing and Healing The Guild of Health and the Guild of St Raphael have forms for the Laying-on of Hands and Anointing with Holy Oil. Michael Botting, *Pastoral and Liturgical Ministry to the Sick*, Grove Booklet 59, 1978, has a selection of suggested services.

The Blessing of Civil Marriage: This matter is under discussion in the dioceses and Synod of the Church of England.

Children's Eucharists The General Synod decided not to include in Rite A a thanksgiving prayer for communion services at which children were present but did not receive communion.

Compline A form of Compline in modern English is available under the title *A Late Evening Service*, Grove Worship Series no 72. Another form is published by Mowbrays.

Exorcism The forms of prayer from the 1974 Archbishop of York's report 'The Christian Ministry of Deliverance and Healing' are reprinted in John Richards, *Exorcism, Deliverance and Healing*, Grove Booklet 44, 1976.

Family Services It is quite possible to base a Family Service on the shortened form of Morning Prayer, or on the first part of the Holy Communion Rite A (see note 24 to that service). Alternatively, it is quite in order for the minister to invent his own service or to use, for example, the Church Pastoral-Aid Society Family Service, *Family Worship*, CPAS 1971.

Harvest Festival

Holy Week See the Joint Liturgical Group's *Holy Week Services*, ed. Ronald Jasper, SPCK and Epworth, 1971; Peter Akehurst, *Keeping Holy Week*, Grove Booklet 41, 1976; J.T. Martin, *Christ our Passover*, *The Liturgical Observation of Holy Week*, SCM. USPG produce a Good Friday service, *The Lord of Love*.

House Blessing See the Church of South India Book of Common Worship Supplement, OUP 1967, p. 211. SPCK publish an Order for the blessing of a house.

Inaugural Services Some general principles and examples of dedicating a building and opening a bookshop are in Colin Buchanan, *Inaugural Services*, Grove Booklet 32, 1974. Other examples, but in older language, are in Bishop Leslie Hunter, *A Diocesan Service Book*, OUP 1965.

Institution Services See Trevor Lloyd, *Institutions and Inductions*, Grove Booklet 15, 1973.

Mothering Sunday Services Many different versions are available. Some are published by Church Information Office, Mothers' Union and Home Words. Good material can also be found in the CIO book of services, *Our Mum*.

The Preface

Every prayer book of the Church of England has had a Preface introducing its contents. In Cranmer's Prayer Books of 1549 and 1552 the Preface was the introductory material which in the 1662 Book is printed under the title 'Concerning the Service of the Church'. This discussed how the bible could have its rightful place in public worship, and how the services could be made simple and easy to follow. It stood as the Preface in 1559 and 1604, and was then relegated to second place (and given its new title) when another Preface was written to introduce the revision of 1662.

This new 1662 Preface stands at the front of the 1662 Prayer Book today. (By law, the 1662 Prayer Book is supposed to start with the Act of Uniformity of 1559, but printers seem regularly to omit it. It is full of the atmosphere of triumph of the churchmen who were ousting the puritans after the Commonwealth period, glorying in 'His Majesty's happy Restoration', and hinting strongly that all parliamentary action taken without the Royal Assent since 1645 was illegal. The Book itself was little changed from 1552 or 1604, but the Preface explains the minor verbal changes and commends some additions.

In 1549 and 1662 the Preface introduced new services. In 1552 the existing Preface from 1549 introduced another set of new services. But with *ASB 1980* the Preface introduces no new services – all were authorised for use some time before *ASB 1980* itself appeared in print. What this Book does is to *collect* the new services together between one set of covers, and the Preface introduces the collection. There is some variation within the collection – some editions have a psalter in them, some not. But there has

also had to be an actual choice of what should be included, and what excluded. Thus no materials authorised or in print in the 1662 Book are included (save for some canticles printed at the end of Morning and Evening Prayer, and some parts of the Order for Holy Communion Rite B). The Thirty-Nine Articles, for instance, are no part of 'alternative services' and do not appear. And the Book as a whole does not have the status of 1662 – clergy and others being licensed say they will use the forms authorised by Canon (which includes the services in *ASB 1980*, but also includes many others), and do not mention any particular book.

Nevertheless the Preface does point out that this collection of services expresses 'the mind of the Church of England in the last quarter of the twentieth century'. This implies the use of the Book for teaching as well as worship, for preparation, study, and private devotion, and as a handbook with some permanence which all should have.

The services, as the Preface says, have been prepared and revised by the Liturgical Commission, and by the Convocations, House of Laity, and General Synod, over a period of fifteen years of non-stop activity. The Preface itself, not being a 'service', has not been seen in General Synod, but stems from the Bishop of Durham's working-party which has handled the presentation and production of *ASB 1980*. The Preface of 1549 and 1552 is associated with the name of Thomas Cranmer; that of 1662 with the name of Robert Sanderson; that of 1980 with the name of John Habgood. The *style* may well derive from the authors – but the *contents* of each Preface are dictated by the contents of each book.

> The provision of alternative services is to be welcomed as an enrichment of the Church's life rather than as a threat to its integrity.
>
> *ASB 1980*, Preface

> I ... declare my belief in the faith which is revealed in the holy scriptures and set forth in the catholic creeds and to which the historic formularies of the Church of England bear witness; and in public prayer and administration of the sacraments, I will use only the forms of service which are authorised or allowed by Canon.
>
> 1975 *Declaration of Assent*

> Hence those who seek to know the mind of the Church of England in the last quarter of the twentieth century will find it in this book.
>
> *ASB 1980*, Preface

> But words, even agreed words, are only the beginning of worship. Those who use them do well to recognise their transience and imperfection; to treat them as a ladder, not a goal; to acknowledge their power in shaping faith and kindling devotion, without claiming that they are fully adequate to the task. Only the grace of God can make up what is lacking in the faltering words of men. It is in reliance on such grace that this book is offered to the Church.
>
> *ASB 1980*, Preface

The Calendar and Lectionary and Rules to Order the Service

The Calendar
Why have Holy Days?

Most people are fortunate and glad enough to enjoy holidays from time to time as a break from work. In the past, however, 'days off' were allowed so that labourers should have an opportunity to go to church: holidays originated as holy days, and were therefore in the nature of extra Sundays. Human need for rest and recreation undoubtedly forms an element in the traditional Christian observance of Sunday, as also in the Jewish Sabbath. But this man-centred interpretation of their purpose does not go to the heart of their significance, which has to do with the believer's attitude to time.

As part of life itself, time needs to be regarded as a gift to be acknowledged before God, who is its author and creator. The Old Testament principle for making such acknowledgement was to set aside a part to represent the whole. Just as a person was expected to offer a tithe of his income (Deuteronomy 12.4-7), so a proportion of time was set aside for God by the offering of sacrifices at the daily hours of prayer, on the weekly sabbath, at the monthly new moon festival, and at the new year (Numbers 28-29). By this means of dedicating a part of one's time, as of one's possessions, to God, the whole was acknowledged as a gift from him. This Jewish tradition has had a very strong influence on Christian worship, especially in the case of the sanctification of time, through the daily hours of prayer and the keeping of Sunday as a Christian sabbath.

FESTIVALS OF CREATION AND OF HISTORY

Numbers 28-29 mentions other holy festivals in addition to those which mark the passage of time. The purpose of these must be considered. The seasons of seed-time and harvest, and man's basic need to gather the fruits of the earth are taken account of in all religions, but the Old Testament emphasis is that the children of Israel would be blessed with abundant crops by keeping the laws of Yahweh rather than by making special prayers or offerings during the season of sowing. When the harvests were gathered in, however, it was a different matter as once again there were divine gifts to be acknowledged with gratitude. So the various harvest festivals, beginning with the firstfruits as a token that God would fulfil his promise, were regarded as times for celebration and thanksgiving (2 Chronicles 8.13). In Israelite worship, however, these creation or nature festivals were overshadowed by the annual commemoration of a historical event, the mighty act by which they had truly become identified as the people of Yahweh: the Passover deliverance from Egypt. This supreme festival may be regarded as a celebration of salvation-history.

In this last respect the Christian Church has received an inheritance from Judaism which it has developed extensively. By contrast, nature festivals have not occupied a significant place in Christian liturgies despite the local influence of

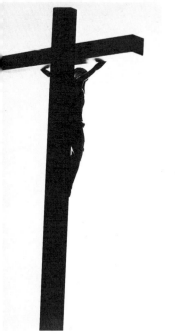

the various pagan cultures into which Christianity has been introduced. Harvest festivals find no place in the Book of Common Prayer!

Since the Passover festival was the season of Christ's crucifixion and resurrection and provided a great deal of symbolic material for the Christian theology of salvation it is not surprising that there developed from earliest times a three-day, Friday to Sunday, celebration of salvation-history linked to the Passover as the heart of the Church's year. At first there was a good deal of controversy as to whether the crucifixion should always be commemorated on the actual day of the Jewish Passover, which can fall on any day of the week. It was clear, however, that the first day of the week had become for Christians a kind of weekly celebration of the resurrection, and therefore the annual commemoration must also conclude on a Sunday.

The date of Easter Day, however, is still calculated according to a formula agreed at the Council of Nicea (325) which ensures that it falls during the Passover moon. The development of Lent as a time of preparation, Holy Week itself, Ascension Day, and the commemoration of the coming of the Holy Spirit at the Jewish harvest festival of Pentecost are all related to the Good Friday-Easter celebration as an annual cycle of Christian salvation-history, providing times for particular observance of the different events each year in the Church's calendar.

An obvious element missing from this pattern was the incarnation. Its inclusion was clearly appropriate, but the humble and obscure birth of Jesus of Nazareth was linked neither to a Jewish festival nor to any particular historical date. As a result the Christmas festival developed much later than the Easter one, and parts of the eastern Church still observe it on 6 January rather than on the western date of 25 December. The twelve days encompassed by these two dates, however, have come to embrace the celebration of events from the birth in the stable to the

visit of the Magi (eastern Christians also remember the baptism of Jesus on the later date).

Given this starting point the Christmas cycle in the Calendar has traditionally been organised to include Advent for preparation, the Circumcision (1 January), the Presentation in the Temple (2 February), and of course the Annunciation (25 March), and even the Nativity of John the Baptist (24 June). All these dates follow from the scriptural evidence. The traditional date for the visit of Mary to Elizabeth, however, has been kept, inconsistently, on 2 July. The Alternative Calendar has now provided a more sensible date of 31 May for its observance in the Church of England.

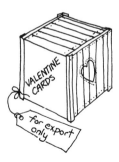

SAINTS' DAYS

In addition to the sanctification of time and the celebration of salvation-history the Christian Church has set aside days for the commemoration of saints. The origin of this practice was connected with the outbreaks of persecution against Christians before the time of Constantine, and during those first three centuries was restricted to a memorial of the witness of those who suffered martyrdom. Church buildings were frequently erected over the tombs of martyrs, and the anniversary of their deaths kept as a reminder of the indissoluble communion of saints, holding both the living and the departed in the unbroken fellowship of Christ. Some of these martyrs were sufficiently well known to be commemorated over a wide area, but in the nature of the case the *sanctorale* (as the calendar of saints is known to distinguish it from the *temporale*, the Church's year, outlined in the previous section) was largely a local compilation, with each diocese having its own list. From the fourth century outstanding Church leaders began to be added to these lists, the supply of martyrs having dried up for the time being. One of the first to be so included was Martin of Tours (died 397), whose feast day on 11 November at one time marked the start of Advent.

THE CALENDAR IN THE BOOK OF COMMON PRAYER

For several reasons the observance of saints' days led to serious liturgical problems arising during the middle ages. The spread of western Christendom meant that the local Roman *sanctorale* (this is, strictly, the variable parts of the services which are proper to each particular saint's day) came to be observed everywhere, thus to some extent destroying the local relevance of such festivals. Perhaps the one exception which proves this rule is the successful promotion of St Valentine! Then the process of adding fresh saints to the calendar inevitably continued, and when the practice for the more important ones of observing an octave (that is, prolonging the special prayers and readings for a whole week beyond the festival) became common, any hope of a systematic daily reading of scripture was virtually lost.

Cranmer's solution was drastic. The *sanctorale* in his first Prayer Book of 1549 provided collect, introit, epistle and gospel for eighteen festivals, all biblical, and also All Saints Day which had to do duty for all the rest, thus reducing the hierarchy of saints to a common fellowship, as the collect points out. In addition the festivals of St Stephen, St John the Evangelist and the Innocents were provided in the traditional place in the *temporale* following Christmas Day. In the second book of 1552 this number was further reduced by one, with the removal of St Mary Magdalene's day. At the same time, however, a few other days were included in the Calendar for which no special prayers were provided. These became known as 'black-letter' days to distinguish them from the former category of 'red-letter' days. They were a reminder that people needed the Church's Calendar for legal and commercial as well as religious purposes. This 'black-letter' list was considerably extended in the 1561 and later editions of the Book of Common Prayer.

The reformation of worship in the Church of England did not affect the structure of the Church's year as a whole. Days of fasting and abstinence were retained during Advent and Lent as well as weekly on Fridays. There was an attempt in Elizabethan times to enforce abstinence on Wednesdays as well in order to help the British fishing industry! The Ember days and Rogation days also continued to be observed.

THE CALENDAR OF THE ALTERNATIVE SERVICE BOOK

The Calendar in *ASB 1980* derives from a scheme of the Joint Liturgical Group. It is used by other churches in England (notably the Methodists). The year is divided into three parts: nine Sundays before Christmas; the 'dominical' season from Christmas to Pentecost; the Sundays after Pentecost.

The pre-Christmas season prepares for the coming of Christ (centering on the Old Testament); the dominical season celebrates Christ himself in the Gospels; the Pentecost season teaches the life of the Church (centering on the Epistles).

The concepts of Lent and Advent are retained, but in a subordinate role. Epiphany also survives.

Within this structure, *ASB 1980* gives a threefold character to holy days:

Principal Holy Days, which consist of Easter, Pentecost and every other Sunday in the year, and also Christmas Day, Maundy Thursday, Good Friday and Ascension Day. These are the days when it is considered reasonable to expect all the faithful to be in church.

Festivals and Greater Holy Days, corresponding to the eighteen Prayer Book 'red-letter' days, together with the three saints' days, Circumcision and Epiphany from the twelve days of Christmas, and the addition of four new festivals: for St Joseph (19 March), St Mary Magdalen (22 July), the Transfiguration (6 August) and the Blessed Virgin Mary (8 September). The Patronal or Dedication Festival of a Church, if not included in the above,

and also Ash Wednesday and the remaining days of Holy Week, are counted in this list. Three of the four new festivals listed here (all except St Joseph) are 'black-letter' days in the Prayer Book Calendar. The date originally proposed for the Virgin Mary by the Liturgical Commission was 15 August, but this was resisted on the doctrinal ground that it was inevitably associated with the Roman dogma of the Assumption, and the practical ground that the many churches dedicated to St Mary did not want to celebrate their patronal festival when a large part of the parish would be away on holiday.

Lesser Festivals and Commemorations, consisting of an extensive revision of the 'black-letter' list. Twenty-three of the Prayer-Book names are retained, although not in every case on the same day. St Alban's day on 17 June was in any case a scribal error: xxii was misread as xvii! Sixty-three new names are provided with the object of making the list more representative of the history of Christianity in Britain, including coverage of the period from medieval to modern times. It is not intended to be exclusive and the addition of diocesan and local commemorations is encouraged. During revision the General Synod felt that the official list should not include post-Reformation figures who had for conscience sake renounced connection with the Church of England and on this ground removed that truly ecumenical figure Richard Baxter, and also the prophetic George Fox and the hymn writer Isaac Watts, while managing to retain John and Charles Wesley. Somewhat inconsistently the Non-jurors William Law and Thomas Ken and the independent Baptist John Bunyan are nevertheless approved. A concern to include a reasonable representation of faithful women produced a controversial decision to add Josephine Butler to those in the Revision Committee's proposals – in which the House of Bishops restored the good lady by a majority of one vote when the whole Synod had previously dismissed her by a majority of three!

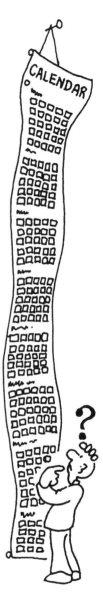

PEOPLE COMMEMORATED IN THE *ASB 1980* CALENDAR

Richard Hooker (3 November, c.1554-1600). The apologist of the Elizabethan Settlement of 1559 and one of the greatest English theologians. His five books of 'The Laws of Ecclesiastical Polity' see the Church as an organic, not a static, institution in which local circumstances and history, as well as scripture, can determine church government and worship, so long as nothing is done which is plainly contrary to scripture.

Thomas ÀBeckett (29 December, ? 1118-70). The picture from a manuscript in the British Museum shows Thomas, Archbishop of Canterbury from 1154, being murdered in his cathedral on 29 December 1170 by four knights inspired by the angry words of King Henry II. He was, for obvious reasons, deleted from the Calendar by Henry VIII.

Charles Simeon (12 November, 1759-1836). A leader of the Evangelical revival. Fellow of King's College, Cambridge and Vicar of Holy Trinity, Cambridge from 1783 to 1836. His biblical preaching and training classes influenced at least 600 future ministers and filled the 900 seats of Trinity Church. He was one of the founders of the Church Missionary Society and founded a body of Trustees, the Simeon Trustees, to administer church patronage.

John Wyclif (31 December, 1329-84). Master of Balliol College Oxford until deprived by Archbishop Simon Langham. Later vicar of Ludgershall and Lutterworth, John Wycliff attacked medieval philosophers such as Duns Scotus and William Occam and opposed the medieval doctrine of transubstantiation, maintaining that the bread and wine remained after the consecration and that Christ was only there as a king is in every part of his kingdom. He encouraged the translation and reading of the bible in English. His followers were known as Lollards.

King Charles 1 (30 January, 1600-49). King of Great Britain and Ireland from 1625. Beheaded on 30 January, the day commemorated with special services of prayer and fasting from the Restoration until 1859. Worked closely with Archbishop Laud against the puritans and considered a martyr because of his defence of the Church and episcopacy against them and the Presbyterians.

Thomas Cranmer (21 March, 1489-1556). Archbishop of Canterbury from 1532 and the greatest single influence on the English Prayer Book. Burnt at the stake at Oxford on 21 March 1556, in the reign of Mary.

Polycarp (23 February, c.69-c.155). Bishop of Smyrna. Said to be a disciple of St John, he had an influence on the date of Easter and was burnt to death in the anti-Christian outburst in the province of Asia about 155.

George (23 April). A picture from a 15th century Greek icon. Little is known of the life of St George and even his existence has been doubted. His meeting with the dragon first appears in a 12th century legend.

William Wilberforce (29 July, 1759-1833). Helped to found the Church Missionary Society and the Bible Society and fought repeatedly in Parliament for the abolition of slavery, which was finally secured a few days before his death.

Jeremy Taylor (13 August, 1613-67). A leading English theologian at the time of the Restoration. He was Bishop of Down and Connor and First Chancellor of Dublin University. His devotional writings, *Holy Living* and *Holy Dying*, exercised great influence on the development of Anglican spirituality.

Francis of Assisi (4 October, 1181-1226). Founder of the Order of St Francis, for whom he wrote a simple rule of life based on sayings from the gospels. His simple and direct faith and love of nature and his humility have endeared him to modern man.

Rules to Order the Service

Rules are provided to give guidance in which 'propers' (i.e. prayers, psalms and readings appropriate for a particular day or season) are to be used when, for example, a fixed festival coincides with a moveable one, or with a season such as Holy Week or Easter Week. Some principle of choice is needed, but those who venture very far into this subject are liable to become either bewildered by its complexity or bored by its punctiliousness. Most will be content to follow the list of 'praetermissions and transferences' of holy days as indicated in the published Lectionaries for each particular year. One trend towards simplicity introduced with the Alternative Calendar is a principle of using whenever possible no more than one collect at any service, although the Advent Sunday and Ash Wednesday

collects might still be read as additions to the relevant Sunday collect until the days before Christmas Eve and Palm Sunday respectively.

However desirable it may be to have alternative services available for use in the worship of the Church of England, there are undoubtedly problems about having alternative Calendars. It has been possible to reform the Calendar only on this basis, but the consequences mean, for example, that St Matthias' day may now be either 24 February or 14 May, and St Thomas' day either 3 July or 21 December. Perhaps more important, in view of their significance as ordination seasons, the Ember Days vary in the two Calendars. The hope must be that eventually one Calendar will be agreed, even if alternative lectionary schemes continue in use.

The Lectionary

It is clearly important that a Christian congregation should give attention to the 'whole counsel of God' in its worship, and for this purpose a definite scheme of scripture reading is likely to prove more satisfactory than a random selection of passages. Evidence is too scanty to establish how far the lectionary had developed in Jewish synagogue worship in the time of Jesus and Paul (cf Luke 4.16-21; Acts 13.15). Readings of Paul's letters would naturally have taken place when congregations met together, and these and other apostolic writings came to form an additional reading to the traditional recital of the law and the prophets on the synagogue model used in early Christian worship. It was customary to commence such readings from the point which had been reached on the previous occasion. As the various festivals and seasons of the Church's year developed so it became settled that particular readings should be used on certain days. This progressively reduced the scope for continuous readings through different books of the bible.

The readings provided for the Alternative Calendar have been produced under three main influences. The first has been that of an ecumenical body known as the Joint Liturgical Group. In its publication entitled *The Calendar and the Lectionary* (1967) the Sunday readings were arranged on a two-year cycle with a particular theme for each Sunday. Three lessons were provided for each Sunday eucharist, but the themes chosen meant that during the nine weeks before Christmas the Old Testament reading was the 'controlling lection'; between Christmas and Pentecost the Gospel passage assumed this position; and from Pentecost the themes became those of Acts and the Epistles. A consequence of this arrangement was that if two readings only were to be used at a particular service then the 'controlling lection' must be one of these. The essentials of this scheme are now incorporated in the new lectionary to provide readings for each Sunday eucharist; and also for Evening Prayer, using the readings provided for

'Synagogue worship was the norm of Christian worship in the days of the apostles, even to the response "Amen" by the people at the close of every thanksgiving.'

C.W. Dugmore, *The Influence of the Synagogue upon the Divine Office.*

the alternate year of the two-year cycle. The Sunday themes have now been removed from the main body of the Lectionary, and appear in a table at the end of the book.

The second influence has been that of the 1961 Table of Lessons, used for Sunday Morning Prayer but re-arranged to fit where possible the Sunday themes introduced from the work of the Joint Liturgical Group, and also followed to a considerable extent in providing the readings for weekday Morning and Evening Prayer. By this route some much older lectionary traditions have been retained, such as reading Isaiah in Advent and the Joseph cycle from Genesis in Lent.

In addition, the House of Bishops asked the Liturgical Commission to produce a daily eucharistic lectionary, providing readings for all weekdays for which no separate provision had already been made. In the consideration of this lectionary in the House of Bishops in November 1976, the Commission's Lectionary was thrown out and the Roman Catholic daily eucharistic lectionary preferred. The Commission was later asked to adapt the Roman Lectionary to the *ASB* Calendar. So the daily eucharistic material in the Alternative Lectionary reproduces the Roman Lectionary.

Every single day of the year is now furnished with at least six readings from scripture: two for the Eucharist and two each for Morning and Evening Prayer.

WHICH LECTIONARY

The following lectionaries are authorised for use in the Church of England:

- 1871   as printed in the Book of Common Prayer.

- 1922   as revised in 1928. This is authorised by Parliament.

- 1955   authorised by the Convocation in May 1961.

- Those attached to Morning and Evening Prayer (Series 2 revised); Holy Communion (Series 3).

- The Alternative Lectionary, approved by the General Synod in July 1978 and as adopted in July 1979. (It is important to realise that, when the Alternative Lectionary is being used, the *ASB 1980* collects should also be used.)

An early bible – possibly by William Tyndale

On certain days there are alternatives to choose from. It must be remembered, however, that the weekday morning readings for one year are read at Evening Prayer the next year, and vice versa. On Sundays too, as has been already mentioned, there is a similar interchange between Holy Communion and Evening Prayer. Anyone who uses the daily Old and New Testament readings either from the morning or the evening table will read virtually the whole bible at least once in the course of two years.

The Psalter

Particular psalms have been chosen to fit the themes for Sundays and other holy days, but on other weekdays the traditional method of reading through the psalms in numerical order is retained. The pace is slower, and the daily ration therefore smaller, than in the Book of Common Prayer. The psalter is read through in about ten weeks, but not exactly, so that the same psalms do not always occur on the same day of the week or invariably at either Morning or Evening Prayer.

The Liturgical Psalter is incorporated into some editions of *ASB 1980*. See p.244 of this book for more comment on the psalms and how the General Synod came to the decision, after much debate, to include the Liturgical Psalter in the Book.

General Notes

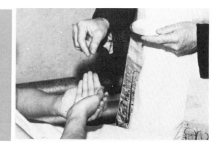

History

Sometimes in the Prayer Book there are extended rubrics at the beginning of a service. The same idea was followed in 1928 and in Series 1 and 2 services. But these were always *rubrics*, giving directions to the minister. 'Notes' are a different concept, and they were first found in Series 3 Communion, published in report form in 1971, and (slightly amended) authorised from 1 February 1973. Although these Notes contained a few directions, like the old opening rubrics, their main function was to permit more elasticity in the use of the service, to allow variations which would have too much prominence if printed in the text, and yet should be allowed, and to make suggestions about the conduct of the service. Since 1971 all the new services authorised by General Synod have had 'Notes' at the beginning.

Purpose

The character of the Notes indicates their purpose. Really, they are 'pastoral' – allowing that elasticity and flexibility which will make the service fit the people and surroundings in which it is conducted. The aim is to domesticate the liturgy in each particular place, and this means not a large number of special instructions, but a pattern of variations which do not clutter the main text of a rite. They 'enable' congregations to worship within their own tradition and without any suspicion that they are somehow in breach of a 'law'. Notes are a canonisation of common sense, and an escape from legalism. Their very presence indicates that the services which are authorised are to be followed in the spirit rather than in the letter.

Particular and General

Each of the Series 3 services of the 1970s had its own provision of Notes, largely relating to the specific possibilities and character of the particular service. However, once the principle of Notes was admitted, certain very general Notes had to be repeated from one service to another through the whole range of booklets. So, when *ASB 1980* was being compiled, it became desirable to extract the 'General' Notes, and set them out once for all at the beginning of the whole Book, so that they would not have to be repeated for each service. In the event there proved to be relatively few of them. Their removal from the specific services means that the Notes at the beginning of each service, whilst still fulfilling the purpose of giving elasticity and allowing the services to be authentic to the particular people and places where they are used, are now all related to that particular service.

WHAT GENERAL NOTES ARE THERE?

The answer is 'ten in all'. Each is worth a mention here.

Distinctions in the text

The use of blue and black (or italic and roman type in a one-colour edition) is part of the original design of Series 3 booklets from 1971 onwards, following the layout of the designer Keith Murgatroyd. On the other hand, both the Liturgical Commission and the General Synod have usually handled one colour printings only. Thus the detailed use of the two colours has been provided by the editorial teams which have seen the ser-

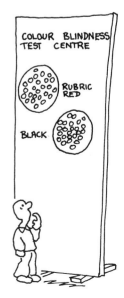

vices (and in this case the whole *ASB 1980*) through the press, and it is they who have drawn up this first General Note to explain what they have done. In general the particular *addition* to the approved texts which they have made is the giving of a colour to the marginal numbers – blue for optional material, black for mandatory. The difficulty is when there is a mandatory part within an optional one . . .

Rubrics are now always in blue, and spoken text in black. The original meaning of the word 'rubric' is 'red', and that is the colour used in the handwritten medieval rites. When printing came, the Prayer Books were printed in black throughout, but the directions were still called 'rubrics', and so they have remained. Roman Catholic liturgical publications, as well as *The Methodist Service Book* and *An Australian Prayer Book* (to mention but a couple), have reverted to red, and the 'bluebrics' of *ASB 1980* are very distinctive of the Church of England.

Saying and singing

It would be tedious to insert 'or sung' every time the word 'said' occurs in the rubrics, or to have everywhere such instructions as 'A psalm may be *used* here'. So 'said' is taken to include 'sung' and vice versa. This not only ensures that no one gets caught in a legalistic trap, but it is also a charter to composers to experiment with settings for any parts of *ASB 1980* that might be singable. It is to be hoped that there is widespread experiment in line with the charter.

Posture

The lack of directions about posture in the rubrics of the services allow much greater freedom than in the Book of Common Prayer.

Biblical passages

A list of the authorised versions is set out on page 66 above. Not all the sentences within the services or the propers are taken word for word from such versions (see the fourth 'Comfortable Word' for

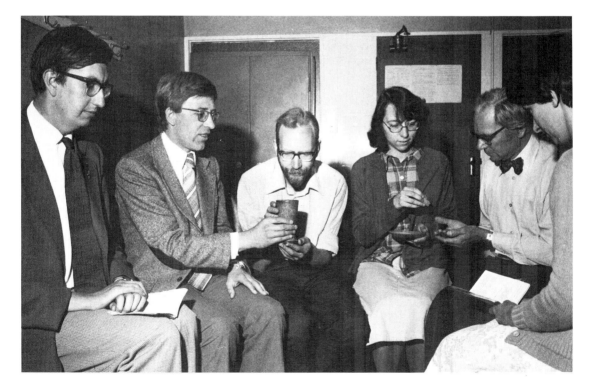

instance), but even they can be read from actual versions if wished. All psalm passages used in the services are from the Liturgical Psalter, which appears at the end of some editions of *ASB 1980*. As ministers can in any case make changes of no substantial importance in the conduct of services, they can presumably try out new versions of the bible, or offer their own translations of the original, without offending. The Note here is 'enabling', *not* restricting.

Prayer Book texts

This Note continues a discretion allowed throughout the period since Series 3 services have been used. By allowing canticles and anthems to be sung to traditional settings – and thus with traditional words – it has enabled some congregations to take nervous steps into modern language worship, whilst still keeping much familiar singing going.

In *ASB 1980* the words of traditional material for the communion service are set out in Rite B, whilst the canticles used at Morning and Evening Prayer are found in traditional form at the end of that part of the Book.

The Lord's Prayer

This Note allows the Lord's Prayer to be used in any of the three current forms (modern, modified, and traditional) in any service. It is worth noting that the differences in the first line enable a congregation to know *which* version they are using immediately a lead is given:
'Our Father in heaven' – modern form (Rite A)
'Our Father who art in heaven' – modified form (Rite B)
'Our Father which art in heaven' – traditional form (BCP)
The modern form is always used with a doxology in *ASB 1980*, and those using other forms would best conform to *ASB 1980* by using the doxology always with them also.

Collects

The permission here to use only one collect when more are provided is written this way round because it is intended to drop a broad hint that one collect is enough. Collects relate to the themes of lessons, and as only one set of lessons is read, only one collect is appropriate. At communion congregations sit for a reading after the collect, and are far better off if they know there will only be one!

Collect endings

This Note allows the minister to add a longer ending to any collect which ends in 'Christ our Lord'. It will help if those who take advantage of this permission so inflect their voice and measure their speed that congregations know when to respond 'Amen'.

Chanting psalms and canticles

Because *ASB 1980* differs from 1662 in introducing pointing for psalms and canticles, the General Notes have had to include an explanation of the way in which this pointing (along with asterisks, spacing, and lining out) has been done to facilitate congregational singing and chanting. The intention is that congregations should really join in meaningfully and heartily, rather than trailing despairingly behind those sorts of choir which are either unwilling or unable to share the secrets of chanting with the other worshippers.

The note also includes reference to the omission of bracketed parts of psalms, usually those parts which call upon God for vengeance upon the enemies of Israel (or of the psalmist). David Frost, in his own discussion of the psalter at the very end of this Guide, says wise words about how to understand these passages and to use them.

Morning and Evening Prayer

You make darkness and it
is night,
in which all the beasts of
the forest move by
stealth.
The lions roar for their
prey,
seeking their food from
God.
When the sun rises they
retire,
and lay themselves down
in their dens.
Man goes out to his work
and to his labour until the
evening.
How many are your works,
O Lord!
in wisdom you have made
them all.

Ps 104.22-26

'In vain you rise early
and stay up late,
toiling for food to eat
for he grants sleep to those
he loves.'

Ps 127.2

The response of the
prophet Amos is a shout of
praise:

'He who made the Pleiades
and Orion,
who turns blackness into
dawn
and darkens day into night
–
the Lord is his name.'

Amos 5.8

Most Church of England worshippers think of Morning and Evening Prayer (Matins and Evensong as they are often called) as Sunday services but in the Alternative Service Book, as in the old Book of Common Prayer, they are in fact daily services. They take on a special character on Sundays because Sunday is a special day, held in honour by Church and state as the day of Jesus' resurrection. The services stand in a long tradition of Christian daily prayer. A colourful example is the hymn *O gladsome light* (*ASB 1980*, section 32) probably better known as *Hail, gladdening light*, which was already spoken of as 'ancient' in 374 AD and was sung in the eastern Church when the evening lamps were lit. This tradition of daily prayer has developed differently in different parts of the Church, and before looking at the particular services of the new book it is worth asking the question why the idea of daily prayer should exist at all.

EACH DAY IS A GIFT

We tend to take a new day for granted and to treat it as arriving automatically, without God playing a part at all. The bible's view is very different. God is the creator who upholds and governs the universe that he has made. Each day is a gift from God and the pattern of days and weeks in which we live out our lives springs from God's goodness towards us. So in Genesis we read:

'God said, "Let there be lights in the vault of heaven to separate day from

night ..." God put these lights in the vault of heaven to give light on earth, to govern day and night, and to separate light from darkness: and God saw that it was good' (Genesis 1.14,17,18).

Life comes to us from God in days. There are other passages in scripture that teach us to see God's hand in this simple event of ordinary life. Jesus uses it as a pointer to God's generous love: 'Your Father makes his sun rise on the evil and the good' (Matthew 5.45). God often seems far from ordinary life because we do not allow the common events of life to lead us back to him in praise.

DAWN AND DUSK

Light and darkness, day and night, are part of the world we experience all the time but we become aware of them at their moments of passing. Times of change or transition are important to us as human beings and we need to respond to such a moment in a concrete way. In the rhythm of daily life morning and evening are moments of change in which our hearts should move towards God in praise, in confession, and in the renewal of our love. The Christian tradition of morning and evening prayer has its roots in this Godward response at the great moments of dawn and dusk.

One reason why it is easy to take the repeating rhythm of day and night for granted in England today is the availability of electric light. 'What I am having to get used to is the dark', writes a young Englishman spending his first nights in an African village. This is that almost total darkness that cannot be dispelled by the flick of a switch. It is the darkness known throughout history until the 20th century; the darkness of 'Lighten our darkness . . .'. Basil the Great (c.330-79), the Christian bishop who first mentions the hymn *O gladsome light*, comments:

> 'It seemed fitting to our fathers not to receive the gift of the light at eventide in silence, but, on its appearing, immediately to give thanks.'

The popularity among some Christians of the late evening service of Compline shows that bed-time is now a more significant moment than dusk. Modern technology has softened the meaning of evening and has given western men the impression that the world is theirs to command. But the God-given framework of our daily life remains unchanged, and the only antidote to destructive arrogance is

to build into our lives a framework of prayer and praise. The services in *ASB 1980* represent one attempt to provide such a daily pattern of prayer.

The History of Morning and Evening Prayer

Reading from the scroll in the synagogue

IN THE NEW TESTAMENT

We read in Acts a vivid picture of the life of the Church in the earliest days immediately following the resurrection of Jesus. The believers, we are told,

> 'devoted themselves to the apostles' teaching and fellowship, to the breaking of bread and the prayers . . . day by day, attending the temple together and breaking bread in their homes' (Acts 2.42,46).

This familiar passage of scripture tells us that the worship of the earliest Christians followed the traditional worship of the temple in Jerusalem. Elsewhere the synagogue provided a pattern for Christian worship. Prayers, psalms, readings from the Old Testament and explanations of those readings comprised the ingredients of daily worship which took place at least every morning and in the evening when the lamps were first lit.

Emperor Constantine (c.274-337)

IN THE EARLY CHURCH

Hippolytus (c.170-236), an important leader of the Church in Rome, gives us a glimpse into early Christian habits of prayer.

> 'Let every faithful man and woman, when they have risen from sleep in the morning, before they touch any work at all, wash their hands and pray to God, and so go to their work.'

If Christians are at home they are to pray aloud, or elsewhere secretly, also at the third, sixth and ninth hours (9 am, 12 noon and 3 pm), before they go to bed, at midnight with their wives and at cock-crow. In addition to these seven times of private prayer, the Church met for corporate prayer in the morning and at the lighting of the evening lamps. Hippolytus encourages Christians to be present.

One part of that evening worship service still survives in our new service. The canticle *O gladsome light* or *Hail, gladdening Light*, has been said or sung by Christians for at least seventeen hundred years.

A day in the life of a monk

Rise

12 Midnight	Mattins
1 a.m.	Lauds

Reading

7 a.m.	Prime

Breakfast and Chapter Meeting

9 a.m.	Terce

Work

3 p.m.	None

Dinner

5 p.m.	Vespers

Supper

7 p.m.	Compline

Bed

MONASTIC DEVELOPMENTS

The conversion in 313 of the Roman Emperor Constantine (c.274-337) led to a dramatic reversal of the Church's fortunes. Instead of being the faith of a persecuted minority, Christianity became the official religion of the state. Christians now worshipped openly in great churches and cathedrals where Morning and Evening Prayer became the regular and public services.

Meanwhile some Christians sought a greater degree of commitment to Christ by shutting themselves off from the rest of the world in separate communities where, without other distractions, they could be free to devote their time to prayer and the worship of God. These communities became known as monasteries and convents and the people who joined them as monks and nuns. They attempted to sanctify the whole of each

day by making use of the hours of devotion, recommended by Hippolytus, for the recitation of the psalms in order and the consecutive reading of bible passages. A day in the life of a monk would have worked out something like the table on this page.

Naturally this pattern of worship was quite impossible for the ordinary layfolk, who centred their worship on the weekly Sunday mass which stood at the heart of pre-Reformation religion. The clergy who were not monks would also adapt the monastic pattern to suit their own daily timetable.

REFORMATION CHANGES

When Thomas Cranmer was archbishop he found much that called for correction in the worship of the Church. An English peasant would know something of the sayings of Christ and many of the Old Testament stories, which he learnt from sermons in his parish church. He also had a deep fear of God's judgement enhanced by the wall-paintings and colourful reminders of the rewards of the virtuous and the torments of the damned depicted on the wall above the screen which divided the chancel, where the clergy worshipped, from the nave, where the people stood or knelt on the bare floor. But he could understand little of the services which were whispered, said or sung in Latin. The bible was, for him, a closed book. In short, he was an isolated observer of a strange and involved clerical ritual.

It was Cranmer's aim to make the services of the Church the worship of the people. In the Preface to the Prayer Book, which still appears in all editions, he sets out his intentions. The book is to replace the many local variations in use throughout the kingdom and to simplify the complicated rules by which they are governed. The daily services are reduced to two and they are to include regular recitation of the psalms and consecutive readings from the bible. Above all he wants worship to be conducted in the language people understand.

We may list Cranmer's achievements:

● He reduced eight daily services in Latin to two daily services in English – incorporating material from no less than five of the old services. Everyone could now understand and follow the order of service.

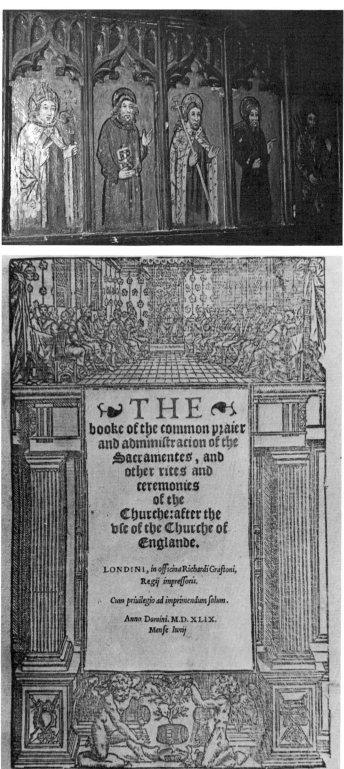

above
Pictures on the gallery in
Lower Strensham Church
below
The title page of the 1549
Book of Common Prayer

CRANMER'S ORDER OF SERVICE

Morning Prayer *incorporating*		**Evening Prayer** *incorporating*	
Lord's Prayer	Matins	Lord's Prayer	Evensong
Versicles		Versicles	
Gloria		Gloria	
Venite		Psalms	
Psalms		O.T. Lesson	
O.T. Lesson		Magnificat	
Te Deum			
N.T. Lesson	Lauds	N.T. Lesson	Compline
Benedictus		Nunc Dimittis	
Kyrie	Prime	Kyrie	Evensong
Creed		Creed	
Lord's Prayer		Lord's Prayer	
		Preces	
		Collect of the Day	
		Collect for Peace	
Preces	Lauds	Collect for Aid	Compline
Collect for the Day			
Collect for Peace			
Collect for Grace	Prime		

● The psalms were to be repeated entirely in the course of each month. Hitherto the regular recitation had been so interrupted and confused that psalm 119, for instance, was read daily while other psalms were read not at all.

● The bible was to be read consecutively at both daily services in a way which ensured that worshippers would read the Old Testament once and the New Testament thrice each year.

● The two services were designed to promote understanding and godliness in the congregation. Simple rules, a clearer shape to the services and the daily hearing of the scriptures aided the communication of the truths enshrined in the Church's worship and the edification of the worshippers.

● Cranmer wrote beautiful and generous prayers. The Litany (1544) and the collects bear the mark of his literary skill and deep spiritual insight even where some have been copied or adapted from older models.

DEVELOPMENTS TO THE PRESENT DAY

Thomas Cranmer hoped that people would come daily to church for Morning and Evening Prayer and on Sundays to Morning Prayer, Litany and Holy Communion. As it turned out he was unable to persuade any but the clergy to worship daily and the people would only come to Morning and Evening Prayer on Sundays. They were unwilling to receive communion each week. Since 1662, the date of the last authorised Prayer Book, Morning and Evening Prayer have become main public preaching services of the Church of England.

From the 19th century pressing pastoral needs and a revival of interest in pre-Reformation worship led to a number of attempts to modify the Prayer Book services. In 1872 the 'Shortened Services Act' allowed, as the title suggests, abbreviated services for daily use and for any third service, perhaps an evangelistic one, on a Sunday. In the 1928 proposed Prayer Book the appendix includes the old Hour Services of Prime and Compline.

The Shorter Prayer Book (1947) included many of the most popular suggestions of the 1928 Prayer Book, for example an alternative exhortation, confession and absolution at Morning and Evening Prayer.

More radical changes had to await the production of *The Daily Office* by the Joint Liturgical Group in 1968. This attempt by representative Christians of many denominations deeply influenced the revision of Morning and Evening Prayer. We have largely to thank this group for a wider range of seasonal material, a new way of reading the psalms regularly, a variety of new canticles and some modern collects, which have found their way into Anglican services.

The Daily Pattern of the Office

Whether the *use* of Morning and Evening Prayer daily through the week is widespread or not, the principles on which the services are constructed are very clearly for daily use. This was particularly clearly seen in Cranmer's original concept, where no provision was made for Sundays at all, but the services ran on through the civil year in a continuous pattern without regard even to the *existence* of weeks! Special provision was made for the days around principal holy days, and that was all. In 1662 a further minor concession provided 'proper' lessons (from the Old Testament only) which would override the daily consecutive readings every Sunday. Thus Sundays became recognised as a separable

cycle from the other days of the week – but the daily cycle was primary, and Sundays an interruption of it!

The great principle of daily use of the offices is the principle of continuous reading of scripture, and continuous recitation of the psalter. It is probably these considerations which led the reformers to insist that the clergy should continue to say the services privately when they could not get congregations to worship with them twice daily – they were getting a continuous diet of scripture.

The ASB offices are therefore to be seen as providing this daily fare, for daily use. Sundays have been separated entirely from the weekday use, giving two

> Jesus, Saviour of the world, come to us in your mercy:
> we look to you to save and help us.
>
> From
> *The Daily Office*

'We have come
together as the
family of God in our
Father's presence
to offer him praise and
thanksgiving,
to hear and receive his
holy word,
to bring before him the
needs of the world,
to ask his forgiveness
of our sins,
and to seek his grace,
that through his Son
Jesus Christ
we may give ourselves
to his service.'

ASB 1980,
Morning Prayer

different cycles – a daily one of continuous reading, and a Sunday one of an 'anthological' kind, often related to the 'theme' of the eucharistic lessons. The weekday cycle includes reading the psalter five times during the year, and covering the main books of the bible (even if sometimes excerptively) once in the year, provided that two readings are used in the morning, two in the evening. However, the actual pattern of the daily lectionary allows other approaches to the continuous reading.

(a) It is possible to use an office in the mornings only, or in the evening only, and then the lectionary provision will last two years.

(b) It is possible, using the shorter forms (which are clearly meant for daily weekday use), to read *three* lessons in a day – in which case the Old Testament provision will take two years to read, but the New Testament will take only one year, and will be read entire again in the second year (with Morning and Evening interchanging provision).

Well, then, the reading of scripture is the heart of the office – what material should flank it? To answer this, we work from the heart outwards, not from the beginning to the end as one might expect.

Firstly, *the canticles.* They have been used traditionally as a call to worship (see the traditional Venite in the morning – including the call 'If only you would hear his voice today' and note how in the longer form for the evening there is now a choice of canticles meant to 'move' us to worship before the psalm), and as responses to the readings. In the purest pattern of responses – that in Cranmer's Evening Prayer – the Magnificat, Mary's song of response to God's promise, was the response to the Old Testament, that is, to the book of God's promise, and the Nunc Dimittis, Simeon's song of response to God's fulfilment of promise, was the response to the New Testament, that is, to the book of God's fulfilment of his promise. A similar, though more flexible, plan is found in the longer forms today. In the shorter forms a new principle is used – that is, that the canticles are themselves treated as a cycle of readings, and twelve different ones follow the readings in the two services of each day from Monday to Saturday.

Secondly, *the prayers*. The Lord's Prayer is a staple feature of the diet, and introduces a period of prayer. The collect of the week links the offices with the Sunday eucharist, and provides a daily reminder, as all else goes in cycles, of the underlying relation between the Sunday and its weekdays following. The other collects are especially meant to mark out the morning or the evening as such. More prayers can, and often should, be added according to the needs of the day, and of the time of day.

Thirdly, *penitence*. For daily purposes, penitence may be omitted as a liturgical form, though it is still needed as an attitude of heart. If it is used, then for obvious reasons it is more appropriate in the evening, and in the shorter forms is only printed out for the evening.

Fourthly, the *creed*. This is used as a different sort of response to the reading of scripture, and, to balance the penitence in the evening, it is provided in the shorter form in the morning only.

When saying offices daily, whether on one's own or in a small group, it may well be helpful to find the place in the psalter and the bible before starting the office, and it can then be read through without extra directions. Informal prayer or hymn singing may be added at the end. On the other hand, groups may wish to study a passage, and they can do this informally either by stopping the office when it is read as a lesson, or, better, by noting in advance that they will return to it, then reading it formally in its place, and returning to it informally later.

The Sunday Use of the Offices

History has given many parishes an understanding of Morning and Evening Prayer as main Sunday services, and very often the Sunday worshippers have little or no appreciation of the daily purpose of the offices. Why should they have? Their daily use is *not* the average layman's business!

How then are they to be used as Sunday services? The principles laid out above give the clue. There is a two year provision of lessons, related to the themes of the Sundays in the eucharistic lectionary, and a similar special choice of psalms to go with the lessons. The longer forms of the services should be used, and the canticles used as responses to the lessons, not as importing separate themes of their own on their own cycle. Thus the intention is to enable the Sunday services to group round a theme rather more than is possible with a daily one. The sequence from one service to the next is not as strong on a Sundays-only pattern (how could it be?) but the unity of material within the service is slightly more emergent.

History also dictates that the Sunday services are more than skeletal offices. They have an office structure, but they also have expectations which run far beyond the rubrics – of hymns, and preaching, and prayers, and even a collection. Each service is then built up into a totality with its own integrity, fulfilling the expectations of those who are regular attenders, and reckon themselves to be worshipping within a 'cycle' appropriate to them – yet also with a self-contained character for the occasional worshipper. To keep in line with the old 1662 Prayer Book there is even a spoken 'table of contents'.

SUNDAY WORSHIP

The first day of the week has always been special to Christians. From the earliest days of the Church, Christians have gathered together on this day (Acts 20.7.) It soon came to be called the Lord's Day – associated with a celebration of Jesus' resurrection (Mark 16.2). We read of collections every Sunday in Corinth (I Cor 16.2) and on 'the Lord's Day' John received a vision from God (Rev 1.10). Later, Sunday became the corner-stone of the Christian Calendar. Many churches, following early tradition, make a service of Holy Communion the central act of weekly worship. This, however, is a late development in the history of Anglican worship since the Reformation in the 16th century. Until our generation most lay people were more accustomed to worshipping at Morning and Evening Prayer.

HOW TO USE THE *ASB 1980* SERVICES ON SUNDAYS
Choral Matins and Evensong

By the time the Prayer Book was authorised in 1662, Morning and Evening Prayer had become the weekly diet of Anglicans on Sunday. At that time the somewhat bare service compiled by Cranmer for daily worship was enriched by anthems, more prayers and, when it became separated from ante-communion, a sermon tacked on the end. Later, in the 19th century, clergy and robed choirs began to introduce hymns and, at the beginning of this century, ministers widened the range of prayers still further.

If you go to a cathedral or parish church on a Sunday you may still find the worshippers using Morning and Evening Prayer, often sung by the choir who may use beautiful, if difficult, musical settings for the canticles and other sung portions of the service. While some cathedrals and churches will persist with the much-loved Prayer Book with its familiar rhythms, others will be using the new services.

Family evangelistic services

Increasingly in the 20th century the Church in western christendom has found herself in a missionary situation. People have grown up in ignorance of the basic christian truths and apart from the local Church. As a result churches have to introduce strangers to the Anglican way of worship. Often newcomers find it easier to begin by coming to a family service, which involves less commitment than a holy communion service. Moreover the new services allow for a very warm and participatory form of worship in which the whole family can take part. They allow freedom within the traditional outline of Anglican worship.

In one place in the North of England, everyone comes to the local pub at 9.15 am on Sunday. The Christians transform the bar into a centre of worship and families from the local housing estates

crowd in. The service starts with a hymn, the Introduction and the Confession, then one of the congregation leads everyone in songs and hymns accompanied on the pub organ. They usually celebrate birthdays, give the notices and welcome newcomers before the lessons and a canticle are read. After another hymn, the congregation breaks up for all-age Christian education. The adults gather round the pool table and sometimes the sermon leads to questions and discussion before the worship hour ends with intercessions, the blessing and coffee! For many the service provides a good way in to the full life of the local Church.

An introductory act of worship before a special activity

The Canons, or regulations, of the Church of England state that Morning and Evening Prayer shall be said or sung on every Sunday in each Parish Church 'except for some reasonable cause approved by the bishop'. Sometimes a parish plans a series of special lectures, debates or discussions to take the place of a sermon. Obviously, the subject demands more time than is available in a normal service. The clergyman may then decide to use a shortened form of Morning or Evening Prayer as an opening act of worship. It need only last a few

minutes and in the evening, could include as little as the versicles and responses (the opening act of praise), the psalm appointed, the New Testament lesson, a canticle, the Lord's Prayer and the evening collect. You may find that Morning or Evening Prayer is used as introductory worship on such occasions as a quiet day, a deanery synod, an Archdeacon's visitation, a series of Lent Studies and an act of experimental worship or drama.

HOW TO USE THE *ASB 1980* SERVICES ON WEEKDAYS

A daily office for the clergy and parishioners

The regulations or Canons of the Church of England require every minister 'being at home and not otherwise reasonably hindered' to say daily Morning and Evening Prayer and, where possible, these services are to take place in the parish church of which he is a minister.

There is considerable variety in the practice of the clergy. Some fulfil the letter of the canon law. Many say at least one of the daily services at home if not in church. Clergy sometimes shorten the service to allow more time for meditation after the lessons and they widen the intercessions following the set collects. Others use a different pattern of prayer and bible reading. In some parishes clergy prefer to have a daily communion service.

All clergy are charged in the words of the Ordination service *ASB 1980*:

> 'Because you cannot bear the weight of this ministry in your own strength but only by the grace and power of God, pray earnestly for his Holy Spirit. Pray that he will each day enlarge and enlighten your understanding of the scriptures, so that you may grow stronger and more mature in your ministry, as you fashion your life and the lives of your people on the word of God.'

Parishioners often join the clergy in public daily worship and are, of course, always welcome.

A daily act of worship for a ministry team

Many clergy work together in groups or teams and meet daily to dedicate themselves to the work ahead of them and the needs of their people. Morning and Evening Prayer provides a useful framework.

A personal devotion for laymen

In recent years, those who have compiled the new services have recognised that they could provide a valuable aid to the layman in his own personal worship. Many have found the services helpful and have benefitted enormously from the balanced ingredients:

> Penitence – Confession
> Praise – Canticles and psalms
> Hearing God's word – Bible readings
> Prayer and thanksgiving – Intercessions

If you want to try this out, however, you will need to make use of two additional aids. You will need to find the lectionary, or scheme of daily bible readings, to see which psalms and lessons to use. The lectionary is issued each year by SPCK. You will also need to provide yourself with some guidance for the period of intercessions. You might like to try:

> The Diocesan Prayer Cycle
> John Baillie, *A Diary of Private Prayer*, (London: Oxford University Press), 1936
> Any missionary society's Prayer Calendar (write to their headquarters)
> or compile your own list remembering the needs of the world, the Church, those in need and your own family and friends.

OTHER FORMS OF DAILY PRAYER

Not all Christians find it easy to use a set Anglican form of service for their own private devotion. Other possibilities include:

Family prayers

Christian families who gather, perhaps at breakfast or tea, can use a simple service: a bible reading, a short commentary, prayers read by members of the family, including children, and possibly the verse of a hymn or chorus. The Scripture Union, who started producing bible reading aids more than a hundred years ago, publish helpful books of readings and commentaries for families. Books of children's prayers are readily available in Christian bookshops.

Timetable for a team time of prayer.

8 a.m. Meet in church for Morning Prayer
Sentence
Versicles and responses
A canticle
Set psalm
O.T. reading
N.T. reading
Lord's Prayer and collects

8.10 a.m. Prayer Time:
World Needs, often suggested by headlines in the daily newspaper
Diocesan Prayer Calendar
Parish Prayer Cycle
Praise and Prayer for the work of yesterday and today.

8.20 a.m. Discuss briefly the business of the day.

8.30 a.m. Take the children to school.

WEEKDAY WORSHIP

Christians feel the need to worship on weekdays as well as Sundays. For most of us it is impossible to gather together except perhaps in our own families. In communities, schools and colleges, however, worship goes on daily and most Anglican clergy and some laypeople say Morning Prayer, and in some cases Evening Prayer, each day. The daily worship of the Church is called the 'office' which comes from a Latin word which means 'duty'. It is in daily worship that a Christian often discovers what worship is all about and we may think of it in three dimensions.

It is the service we owe to God.

Most Christians have a man-centred view of worship in which we judge the success of a service by how much we enjoy it. Strictly, our worship is directed to God. It is something we do. How much we put into it is the best way to judge its worth.

It is corporate worship.

We join our praises and prayers to those of the Church universal and eternal. All over the world, as well as in heaven, Christians are worshipping God. Through hymns and canticles, through bible readings, which recount the mighty acts of God, and through prayers we add our service to that of the saints of all the ages.

It is an act of individual commitment.

This aspect of worship is particularly apparent on weekdays when there are likely to be few, if any, to join in the service. Not many will admit to enjoying the daily services of the Church, except perhaps when they are sung in a cathedral. Many, however, will testify to the value of the daily services as an opening of oneself to God's word and an offering of oneself in love and service to one's neighbour and to God.

A daily quiet time with God

For some Christians their spiritual life-blood flows from the time they set aside each day to read the bible and to pray. Usually the time varies between five minutes and half-an-hour. A short prayer precedes a reading from the bible. This leads in turn to meditation and prayer. The Bible Reading Fellowship and the Scripture Union publish helpful schemes and explanatory notes.

The new Roman Catholic services

Those who would like to preserve the old traditional acts of devotion may care to consider the new Roman Catholic Services which are designed for the layman as well as the cleric.

Daily Prayer from the Divine Office
  Lauds – Morning Prayer
  Matins - The Office of Readings, which may be used at any convenient hour of the day.
    Little Hour – Prayer during the day
    Vespers – Evening Prayer
    Compline – Night Prayer

Many Anglicans who find this pattern daunting still love to use at least Compline. It is a service in which we commend ourselves to the safe-keeping of God at the end of our work and before we sleep. You will not find Compline in the new book, but it is readily available in leaflets obtainable from Christian bookshops.

The Contents of Morning and Evening Prayer

THE PREPARATION FOR MORNING AND EVENING PRAYER

Approaching God
Christian faith stands on the fact that God has shown himself to us. It is because he has made himself known – revealed himself is the technical term – that we know about him. More than that, we can know him as a person to person. We have a relationship with God. Our best human relationships with parent, child, husband, wife, friend, help us to understand our relationship with God.

God has made himself known
We find the beginning of this process in the Old Testament. It reaches its climax in Jesus Christ, in what he was and said and did. When we share in worship we are, as it were, replying to what God has shown us about himself. This does not happen in a detached way. We are drawn towards him. We give him ourselves just as we give ourselves to another human person whom we know and trust and love. One thing we know as Christians, because God has revealed himself to us, is that he is at work in us. He has given himself to us through Jesus Christ and the Holy Spirit.

We make our own personal response to God in prayer and worship but we are not isolated units. We are, to use St Paul's picture, limbs and organs of a body, the Body of Christ, the Church. Public worship, therefore, is corporate, a word derived from the Latin word *corpus*, which means 'body'. It is common prayer, that is, prayer which we share in common. So we have in our minds the thanksgivings and needs that we share in common. We reach out in sympathy to those members of the body who are ill or in other trouble. We recognise our common failures, to which our own individual sin contributes. We recognise our need as the Church of God for his help to do the work that he wants us to do in the world.

The introduction
The service may begin with a short description of what worship is about (section 1). It is a simple summary of why we are in church or wherever the gathering for worship is being held. It is possible to have acts of worship which are concerned with some special, limited situation, but every form of worship which claims to be Christian and complete needs to have in it a general understanding of worship and of the particular elements that this introduction mentions.

The sentences
The minister may then read a sentence of scripture. Because it comes from the bible it is reminding us of something that God has shown us about himself. It may be about his character or, at special seasons, about something our Lord Jesus Christ was or that he or the Holy Spirit has done or will do. It may waken us to praise or prayer or witness.

Hymns
After these sentences it is good, where possible, to sing a hymn. If numbers are sufficient to give strength to the singing, hymns are a most helpful means for bringing the congregation together in what it is thinking and doing. Each worshipper is then with heart, mind and body sharing the same approach to God as every other.

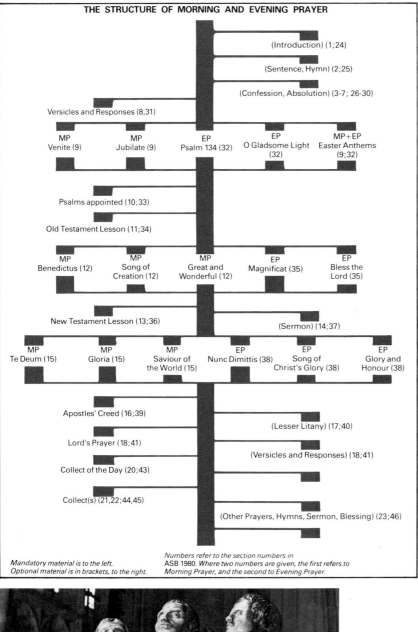

THE STRUCTURE OF MORNING AND EVENING PRAYER

(Introduction) (1;24)

(Sentence, Hymn) (2;25)

(Confession, Absolution) (3-7; 26-30)

Versicles and Responses (8,31)

| MP Venite (9) | MP Jubilate (9) | EP Psalm 134 (32) | EP O Gladsome Light (32) | MP+EP Easter Anthems (9;32) |

Psalms appointed (10;33)

Old Testament Lesson (11;34)

| MP Benedictus (12) | MP Song of Creation (12) | MP Great and Wonderful (12) | EP Magnificat (35) | EP Bless the Lord (35) |

New Testament Lesson (13;36)

(Sermon) (14;37)

| MP Te Deum (15) | MP Gloria (15) | MP Saviour of the World (15) | EP Nunc Dimittis (38) | EP Song of Christ's Glory (38) | EP Glory and Honour (38) |

Apostles' Creed (16;39)

(Lesser Litany) (17;40)

Lord's Prayer (18;41)

(Versicles and Responses) (18;41)

Collect of the Day (20;43)

Collect(s) (21,22;44,45)

(Other Prayers, Hymns, Sermon, Blessing) (23;46)

Mandatory material is to the left.
Optional material is in brackets, to the right.

Numbers refer to the section numbers in ASB 1980. Where two numbers are given, the first refers to Morning Prayer, and the second to Evening Prayer.

From Winchester Cathedral

Charles Wesley, the great hymn writer, said of our attitude to the singing of hymns, 'not lolling at ease or in the indecent posture of sitting, drawling out one word after another, but all standing before God, and praising him lustily and with good courage'.

The Confession

The sentence in section 3 is a fitting transition to confession after a hymn which is about God. If our eyes are turned to him, 'sitting on his throne, high and exalted,' who is adored for his holiness, then we shall more easily say with the prophet, 'There is no hope for me! I am doomed because every word that passes my lips is sinful and I dwell among a people whose every word is sinful' (Isaiah 6.1,3,5). This is not strictly true of every word spoken by the individual Christian disciple, for the good reason that God is at work in us through his grace, but the words of the confession, which are based on this understanding of our position before God, are necessary and true (section 5). Forms of service which claim to be balanced and complete need this kind of acknowledgement of our sinful human condition.

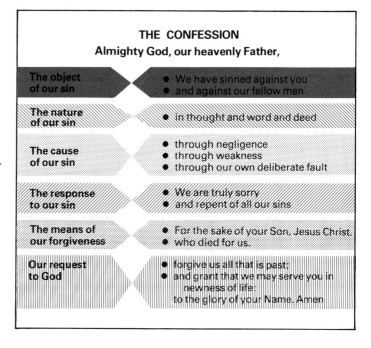

THE CONFESSION
Almighty God, our heavenly Father,

The object of our sin	• We have sinned against you • and against our fellow men
The nature of our sin	• in thought and word and deed
The cause of our sin	• through negligence • through weakness • through our own deliberate fault
The response to our sin	• We are truly sorry • and repent of all our sins
The means of our forgiveness	• For the sake of your Son, Jesus Christ, • who died for us.
Our request to God	• forgive us all that is past; • and grant that we may serve you in newness of life; to the glory of your Name. Amen

THE CONTENTS OF MORNING AND EVENING PRAYER IN *ASB 1980*

*References are to page numbers *ASB 1980*.

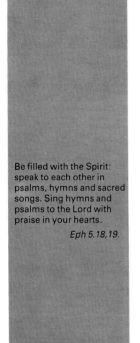

Be filled with the Spirit: speak to each other in psalms, hymns and sacred songs. Sing hymns and psalms to the Lord with praise in your hearts.

Eph 5.18,19.

The Absolution

'If we confess our sins, God is faithful and just and will forgive us our sins.' The truth of the words of scripture which are part of the invitation to confession is stressed again in the words of the Absolution (section 6). Any Christian can speak to another about the forgiveness of God, any preacher can give the good news of it in a sermon, but there are people who need this truth to be spoken with particular authority in direct and official words. So the word of God's forgiveness is usually spoken by a priest or bishop. The absolution is concerned with forgiveness for the past but it also looks to the future because, in God's purpose, forgiveness leads on to new life – deliverance from sins, growth in goodness, and both of these things because we share eternal life, God's own life. It is given to us by him and he keeps us in it.

The opening sections of the service help us to carry out part of the purpose of approaching God outlined in the introduction: 'to ask his forgiveness of our sins, and to seek his grace that through his Son Jesus Christ we may give ourselves to his service'.

THE PSALMS

In using the psalms to worship God, we are continuing the practice of the People of God for at least the last two and a half thousand years. The psalms are a collection of prayers, meditations and songs finally put together after the return of the Jews from exile in 538 BC. Many of the psalms, however, were in regular use long before this, used in the worship of the first temple, or written as personal prayers that later were adopted for use by the whole community.

Although 'itled in the bible 'The Psalms of David', only 73 are actually attributed to him, some are anonymous, whilst others are attributed to Asaph (73-83), the Sons of Korah (84-88), and even Solomon (72, 127) and Moses (90).

The psalms reflect a variety of moods of man's relationship with God. There is adoration (146), thanksgiving (105), penitence (51), pleading with God (143), grief (22), as well as praise of the law (119) and recalling of the mighty acts of God in history (78). Athanasius (c.296-373) described the psalms as 'a book that includes the whole life of man, all conditions of the mind and all movements of thought'. Many of the psalms found their origin in the liturgy of the temple (68), whilst others began as intensely personal prayers that were adopted by the community to reflect their relationship with God. From their use in the temple, the psalms went on to play a central part in the worship of the synagogue and the home, and were inherited by the early Christians, remaining in constant use both for public and private worship ever since.

There have been two basic approaches to the way that the psalms are used. One is to select a psalm to suit a particular occasion. This was the practice at the great festivals in the temple, and is continued today with certain psalms having obvious association with particular days, for instance psalm 22 for Good Friday, or psalm 65 for Harvest Thanksgiving. The other method is to use the psalms in order, irrespective of their theme. This developed in the Church with the rise of the monastic movement, where there is evidence of some communities reciting the whole psalter every day, while many would cover it in a week. In the Book of Common Prayer the psalms are read at Morning and Evening Prayer each day and are allotted by the day of the month – the whole psalter being covered in one month – for example psalms 1-5 are read on the first morning, and psalms 6-8 in the evening. In the Alternative Service Book lectionary the psalms are covered in a ten week cycle on weekdays, whilst on Sundays and holy days they are chosen to fit the theme. The psalms were almost certainly written to be sung, often accompanied by a whole selection of instruments, and they have provided inspiration to composers of every age. There are now many ways in which psalms can be sung, and great variety will be found among different churches. The monasteries developed the use of plainsong, based on many of the Hebrew chants, while the particular contribution of the Church of England has been Anglican Chant, found in use in many churches today.

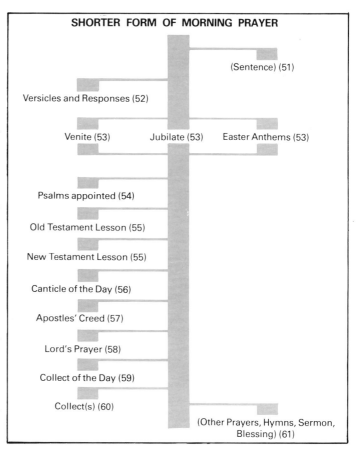

SHORTER FORM OF MORNING PRAYER

(Sentence) (51)

Versicles and Responses (52)

Venite (53)   Jubilate (53)   Easter Anthems (53)

Psalms appointed (54)

Old Testament Lesson (55)

New Testament Lesson (55)

Canticle of the Day (56)

Apostles' Creed (57)

Lord's Prayer (58)

Collect of the Day (59)

Collect(s) (60)

(Other Prayers, Hymns, Sermon, Blessing) (61)

Preacher on pew end in Swavesey Church, Cambridgeshire

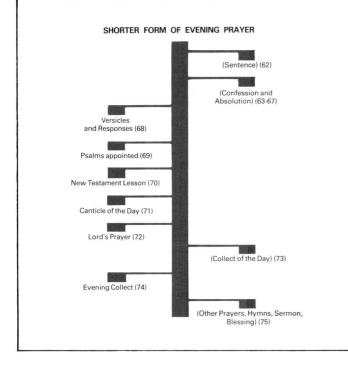

Another popular method of singing the psalms is to paraphrase the words in the style of a hymn, such as 'The Lord's my Shepherd' for Psalm 23 or 'All people that on earth do dwell' for Psalm 100. Recent examples of these metrical psalms are found in *Psalm Praise*, whilst the chants of Joseph Gelineau are a modern derivation from plainsong.

A question that is often raised concerning the use of psalms in worship is to query how far poetry that is the product of Jewish culture is appropriate for use by Christians to worship God. In the fifth century, the Gloria – 'Glory to the Father, and to the Son and to the Holy Spirit . . .' was added to the end of each Psalm in order to state the Christian context.

How to make sense of the psalms

Not only are the psalms difficult to sing, they are also hard to understand and to read sensibly in Christian worship. Most Christians find that the value of the psalms increases with age, experience and constant use. Here are some clues which may help you to find your own key with which to unlock their treasures.

● **Jesus made the psalms his own prayers**. He knew the psalms intimately and quoted from them at critical moments of his life and ministry. On the cross, for example, he uses the words of Psalm 22 to express his agony. When we say the psalms we are using words which were very precious to Jesus because they put into words so much of what he felt and experienced.

● **The psalms are deeply human**. They have stood the test of time. Through the centuries Christians have found that the psalms often reflect those human emotions, so hard to articulate, of praise, thanks, petition, despair and even anger. In every chapter of human experience there is, it seems, a suitable psalm which enables us to offer it to God.

● **The psalms are the historic worship of the Church**. As we sing the psalms we join our praises to the songs of Christians down the ages. We acknowledge that the Church has always seen the psalms as pointing forward to Jesus Christ. In him they find their fulfilment and many of their anomalies, for example their bitter condemnation of evil men, find their resolution in the cross and are balanced by Jesus' teaching in the New Testament. In the mind of St Paul, for instance, the Christian obligation to love one's neighbour does not conflict with God's determination to judge sin and overthrow oppression. 'Do everything possible on your part to live in peace with everybody. Never take revenge, my friends, but instead let God's anger do it' (Romans 13.19). The Church has been able to accept tensions like this and gladly to sing the psalms believing that they tell us difficult but eternal truths about God.

● **The psalms are God-centred**. Even those which retell the history of his people are recounting his mighty acts with a purpose. They trace God's hand in the history of Israel as an indication of his will to redeem his people, a determination which found its culmination in the saving death of his Son, Jesus Christ. The same may be said of those psalms which express horrific sentiments: 'Happy shall he be who takes your little ones and dashes them against the rock' (Psalm 137.9). In each case the writer and the worshipper is reflecting a cry for justice which respects the fact that justice is God's concern. In other words we are talking less about our enemies than about God's and we are praying for the fulfilment of his will and purpose and not our own. We are squeamish about judgement today in a way our fathers never were. Although psalms, or verses of psalms, which seek God's judgement upon Israel's enemies are often omitted, many Christians justify their continued use on the same grounds as they justify those which seek God's blessing on his people. They display a profound, if paradoxical,

faith in his justice and his mercy.

● **The psalms point to Jesus as king**. It is easy to recite the psalms without ever noticing that the central character of many psalms is not just an ordinary individual but the king (Psalms 2,18,20,21 etc.). In other psalms which do not mention the king specifically, it appears that the speaker is royal (e.g. Psalm 118). This is the king of David's line with whom God has made an everlasting covenant (Psalm 132.11) and whose reign will bring blessing to his people (e.g. Psalm 72) and justice to the world (Psalm 72). These hymns and prayers may have been used by a number of kings of Judah but in their strong and full language find their obvious fulfilment in Jesus. The writers of the New Testament refer to them in this sense (for example Psalm 2.7 in Acts 13.33, Psalm 16 in Acts 2.25ff, Psalm 110 in Mark 12.36, Psalm 118.22 in Mark 12.10 and 1 Peter 2.7, Psalm 118.26 in Mark 11.9).

THE BIBLE READINGS
At the heart of Morning and Evening Prayer we listen to the word of the Lord in the readings from the Old and New Testaments.

The services in *ASB 1980* introduce nothing new in this respect. Slight modifications are to be found in the shorter forms of service where the two readings at Morning Prayer are not separated by a canticle and where only a New Testament lesson is provided at Evening Prayer. The norm, however, continues to be an Old and New Testament reading, standing in the relation of promise and fulfilment, as the canticles make clear.

The continuous reading of scripture

The story of daily bible reading in the Church
The early Church followed the practice of the Jewish Synagogue, where the daily readings continued each time from the point which had been reached on the previous occasion. Daily readings depended, in a day when individuals did not possess copies of the scriptures, upon

the ability of believers to meet together. In the monasteries the conditions for regular, corporate bible reading were available to encourage the development of systematic daily readings.

Unfortunately, in the pre-reformation Church, these regular readings were constantly interrupted by special passages to mark the increasing number of Saint's Days – including legends of the many post-biblical saints. Except for the night office of Mattins, the readings were reduced to very short, seasonal verses. Cranmer re-arranged the daily services around a comprehensive lectionary, or list of lessons to be read at the services, which covered most of the Old Testament once a year and nearly all the New Testament three times. He allowed only the minimum of variation from the regular course of reading to take account of major festivals. Sundays were included in the general scheme since the Prayer Book was intended to provide a daily pattern of devotion for all Church members.

The expectation that lay people would worship in Church daily proved to be hopelessly idealistic. In 1559, therefore, some lessons were appointed for use on Sundays, and this marked the start of a separate Sunday Lectionary.

In the Alternative Lectionary, published to accompany *ASB 1980*, the chosen Sunday readings now fit the same themes as the readings used in the holy communion service. On weekdays, on the other hand, the lectionary uses readings which, though not always continuous, do follow the thread of meaning in each book of the bible.

Why do we read the bible in worship?

It is important to recognise that bible readings have a dynamic and creative part to play in the whole service, which is in no way undermined by the fact that today numerous modern translations are available in cheap, paperback editions which can easily be read at home, on the way to work, or in hotel bedrooms.

● *The bible readings link the congregation to the Christian tradition.* It is the bible

which enables us to identify the Christ who is the object of our adoring faith with Jesus of Nazareth who lived and died and rose again. Today's worship is, moreover, linked to the Christian Church through time and space by means of this common tradition about Jesus. Nothing can replace this.

● *Bible reading imposes upon the worshippers the duty of listening.* This, after all, is the appropriate attitude to adopt in God's presence. All the prayers, music and ceremonial are pointless if we do not pay attention to God who is addressing us. 'If only you would hear his voice today,' the Venite reminds us as we prepare for the readings at Morning Prayer. Silence is recommended after one or both of the readings. On weekdays, when the lectionary is by implication a course of bible study, longer meditation is called for. It helps if you can follow the reading in a bible.

● *The readings enable the worship service to become a proclamation of the saving power of God in Christ.* To worship without the readings would be like joining a cheering crowd without having heard what the announcement was about. The scriptures recount the acts of God and the biblical theme and imagery are caught up and alluded to in the hymns and prayers. It follows from this that all the great themes of scripture must be covered in any adequate lectionary. When the bible readings are allowed to affect the rest of the service our worship becomes a true proclamation of God's word for that occasion, place and people.

How to read the bible in worship

Here is a valuable ministry in the Body of Christ for those with gifts and skills in reading and voice production. It must not become the prerogative of the churchwardens, nor should everybody be expected to take a turn. The most effective reader will always be the one who gives the impression that he is himself addressed by the words he reads. Wonder and humility will communicate more

CANTICLES

As with the psalms many of the canticles are very ancient. Many are biblical passages mainly from the New Testament, which were first used as songs, while others are ancient hymns written either in Latin or Greek in the first centuries of the Christian Church.

16 different canticles are provided for use at Morning and Evening Prayer.

CANTICLES FOR USE AT MORNING AND EVENING PRAYER

Morning Prayer

Venite   An invitation to worship and to listen to God. Psalm 95.1-7, Psalm 98.9.

Jubilate   A call for all people to praise God. Psalm 100.

The Easter Anthems   In praise of the resurrection of Jesus from the dead. Particularly suitable for use at Easter and on Sundays. Verses from 1 Corinthians 5.7,8: Romans 6.9-11; 1 Corinthians 15.20-22.

Benedictus, The Song of Zechariah   In praise of the salvation which is brought by Christ. Originally sung by Zechariah at the birth of his son John the Baptist. Luke 1.68-79.

A Song of Creation   A call for all that God has created to praise him. Often called the Benedicite, it is found in the Apocrypha in the Song of the Three Children 35-64 (adapted).

Great and Wonderful   Praise of God for his works and his holiness. Part of the worship of heaven described in Revelation 15.3-4.

Te Deum   A Latin hymn, written in the fourth century, in praise of the Father and the Son, and concluding with a prayer for help and mercy. It is often used on occasions of thanksgiving.

Gloria in Excelsis   A Greek hymn from the fourth century, which has commonly been used in the Eucharist. A celebration of Christ, based on the worship of the angels in Luke 2.14.

Saviour of the World   A prayer to Christ for help and for the deliverance that he gained for his people on the cross. The canticle is appropriate for use in Advent or Lent. Written by a nineteenth century Congregationalist, Dr Henry Allon, and now modernised.

Evening Prayer

Psalm 134   An evening psalm, calling God's people to worship.

O Gladsome Light   A third century Greek evening hymn, celebrating Christ, the light of the world.

The Easter Anthems   as at Morning Prayer.

Magnificat. The Song of Mary   A celebration of God's care and goodness to the humble and needy. Sung by Mary when Elizabeth visited her, in celebration that she had been chosen to be the mother of the Messiah. Luke 1.46-55.

Bless the Lord   A song praising the majesty and holiness of God. Song of the Three Children 29-32 from the Apocrypha.

Nunc Dimittis. The song of Simeon   A song celebrating that Jesus is the longed for Messiah. Sung by the aged Simeon, when Jesus was presented in the temple. Luke 2.29-32.

The Song of Christ's Glory   In praise of the humility of Jesus and of his exaltation. Taken from Philippians 2.6-11.

Glory and Honour   Part of the worship of heaven, in praise of God the creator and of Jesus, the Lamb of God. Revelation 4.11; 5.9,10,12,13.

of the Word of God than a theatrical rendering or a superlative sense of timing.

Dialogue readings, group readings, musical accompaniment of the spoken word, the whole congregation reciting together and full-scale dramatisation are helpful alternatives to one person holding forth from a lectern.

THE SERMON

The sermon should stir and nerve and challenge and thrill the congregation into worship and action. In a good sermon the preacher enters into a real dialogue with the congregation – that is, preacher and people struggle together to understand what is the word of the Lord for them.

Visual aids, interviews, actual dialogues, filmstrips, mime, dance, drama and small group discussions often sup-

plement the traditional lengthy monologue in today's Church. But they do not dispense entirely with the sermon which is a very good means of encouraging commitment, reaffirming faith and renewing vision.

In the new services the sermon may follow directly upon the readings and obviously this is a help when, as should usually be the case, the sermon is related to one or both of them. Whether it is placed here, however, or in its traditional position following the hymn after the notices, deliberate thought should always be given to the appropriate sequel to the sermon, whether it be intercessions, a time of silence, a particular hymn, a baptism, or even a collection. The sermon is an integral part of the worship service and a springboard for Christian understanding and service in the world.

HOW TO LISTEN TO A SERMON
● *Believe that God has something to say to you.* Many distractions divert our attention from what the preacher is saying. His voice, manner or style of delivery may annoy us. Our own pre-occupations with work, family or pleasure may drive our thoughts off at a tangent. We may have prejudices or blind spots which make it impossible for us to hear what he is saying. The Church, and all it stands for, may provide an institutional barrier. Yet if we believe that God will speak to us hc usually does, and it will help if we go to Church expecting him to do so.
● *Work out one point or thought to take away from Church with you.* A good preacher will probably endeavour to teach only one major truth in each sermon he preaches. Experience shows that not all the congregation will take the same point, but it is important that we shall not be distracted from looking for it. We need to beware especially when a sermon is entertaining, colourful or full of illustrations. The purpose is not to amuse but to change us into Christian men and women.
● *Turn the point of the sermon into a prayer and a commitment.* Usually the sermon ends with a prayer. If this is not taken as an opportunity to help the congregation apply the message to themselves, it is useful to take time at the end of the service, following the blessing, to offer ourselves to God – as the sermon suggested – for the work and witness of the coming week. Some ministers helpfully underline the main point of the sermon in the first part of the blessing which concludes the service.
● *Aids to concentration.* Take notes as the preacher speaks. Follow the argument from a open bible. Discuss the sermon, not the preacher, afterwards with friends.

THE APOSTLES' CREED

This statement of Christian faith follows, as a fitting conclusion, the section of the service in which we hear the word of God in the readings from the scriptures and possibly the sermon. The apostles did not write it but, by the end of the fourth century, it had gained its title, presumably because it was thought to reflect the teaching of the apostles and was true to their faith.

Those who were baptised in early days professed their faith in the words of a creed and the practice is related to the passage in Matthew 28.19 where Jesus tells his disciples to baptise all nations, in the name of the Trinity. In its present form the Apostles' Creed developed from that used by Christians in Rome at their baptism, falls into three sections. We confess our faith in God the Father, God the Son and God the Holy Spirit. The saying of this creed, essential at baptism, has for the last thousand years been a regular feature also of the Church's daily worship. In the new services, however, the shorter form of Evening Prayer omits the creed.

Two phrases call for further explanation:

● *He descended to the dead.* It was easy for Christians to misunderstand the old phrase, 'He descended into hell'. The words at first sight suggested that Jesus, when he died, went to the place of eternal punishment. The creed never intended such an interpretation. The new translation, which has been agreed by all the major denominations, makes this clear. The clause was probably inserted into the creed to emphasise that Jesus experienced the full reality of death. Many Christians have seen here a reference to Jesus proclaiming his victorious death to the departed so that those who lived before his birth might have the opportunity to believe in him. People who hold this view point to 1 Peter 3.19,20 but it is more likely that the 'spirits' in this passage refer to angelic powers in rebellion against God (as in Genesis 6) and that Peter is referring to Christ's triumphant announcement that their power had finally been broken. On this interpretation, 1 Peter 4.6 refers to those Christians who believed the Gospel and have since died.

● *I believe in ... the holy Catholic Church.* Some Christians have been tempted to think that they are expressing, by this phrase, a faith in the Roman Catholic Church. This would be a contradiction in terms for the word 'catholic' means 'universal'. We profess our belief in the world-wide Church of Jesus Christ which includes all Christians who repent of their sins, believe in the good news of Jesus Christ and are baptised (see Acts 2.38).

COLLECTS AND PRAYERS

What is a collect?

A collect is a type of prayer that has been traditional in Roman Catholic and Anglican worship. The Latin word *collectio* means a 'gathering together' and was used of these prayers either because they were prayed when people gathered together or because the prayers themselves gathered together the people's prayers. The early Church, for example, used such prayers for intercession. The presiding minister would suggest a sub-

THE COLLECT OF THE SECOND SUNDAY AFTER EPIPHANY

Almighty God,
by whose grace we are accepted
and called to your service,

strengthen us by your Holy Spirit
and make us worthy of your calling,
through Jesus Christ, our Lord,
Amen.

- The address to God and the divine attribute upon which we base our petition
- A short, simple and definite request
- A concluding doxology
- The people's affirmation

ject for prayer, there would be a time of silence for the congregation to pray, and then he would sum up the prayer with a collect. In Anglican worship there is a special collect for each Sunday or holy day which is used at the end of the opening section of the communion service to express the theme of the day. The same collect is then used at Morning and Evening Prayer to give continuity to the day's, or the week's, worship. Morning and Evening Prayer also have daily collects to follow the collect of the day. In the shorter form of these services normally only one of these daily collects is used. On Sundays, or with the full services, the minister will probably use two or more. The morning collects ask for God's protection and strength to serve him. The evening collects look for God's peace and defence as we take our rest.

The structure of a collect

Collects are short and compact and they follow a pattern made up of four parts:

- The calling upon God's name, usually including a clause telling us something about God.
- Our request and perhaps the reason why we ask.
- The ending, usually mentioning Jesus and sometimes also the Holy Spirit. This reminds us that our prayer goes to the Father through Jesus who is a bridge between us and the Father.
- The Amen. This is a very important part of the collect. It is the congregation's part of the prayer, the way in which they can say, 'Yes. That's what we want.'

Prayers in church

When we worship with other people in church we are taking part in a united action. The fact that several people are sitting together in the same place at the same time saying their private prayers does not constitute an act of worship. Our prayer is corporate and that means that the whole congregation prays together. Whenever people do things together they have to agree on a way of doing it. If twenty-two men decide to play a game of football there must be some set form to the game upon which they all agree and in which they can all take part. There would be chaos otherwise. In the same way if we are truly to unite in our prayers there must be some sort of set form in our prayer time, some sort of framework in which to pray.

There are many different kinds of framework. There is the use of 'biddings'. The leader mentions a particular item for prayer, there is time for silent prayer and then the prayers are summed up in a short sentence or a longer written prayer. There is the responsive form of prayer, in which the congregation are required to respond to the leader's words using a repetitive form, for example, Minister 'Lord, in your mercy,' Congregation 'hear our prayer.' A large measure of freedom is allowed in a framework in which the subject for intercession is announced and the congregation pray freely aloud around that subject. Most commonly, however, during the prayer time, the minister or one or more members of the congregation will read prayers of intercession around a particular theme. Many congregations use lists of intercessions produced by dioceses or missionary societies which specify particular prayer needs for a particular day. There are many excellent books of prayers which may be used in this time. Here is a selection:

Christopher Campling and Michael Davis, *Words for Worship*, (London: Edward Arnold, 1969); Frank Colquhoun, *Contemporary Parish Prayers*, (London: Hodder and Stoughton, 1975); Dick Wil-

liams, *Prayers for Today's Church*, (London: CPAS Publications, 1972); Caryl Micklem, *Contemporary Prayers for Public Worship*, (London: SCM Press, 1967); Norman W. Goodacre, *Prayers for Today*, (London: Mowbrays, 1972).

What sort of prayers shall we use?

● *Liturgical prayers* Collects and other prayers which do not change but are read in a set form are called liturgical prayers. The new services include prayers for the Royal Family and for the congregation together with a general intercession and a general thanksgiving. The leader of the service may select from these or use one or more sections of the litany (see below). Liturgical prayers save the congregation from being at the mercy of the mood of the one who is leading. Worship remains orderly, dignified and God-centred. On the other hand, much repetition of the same words can make them stale. And what room is there for the prompting of the Holy Spirit?

● *Free prayer* Free prayer does not have a fixed form, but is chosen or composed by the person leading the prayers. In the intercessions after the third collect there is room for free prayer, which may well include prayers of thanksgiving and praise. Free prayer need not be written down, but it is not entirely spontaneous. A good deal of preparation goes into free prayer – in the form of meditation before the service. During this time the person leading the prayers will spend time with God, until he or she knows what to pray for. In free prayer the leader can respond to the Holy Spirit as he feels led and this may help the congregation to feel that they really are communicating with God. As a lady said of a certain minister, 'Mr X. talks to God when he prays. You can't often say that these days.' But there are real dangers in free prayer. The minister sometimes lectures the congregation, addressing the prayer to them instead of to God. Free prayer can become local and in-ward-looking. It can become almost as stale as repeated liturgical prayer – the

same well-worn phrases being used over and over again. In a cathedral or a large city church which serves a varied community there may be a need for very formal services in which free prayer plays a small part. More usually, however, in a smaller fellowship, free prayer will have a larger place.

Extempore Prayer

Extempore prayer is spoken prayer which is unprepared and spontaneous. It has never played a large part in Anglican public worship, but increasingly time is being allowed for extempore prayer after the third collect. It works best when the minister first gives the congregations some guidance on subjects for prayer.

Extempore prayer can be disorderly, repetitive and extremely lengthy! Sometimes it is centred on man and his problems, rather than upon God, sometimes it is very personal and out of place in a large congregation. Often it cannot be heard over the whole church building, so that a part of the congregation is unable to make the prayer their own. Extempore prayer is generally more suited to a prayer meeting or a small group gathered for informal worship.

Writing prayers

One of the most rewarding ways in which lay people can play their part in worship is by writing prayers for use in church. Writing prayers is not easy, but a prayer written and prayed by a person in touch with a particular situation can be much more appropriate and meaningful than one found in a general book of prayers. When we write prayers there is no need to use special language. When Jesus prayed he called his Father 'Abba' – 'Daddy'. We can be just as familiar with God and use language which is just as simple and effective. We need not address him as 'Thou'. That is stilted and extraordinary today. Nevertheless our prayers are addressed to God and should be expressed in language which is as beautiful as we can make it. Prayers should be short. There is often a temptation to ramble and lose the concentration

What Morning Prayer means to me

I live and work in North London surrounded by noise, by dirt and, all too often, by suffering and despair. What has that to do with Morning Prayer? How can the two possibly go together? The answer is that prayer overcomes despair. Monday morning on a wet winter's day can be pretty miserable in a place like this; to offer prayer and praise to God the Father, Son and Holy Spirit can sometimes be the very last thing I feel like doing. That is when the constant rhythm of Morning Prayer becomes such a blessing.

O Lord open our lips:
 and our mouth shall
 proclaim your praise.

God answers that prayer and many more. Not only does he open my lips to praise him but he speaks to my heart through the psalms, canticles and readings. I go on my way strengthened and rejoicing, 'Jesus is the same, yesterday, today and forever.' It doesn't matter how bleak things around me may be, I know that God is in charge.

Christian Merivale

Christian Merivale was a farmer before he was ordained. He lives with his wife, Jane, and two children in a flat in Highbury, North London, where he is a curate.

By the mystery of your holy incarnation ... by your cross and passion ... by your mighty resurrection ... by your sending of the Holy Spirit, *Good Lord, deliver us.*

ASB 1980, The Litany

The litany ends with a celebration of the greatness of God upon whom we depend for everything:

'Holy God,
holy and strong,
holy and immortal,
have mercy upon us.'

of the congregation. The use of silence is important. It allows the congregation to join in and make the words which have just been spoken their own.

THE LITANY
What is the Litany?

The Litany is a fixed form of prayer which consists of petitions offered by the minister to which the congregation respond. The word 'litany' comes from a Greek word which means 'supplication'. The Litany is a form of liturgical prayer which enables the whole congregation to participate.

The Litany in *ASB 1980* (p.99) is a general and all-embracing prayer which is always God-centred. The Litany is divided into six sections of which the first and last must always be used.

● *Section I* sets the scene for our prayers as we come before God – Father, Son and Holy Spirit – to ask mercy of the 'Holy, blessed and glorious Trinity'.

● *Section II* is about God and us. We face up to the full extent of our sin and the sin of the world and ask God to deliver us by the good news of Jesus Christ.

● *Section III* brings to God in prayer the Church and all she is called to be and to do.

● *Section IV* prays for the nations of the world and particularly for the queen, parliament, the officers of the law and our use of the land.

● *Section V* centres upon the needy, near and far, not forgetting those who malign us and ending with a thanksgiving for those who have died 'in the peace of Christ'.

● *Section VI* is about 'me'. The repentance and the amendment of life for which we pray is a miracle God works in each person individually.

Where did the Litany come from?

The Litany was the first part of Cranmer's Prayer Book to appear in English.

In 1544 this was a revolutionary move intended to help the people, as the Preface put it, to pray 'in their hearts the same petitions which do enter in at their ears so that with one sound of the heart, and with one accord, God may be glorified in his Church'. In compiling the Litany Cranmer was following a traditional form of prayer which seems to have had its beginnings in the Church in the fourth century. The Litany always has been, and still is, a popular way of praying in the Orthodox Church. Cranmer's Litany bears the marks of Eastern influence, Luther's Litany (1529) and, of course, the old Roman form. Like its predecessors the Prayer Book Litany was originally designed to bc said or sung in procession around the church.

Using the Litany

In the new services the Litany may be used instead of the Prayers. Traditionally the Litany has been used at ordinations and according to the Prayer Book, 'after Morning Prayer upon Sundays, Wednesdays and Fridays'. Before the Reformation the Litany was used daily in England during Lent and Rogationtide, which comprised three days of fasting before Ascension Day. Christians today seem either to hate or to love the Litany. For some it is too long, wordy and general in its petitions. For others, however, it is an unparalleled aid to public and private devotion – rich, generous and redolent of ancient Christian prayers.

The Order for Holy Communion

HOW IT BEGAN

The New Testament gives us four accounts of Jesus' institution of the eucharist, in Matthew 26, Mark 14, Luke 22, and 1 Corinthians 11. In addition John 13 records the same supper, but does not mention the institution. The general picture which emerges is that there was a 'last supper' which Jesus held with his disciples after nightfall on the Thursday evening, and in the course of that meal Jesus took bread, gave thanks, gave it to his disciples, and said to them 'Take, eat; this is my body which is for you'; and then following the supper, similarly took a cup of wine, gave thanks, and gave it to the disciples with the words 'Drink this, all of you: for this is my blood of the new covenant'. The meal appears from the first three Gospels to have been a passover meal, with all the overtones the passover has of God's redemption of his people from bondage through the shed blood of a lamb. In John's Gospel the last supper is not so clearly a passover meal, but the account can be reconciled with those in the other Gospels so as to leave the passover probability still very strong.

Although John does not have an account of the institution it is clear from his use of 'eucharistic' terminology in chapter 6 that he was well acquainted with the institution, and traced it back to Jesus himself. This tallies very well with the passing hints in Acts that from the beginning the infant Church was steadfast 'in the breaking of bread' (Acts 2.42), and with the explicit account in 1 Corinthians 11 where Paul claims to be handing on what he received 'from the Lord'. He further adds that Jesus actually commanded 'Do this in remembrance of me', and the invariable practice of the Church from the beginning reflects this sense of acting under the Lord's command.

The actual account of Jesus' institution of the eucharist seems to have acquired a set shape, differing slightly between Matthew/Mark on the one hand and Luke/Paul on the other. It is very likely that the set shape derives from continual repetition of the narrative of institution, more or less from memory (which accounts for slightly varying texts), probably within the eucharist itself as part of the pattern of worship. Certainly by the time of Justin Martyr (died 160) we find other authors quoting this narrative, again as if from memory (as though it were said aloud in worship). The first full text of a eucharistic prayer which we have comes from Hippolytus of Rome around 215, and there there is a narrative of institution embedded within the prayer, roughly as it is found in *ASB 1980*. It is clear that originally its role was to relate the particular celebration to our Lord's general command, and it stood as a relative clause within the eucharistic prayer to fufil this purpose. Its final command 'Do this . . .' then led into our

---

Note: All references to the 'rite' or 'service' in this chapter are to Rite A unless otherwise stated.

Consecration

statement of our response 'Therefore we [do this] ...' usually called the 'anamnesis' because it tells how we intend to keep the remembrance (Gk. 'anamnesis') of him. The narrative of institution was not therefore originally a 'formula of consecration', and the new orders in the Church of England have gone back to the original concept and do not lay any great weight of special solemnity upon our saying 'This is my body' and 'This is my blood'. The narrative gives us our warrant for celebrating the eucharist, but it is *not* a series of rubrics telling us when to pick up or put down the bread and wine.

THE SHAPE

Jesus instituted the eucharist by a series of specific actions within the last supper, which we have thought was probably a passover. These actions were:

During supper
1 *He took bread*
2 *He gave thanks*
3 *He broke it*
4 *He gave it to his disciples*

After supper
5 *He took the cup*
6 *He gave thanks*
7 *He gave it to his disciples*

When the actions with the bread and the cup are separated from each other by the meal, then they naturally form these seven actions. However, in the second century the meal context started to fall away, and the two sets of actions started to merge into a single set. These can then be set out as:

1 *The President takes the bread and cup*
2 *He gives thanks over both bread and cup*
3 *He breaks the bread*
4 *He gives the bread and the cup to the worshippers*

It is clear that these actions, whilst they give a clear structure and shape to the meal, are not of equal weight with each other. 1 and 3 are preliminary to 2 and 4, and 2 and 4 are the great indispensable parts of the meal. This can be seen in the cross-headings before sections 36, 38 and 42 in the service today.

The 'preparation of the gifts' is a preparatory action, comparable to that of the disciples who went ahead to prepare the passover room for Jesus. It is not part of the dominical action, and can in fact come earlier in the service if desired.

From the time of Justin Martyr onwards, there is a fairly clear picture discernible that the meal was preceded by readings from the bible (with exposition), followed by prayers of intercession. Finally, before the meal itself began, the participants greeted each other with the 'kiss of peace'. Thus the overall structure became:

Bible readings and sermon
Prayers
Kiss of Peace
Sacramental meal:
 Taking
 Giving thanks
 Breaking the bread
 Sharing the bread and cup

This 'shape' can easily be followed in the new order.

THE PRESENCE OF CHRIST

When Jesus explained the feeding of the five thousand, according to the account in John 6, he referred *both* to eating him himself (e.g. John 6.57) *and* to eating his flesh (John 6.52). It is clear that there is in this a description of the eucharist, and John's first readers in around 100 AD would have been bound to read it that way. The Gospel account was here teaching that which was their weekly, if not daily, experience. They fed on Christ, they ate his flesh and drank his blood.

The accounts of the last supper itself confirm this. Jesus calls the bread his body and the wine his blood, and commands his disciples to eat and drink them. This is the language which is found in all the accounts of early Christian worship, and in all the actual liturgical texts from the early centuries. The bread 'is' his body; the cup 'is' his blood. Ignatius of Antioch in the first years of the second century AD could say that a certain group (called Gnostics) were

heretics precisely because 'they allow not that the eucharist is the flesh of our Saviour Jesus Christ, which flesh suffered for our sins ...'.

So Christians have always been committed to saying that *in some sense* the bread is Christ's body, the cup is his blood. It is obviously not a physical or material sense – this is no cannibalism, and the idea that it might be does not seem to have troubled the disciples' minds. It is difficult to take Jesus' words wholly literally, and it would be somewhat wooden to do so. He was present in his flesh and blood, and preparing to suffer death in his earthly body, when he declared at the last supper that the bread and wine were his flesh and blood. If it had been true in a literal sense then, then he would have ceased to be like us, to die as one of us and on behalf of the rest of us. It seems clear therefore that he was pointing to the meaning the disciples would have to put on the bread and wine after his ascension.

The Church is surely therefore justified in calling the bread his body and

the wine his blood, without defining closely in *what* sense this is so. It seems that when, in the middle ages, the Church of Rome defined the manner of Christ's presence (by the doctrine of transsubstantiation, which said that the 'substance' of the bread became the 'substance' of his body, though the 'accidents' – the whiteness, texture, etc. – remained those of bread) it caught itself in a web of definitions which went beyond the evidence. The reformers reacted strongly to this, and said that the bread is only the body of Christ to the faithful recipient – rather as the title deeds of a house only convey the house to the right recipient. That is why Cranmer wrote in the 1552 Prayer Book:

> 'and grant that we, receiving these thy creatures of bread and wine, . . . may be partakers of his [i.e. Christ's] most blessed body and blood.'

Nowadays we say in the first three eucharistic prayers

> 'and grant that by the power of your Holy Spirit
> these gifts of bread and wine
> may be to us his body and blood.'

However, in the fourth prayer, and in the prayer from the order following the pattern of 1662, Cranmer's words are retained. Both sets of words teach not so much that an objective change has happened in the elements, as that they have power, in the right context and to the believing recipient, to convey the presence and pardon of Christ. Like the paper and ink of the title-deeds they truly and powerfully *convey* that which they represent.

The question is not so much 'What is there on the table?', but 'What do I receive?' And yet the gift of God, of the presence of Christ, and of the 'benefits of his passion', is not subjective, but is genuinely offered all the time to all who are present. Christ himself, living and reigning, commands believers to assemble at his table, meets with them there, and feeds their inward beings with his riches and his grace – the outward feeding is God's means of grace to effect this gift within.

The Church has always had to face further questions arising from the over-strong belief in a presence of Christ in (or, as is sometimes said, 'under') the bread and wine. Should the consecrated elements be the objects of special reverence and devotion? Should they be reserved for these purposes? How should any remaining at the end of the service be finished up? The new rites give no encouragement to superstition and over-reverence, though the Church of England is considering forms for bringing communion to the sick which will mean that not all the bread and wine is always used up at the particular service in which they are consecrated.

The communicant has to remember that he is there at the Lord's command, that the bread and wine convey to him both Jesus himself and the power of his death which, being alive for ever, he now gives to his people. And as he gives himself to us, he gives not only the 'comfort' (of which the old Prayer Book spoke), but also the demands of his Lordship over us. If he lives in us and we in him, then we go from the supper to live for him.

CONCEPTS OF CONSECRATION

If bread and wine are put on the communion table as merely bread and wine, how do they become the 'body and blood of Christ'? What can the Church *do* which so meets the Lord's command that we then *know* that they are the body and blood of Christ? In other words, what 'consecrates' them?

The Lord's command 'Do this in remembrance of me' is generally taken to include taking-and-thanking and breaking-and-eating. It is when all four actions are done that the Lord's command is fulfilled. Nevertheless, down history the Church has seen the 'thanking', i.e. the thanksgiving or 'eucharistic' prayer as that which 'consecrates'. That can be seen in this rite as at section 43 the president breaks the '*consecrated*' bread –

i.e. it has already been 'consecrated'. So we expect this to occur in the eucharistic prayer before that point.

In the eastern Orthodox Churches they believe that a special calling upon God to send down his Spirit upon the bread and wine, which is a distinct paragraph within the eucharistic prayer, is the way in which the elements are 'consecrated'. In the Roman Catholic Church there grew up, along with the doctrine of transsubstantiation in the middle ages, a belief that the miraculous change was effected by the priest's saying 'This is my body' and 'This is my blood'. Thus the ringing of bells, and the use of genuflection in adoration of the presence of Christ, now thought to be 'there' in or under the bread and wine, became the common practice. And although Cranmer abolished an objective consecration altogether, yet in 1662 both puritans and high churchmen wanted to put such a consecration back. They did this in a way which can seen in the order following the pattern of 1662 (section 65) – little 'indented rubrics' ordered the picking up of the bread and wine, and the laying of the priest's hand upon them, during the account of how Jesus instituted the eucharist. This is the 1662 concept of 'consecration'.

But in the four main eucharistic prayers there is no such provision. There is no point for picking up the bread and cup, and none for laying a hand on them. The best account of this is to say that the whole eucharistic prayer – from the initial greeting to the final doxology – must be viewed as consecratory. That is what Jesus did – he 'gave thanks' over the bread and later over the cup. We give thanks over them, and view them as consecrated not by a single line in the thanksgiving, but by the whole of it.

It is very important to notice that the question 'what effects consecration?' is a different one from the question 'what does consecration effect?' People may agree on the answer to one of these questions, while still disagreeing on the answer to the other.

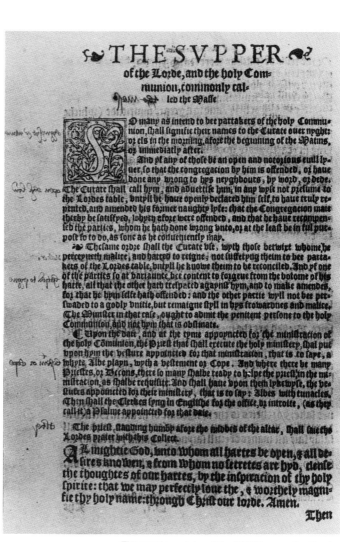

The opening rubrics of the 1549 Communion Service

Then bread and a cup of water and of mixed wine are brought to him who presides over the brethren, and he takes them and offers praise and glory to the Father of all in the name of the Son and of the Holy Spirit, and gives thanks at some length that we have been deemed worthy of these things from him. When he has finished the prayers and the thanksgiving, all the people present give their assent by saying, 'Amen.'

Amen is Hebrew for 'So be it'.

And we call this food 'thanksgiving' and no one may partake of it unless he is convinced of the truth of our teaching, and has been cleansed with the washing for forgiveness of sins and regeneration, and lives as Christ handed down.

For we do not receive these things as common bread or common drink; but just as our Saviour Jesus Christ, being incarnate through the word of God, took flesh and blood for our salvation, so too we have been taught that the food over which thanks have been given [i.e. which has been 'eucharisticised'] by the prayer of the Word who is from him, from which our flesh and blood are fed by transformation, is both the flesh and blood of that incarnate Jesus.

For the apostles in the records composed by them which are called gospels, have handed down what was commanded them: that Jesus took bread, gave thanks, and said, 'Do this for my remembrance; this is my body'; and likewise he took the cup, gave thanks, and said, 'This is my blood'; and gave to them alone.

Justin Martyr 150 AD

THE EUCHARISTIC PRAYER

From the second century onwards there is a single 'thanksgiving' used. The earliest description of this (in Justin Martyr around 150 AD) shows that it was said by the 'president' ('he who presides') and the people responded 'Amen' to show their agreement and their identification with what was said. The Greek word for 'thanksgiving' is 'eucharistia', and from the first post-apostolic writers onwards we find that the whole rite is called the 'eucharist' and the central prayer in it the 'eucharistic prayer'.

The first written text of such a single central eucharistic prayer that has come down to us is to be found in the *Apostolic Tradition* of Hippolytus of Rome and is usually dated around 215 AD. But Hippolytus makes clear that the pattern of Justin's time, whereby the president would make up his own wording in an extempore way, had not ceased in his own time. The written form was merely for convenience, and particularly to help those who had difficulty in producing a sufficiently dignified prayer without preparation of it.

It looks as though the primitive pattern of the eucharistic prayer was based upon Jewish thanksgivings (called *Berakoth*), and the Jewish themes for thanksgivings at meals – not least at the passover – included thanks to God for his work in creation, for his work in redeeming his people out of Egypt, and for the promised land and Jerusalem and God's care for his people. These themes are roughly paralleled in the eucharistic prayers of antiquity in similar thanksgivings for creation, for the work of Christ in redemption, and for the calling into being of a people of God chosen by God to serve him. The text of Hippolytus shown opposite is a good example.

One special feature of the eucharistic prayer is the 'Narrative of Institution'. This is developed from the accounts in the synoptic Gospels and Paul's first letter to the Corinthians, and by repetition has tended to take on a semi-fixed form from earliest times. Indeed the biblical accounts may take *their* form from the repeated use in worship which the accounts already had (but we do not know this for certain). The 'Narrative' of how Jesus instituted the eucharist provides us with the historical peg to which we attach our celebration of the eucharist – that is, we (in the words of Prayer 1, section 38) 'follow his example and obey his command'. It has become usual – and the basic idea of this can be seen in the Hippolytus text – to follow the Narrative, which ends with Jesus' command 'Do this in remembrance of me', with a paragraph known as the 'anamnesis' in which we describe how 'with *this* bread and *this* cup' we obey his command. 'Anamnesis' is the Greek word for 'remembrance', and some reference to 'remembering' or 'remembrance' comes at the beginning of the paragraph.

During Christian history, there developed an idea in western Europe that the reciting by the president of Jesus' words 'This is my body' and 'This is my blood' actually consecrated the elements – almost as though no other part of the prayer but these brief formulae were necessary. But the early Church was more inclined to think that the whole prayer 'eucharisticised' the bread and wine to become the Lord's body and blood, and the idea of a single snap 'moment of consecration' does not give enough weight to the whole pattern of thanksgiving.

Various other regular features appear in the eucharistic prayer over the centuries. In Hippolytus it can be seen that near the end of the prayer there was a request that the Spirit of God would give the benefits of communion to the worshippers, and this led into a doxology. This sequence of thought has been constant down the centuries. However, at an earlier point Hippolytus' text leaves out an

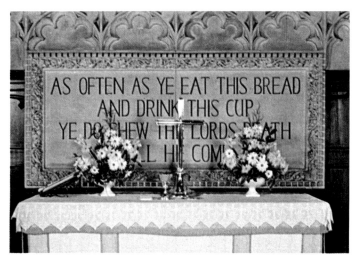

The Bishop, laying his hands on the elements with all the presbytery, shall give thanks, saying:

The Lord be with you;
and all shall say:
  And with your spirit.
Up with your hearts.
  We have them with the Lord.
Let us give thanks to the Lord.
  It is fitting and right.

And then he shall continue thus:
We render thanks to you, O God, through your beloved child Jesus Christ, whom in the last times you sent to us as saviour and redeemer and angel of your will; who is your inseparable Word, through whom you made all things, and in whom you were well pleased. You sent him from heaven into the Virgin's womb; and, conceived in the womb, he was made flesh and was manifested as your Son, being born of the holy Spirit and the Virgin. Fulfilling your will and gaining for you a holy people, he stretched out his hands when he should suffer, that he might release from suffering those who have believed in you.

And when he was betrayed to voluntary suffering that he might destroy death, and break the bonds of the devil, and tread down hell, and shine upon the righteous, and fix a term, and manifest the resurrection, he took bread and gave thanks to you, saying, 'Take, eat; this is my body, which shall be broken for you'. Likewise also the cup, saying, 'This is my blood, which is shed for you; when you do this, you make my remembrance'.

Remembering therefore his death and resurrection, we offer to you the bread and the cup, giving you thanks because you have held us worthy to stand before you and minister to you. And we ask that you would send your holy Spirit upon the offering of your holy Church; that, gathering (it) into one, you would grant to all who partake of the holy things (to partake) for the fullness of the holy Spirit for the strengthening of faith in truth, that we may praise and glorify you through your child Jesus Christ, through whom be glory and honour to you, with the holy Spirit, in your holy Church, both now and to the ages of ages. Amen.

Hippolytus, *Eucharistic Prayer*, 215 AD.

anthem to which all modern worshippers are well accustomed – the Sanctus, 'Holy, holy, holy Lord, etc.'. Because the worship of the Church is to be understood as taking place 'in the heavenly places' (Ephesians 2.5) the prayer starts with 'Lift up your hearts'. It is therefore not surprising that in the years after Hippolytus' time there grew up a tendency to imitate the angels of Isaiah 6 or the elders of Revelation 4 and 'with angels and archangels' sing the heavenly song of adoration. More lately it has become regular in many demoninations to have a further congregational response – the 'Acclamations' – after the Narrative of Institution and before the 'anamnesis' paragraph. The total effect is to give the president the major part in the saying of the eucharistic prayer, but to enable the whole congregation to respond in such a way as to be closely identified with the whole prayer.

The teaching of the Epistle to the Hebrews
'Christ has appeared once for all ... to abolish sin by the sacrifice of himself' (*9.26*).

'Every [Old Testament] priest stands daily doing his service and offering again and again the same sacrifices which can never take away sins. But Christ, when he had offered one sacrifice for sins for ever, sat down at the right hand of God' (*10.11-12*).

'He has no daily need ... to offer sacrifices ... for he did this once and for all when he offered up himself' (*7.27*).

'We have a high priest of this sort, one who is seated at the right hand of the throne of the Majesty on high' (*8.1*).

'He, because he remains forever, has an inalienable priesthood; and therefore he is able to save forever those who draw near to God through him, since he always lives to make intercession for them.' (*7.24-25*)

'Therefore, my brothers, as we have boldness to enter the holy place by the blood of Jesus ... and as we have a great priest over the household of God, let us draw near with a true heart in full assurance of faith ...' (*10.19-22*).

EUCHARISTIC SACRIFICE

The Epistle to the Hebrews teaches that Christ's death was his sacrifice; that his sacrifice was made for our sins; that this sacrifice brought to an end all Old Testament ritual sacrifices (especially those made by the high priest once a year on the 'Day of Atonement'); that this sacrifice was therefore made 'once for all' and could never need to be supplemented or repeated; and that by this sacrifice, because it was perfect and was accepted by the Father, Christ entered into the heavenlies as our high priest, where he lives 'to make intercession for us' – or, as it might be translated, 'to look after our interests'. His sacrifice is eternally powerful and effective, and we come to worship on the basis of his high priesthood – he both died for us, and lives in the heavenly places as our 'forerunner'.

This means that Christians have no sacrifices to make for their sins – it has all been done for them once for all in Christ. The New Testament does speak of 'sacrifices' – i.e. costly gifts to God – which we are to make in response to God's goodness to us, and these have tended to weave their way into the text of our eucharistic liturgy. But they are clearly *responses* to God's gift to us, and Christ's atoning sacrifice for us.

In the second century of the Christian era the habit grew up of calling the eucharist 'the Christian sacrifice' – a form of language which is not to be found in so many words in the New Testament. The Christians then decided that this 'sacrifice' was the fulfilment of a prophecy in the first chapter of Malachi, thus fixing the notion of a Christian sacrifice offered to God by the Church, and also showing how more acceptable to God it is than Jewish sacrifices! The second century Christians tended to express this by saying that they were offering the bread and the cup to God, but they did not well agree with each other as to the *reason* why they offered it to God.

In the third century, Cyprian went further, and interpreted the offering as being the Church's offering of the sacrifice of Christ. The third century also saw the adoption of the titles of the Old Testament Jewish priesthood for Christian ministers (particularly bishops), and this tended to consolidate the idea that the Church, by its 'priests', was offering a real sacrifice to the Father, the sacrifice of Christ.

In the dark ages and in the middle ages the idea was further developed, and the Church came to believe that each eucharist (or 'mass') offered to God had some special (indeed quantifiable) value. This 'mass sacrifice' was able to bring benefits to the living – and to the dead also. It was thus possible to offer a large number of masses for the soul of a particular dead person in purgatory, and the benefit he gained would be in proportion to the number of masses offered. Such a concept tended not only to distort the significance of the eucharist by giving it quite inappropriate values, but also helped crowd out the genuine role of the eucharist as the corporate feast of the redeemed.

The sacrifices Christians offer to God

'Like living stones, be yourselves built up into a spiritual house to be a holy priesthood, to offer spiritual sacrifices acceptable to God through Jesus Christ' (*1 Pet 2.4*).

'I call upon you, my brothers, by the mercies of God to present your bodies as a living holy sacrifice which is acceptable to God and your reasonable service (*Rom 12.1*).

NB (section 53)*
Through him we offer you our souls and bodies
to be a living sacrifice.'

'Through Christ therefore let us offer up a sacrifice of praise continually (that is, the fruit of lips which confess his name); and do not forget to do good works and to share with each other. For with sacrifices like these God is well pleased' (*Heb 13.15-16*).

NB

Section 38: 'Accept through him, our great high priest,
this our sacrifice of thanks and praise ...'
Section 39: 'Through him accept our sacrifice of praise ...'
Section 40: 'We pray you to accept this our duty and service,
a spiritual sacrifice of praise and thanksgiving ...'
Section 41: 'We offer you through him this sacrifice of praise and thanksgiving' (See also section 71).

*Section numbers refer to *ASB 1980*.

The second and third century texts

'From the rising of the sun to the setting of it my name is great among the Gentiles, and in every place incense is offered to my name and a pure sacrifice; for my name is great among the Gentiles' says the Lord of hosts' (*Mal. 1.11*).

'[In Mal. 1.11] God is prophesying about the sacrifices which are offered in every place by us, the Gentiles (that is, the bread and the cup of the eucharist) ...'
Justin Martyr's *Dialogue with Trypho*, c. 135 AD ch. 41.

'Remembering therefore his death and resurrection, we offer to you the bread and the cup.'
From the Eucharistic prayer of Hippolytus, c. 215 AD.

15th century monks at mass

The Reformation period

'Who made *there*, by his one oblation of himself once offered, a full, perfect, and sufficient sacrifice, oblation, and satisfaction for the sins of the whole world ...'
    1552 and 1662 Prayer Books – our italics

NB (*ASB 1980 sections 41 and 65*):
    '... you gave your only Son Jesus Christ
    to suffer death upon the cross for our redemption;
    he made there
    a full atonement for the sins of the whole world,
    offering once for all his one sacrifice of himself ...'

'... the sacrifices of the masses, in which it was commonly said that the priest did offer Christ for the living and the dead, were blasphemous fables and dangerous deceits.'
    Article XXXI of the XXXIX Articles of Religion, 1571.

'... and *here* we offer and present unto thee, O Lord, ourselves, our souls and bodies to be reasonable holy and lively sacrifice unto thee ...'
    1552 and 1662 Prayer Books – our italics.

A modern statement

'Christ's death on the cross, the culmination of his whole life of obedience, was the one, perfect and sufficient sacrifice for the sins of the world. There can be no repetition of or addition to what was then accomplished once for all by Christ ...'

'In the eucharistic prayer the church continues to make a perpetual memorial of Christ's death, and his members, united with God and one another, give thanks for all his mercies, entreat the benefits of his passion on behalf of the whole church, [in communion] participate in these benefits and [in response] enter into the movement of his self-offering.'

    From the *Anglican-Roman Catholic Statement on the Eucharist 1971*, paragraph 5 (the square brackets contain our editorial additions, but the progress of thought in the Statement is perfectly clear).

At the Reformation, all suggestion that the eucharist itself *is* in some sense a sacrifice ceased – and the reformers spoke and wrote hotly against the pre-Reformation teaching. Thus the eucharistic text in the Book of Common Prayer laid great weight upon Christ's one sacrifice for sins for ever, and the structure of the rite looked towards the administration and reception of communion as the great climax and purpose of the service, and excluded this notion of the eucharist as a sacrifice – except of course in the sense that all Christian worship *is* a sacrifice of praise.

In Rite A the emphasis upon the once-for-all nature of Christ's offering of himself on Calvary is expressed in various places. The description (which follows the Narrative of Institution) of what we 'do' in obedience to our Lord's command speaks not of 'offering the bread and the cup to you', but of celebrating Christ's sacrifice and similar concepts. Whilst the modern service lays much more weight upon joy and corporateness and flexibility than did the old Prayer Book rite, yet in all this offering of worship to God, a clear distinction is kept between Christ's one sacrifice for sins for ever and our responsive and continual giving of praise to God, and giving of ourselves in his service.

THE REFORMATION PERIOD

In England the eucharist was almost *the* central question in the Reformation – possibly not *quite* as vital as the authority of the monarch or the pope but very nearly so. For their teaching on the eucharist Ridley, Latimer and Cranmer and many others were put to death in Mary's reign. The new Prayer Books which Cranmer wrote in Edward VI's reign (1547-53) contained revised communion services as their centre-pieces, and these revisions were the hinge on which the Reformation in England turned.

The first stage, in 1547, was the introduction of the use of the English bible into the Latin mass. The Epistle and Gospel were to be read in English.

The second stage was to provide for the people to receive communion: the previous expectation had been that they would only receive communion once a year, and then only in one kind – the bread. So at Easter 1548 'The Order of the Communion' – a short devotion in English, leading up to communion in both kinds (that is with both bread and wine) – was added to the Latin mass. The worshippers were to receive communion after due preparation in English – exhortations, confession, absolution, 'comfortable words', the prayer of humble access, and then communion with English words of administration. Unfortunately, centuries of tradition had fixed people's devotion so that they were not willing to receive communion frequently, and the 1548 'Order', whilst it gave promise of English language worship to come, was of little actual use.

The third stage was the publication of a complete Prayer Book in English, in which the communion service was very important. This Book was to be used from Whitsunday (Pentecost) 1549. The structure of the old mass was kept, but the wording of the eucharistic prayer was subtly altered from the old Roman

canon, and it was followed by the 1548 'Order' leading up to communion.

The fourth stage was an Order in Council in 1550, which led to the breaking down of the old stone altars, and the substitution of wooden communion tables, often trestle tables.

The fifth stage was the publication of Cranmer's great works on the eucharist in 1550 and 1551. These denied transsubstantiation, and affirmed that in the eucharist the body and blood of Christ are only received by faith – that is, by 'worthy' recipients. The books also denied that the eucharist is a sacrifice for sins, because Christ's death on Calvary is

the only such sacrifice, and our 'remembrance' of that death is in no sense an offering of Christ to the Father today.

The sixth stage was the second Prayer Book, which had to be used from All Saints' Day (1 November) 1552. In this Cranmer changed the order of the parts of the 1549 rite, so that the kyries became a response to the ten commandments at the beginning of the service, the intercessions were taken out of the eucharistic prayer and brought into the ante-communion, the penitential material opened the sacramental half of the service, the prayer of humble access was inserted between the Sanctus and the proclamation of the all-sufficiency of Calvary (where the intercessions had been in

LORDS SUPPER

1549 before Cranmer moved them). The long eucharistic prayer was further broken up by being cut short at the end of the narrative of institution, so that it now ended with Jesus' command 'Do this in remembrance of me' – and was followed immediately by the actual doing, the distribution of bread and wine. The Lord's Prayer came after communion along with two long prayers of thanksgiving and the Gloria in Excelsis. This canticle was the only item left which was directed to be sung, and it may have been moved to the end in loyalty to the biblical account that after the last supper Jesus and his disciples sang a hymn before they went out to the garden of Gethsemane.

In the 1552 rite, there was no use of the word 'consecration', and no rubrics or manual acts which suggested a formula or moment of consecration. The bread, for the first time for many centuries in England, was to be leavened *'such as is usual to be eaten'*; no communion could be held without communicants; sermons were commanded (though not all clergy were in fact trusted to preach); the communion table (perhaps that wooden trestle mentioned above) stood in the middle of the people, whether in the chancel or the nave; and the celebrant wore a surplice and no other liturgical garment.

1662

In the period from the beginning of Elizabeth's reign, when the 1552 Prayer Book was restored (in 1559), through until 1645, when the Prayer Book was abolished by law, no changes were made in the communion service. But there was a change in its *setting* – in the early seventeenth century there grew a move to place communion-tables back against the east wall of the chancel, and to put rails round them. Laud (who was Archbishop of Canterbury from 1633 to 1645) was the main enforcer of this move. The result was a separation of table and people,

CRANMER'S 'SHAPE'

The inherited Prayer Book of 1662 kept the structure of the eucharist 1552. This order can largely be seen laid out in sections 57 to 75 of Rite A. In 1662 the full order was:

Ante-communion
1 Lord's Prayer
2 Collect for Purity
3 Ten Commandments (with responses)
4 Collect for the Monarch (one of two to be used)
5 Collect of the Day
6 Epistle
7 Gospel
8 Nicene Creed
9 Notices
10 Sermon
11 Offertory (of money)
12 Preparation of bread and wine
13 Prayer for the Church
14 (When appropriate) Warning Exhortations

Communion
1 Long Exhortation
2 Short Exhortation
3 Confession
4 Absolution
5 Comfortable Words
6 Sursum Corda, Preface, Sanctus
7 Prayer of Humble Access
8 Prayer of Consecration:
    (a) praise for the cross
    (b) petition for 'consecration'
    (c) narrative of institution
9 Distribution
10 (When appropriate) Supplementary Consecration
11 Covering of remains
12 Lord's Prayer
13 Post-communion prayers (one of two to be used)
14 Gloria in Excelsis
15 Blessing
16 Closing rubrics

This shape seems to divide the first part of the eucharistic prayer (Sursum Corda – 'Lift up your hearts' – etc.) from the second, by the position of the prayer of Humble Access. It then stops the eucharistic prayer short after the narrative of institution. It thus does not seem to be one single prayer of thanksgiving – and the 'taking' and 'breaking' are done *within* the narrative of institution. This pattern can be traced in Rite A, sections 57 to 75, though the long exhortations do not now appear, and more options are allowed in the post-communion than under 1662. It can be seen from this that Cranmer's shape, whilst it had its own logic, was *not* the 'fourfold' shape of taking – thanksgiving – breaking – sharing which the biblical pattern presents.

*Archbishop William Laud
(1573-1645)*

'Let the Prayer, Thanksgiving, or Blessing of the Bread and Wine, be to this effect:
... Earnestly to pray to God, the Father of all mercies, and God of all consolation, to vouchsafe his gracious presence, and the effectuall working of his Spirit in us, and so to sanctify these elements both of Bread and Wine, and to blesse his own Ordinance, that we may receive by faith the Body and Blood of Jesus Christ crucified for us, and so to feed upon him, that he may be one with us, and we with him ...'
From the
Westminster *Directory.*

which has endured right through to the twentieth century.

Laud and his friends, by this and many other moves, created great opposition among the puritans, and parliament, in the course of the civil war, abolished the Prayer Book and brought in the Westminster *Directory.* The communion service in the *Directory* was simply an outline: sermon, intercession, exhortation, reading of the words of institution, a 'Prayer, Thanksgiving, or Blessing of the Bread and Wine', a breaking of the bread, then separate distributions of the bread and cup. But the *Directory*, although it suggested the content of the prayers, did not prescribe any set texts.

The Restoration in 1660 led to the Savoy Conference between churchmen and puritans in 1661, and then to the reimposition of the 1552 Prayer Book, with only very marginal changes, in 1662. In the communion service the Lord's Prayer was set out in full, instructions were added after the offertory (which itself was still solely about the giving of money) for the placing of the bread and wine on the table, a remembrance of the departed was added at the end of the prayer for the Church, and a whole pattern of 'consecration' was added to the sacramental part of the service. This included calling the relevant prayer 'the prayer of consecration', adding indented rubrics to the Narrative of Institution to enforce *five* manual acts, making provision for 'supplementary consecration' if the supply of bread or wine is insufficient, and making further provision for the consumption of the consecrated elements which remain unused when the service is over. But otherwise in wording and in order the service remained unchanged from Elizabeth's day. There had been puritans who wanted to pull it in one direction, and liturgical specialists, rather of Laud's sort, who wanted to pull it in the opposite directions, but it ended up very much as before.

THE ANGLICAN TRADITION – OR TRADITIONS

After 1662 the Prayer Book which was then authorised remained the only Book of the Church of England until 1966, and even after alternative services came into use from that year onwards the old Prayer Book retained its status – as it still does today – as a foundation document of the doctrine of the Church of England. The 1662 communion service, with its 1552 structure and wording, remained at the heart of the Prayer Book. And, as shown in our chapter 'Anglican Worship across the World', wherever the Anglican missions founded new Churches anywhere round the world, in the eighteenth and nineteenth centuries, the 1662 Prayer Book and its communion service distinguished those new Churches *as* Anglican.

'Wherever ...'? Well, not quite wherever. In Scotland a very curious alternation between Episcopalians (Anglicans) and Presbyterians in the seventeenth century meant that, when the former were uppermost in the years from 1610 (when the first bishops were consecrated for Scotland) to 1637, steps were taken to provide a Prayer Book for Scotland – and this Book when it was finally produced included a communion service more on the lines of 1549 than of 1552. There was a riot when the Book was first used in 1637, and Presbyterianism came into power for the Commonwealth period. Episcopalians were restored in 1661, but did not have a separate Prayer Book. Then in 1689 the bishops of that Church all became Jacobites and the Presbyterians swore loyalty to William and Mary and inherited the national kirk of the land. The Episcopalians went underground for the most part, and there

experimented with communion services based upon the 1549/1637 model, and not on the English 1662. Finally a text now viewed as the final definitive one was adopted in 1764. It had a 'long canon', similar to 1549, but with a special calling of the Spirit down on the elements (an 'epiclesis').

In America in 1790 a new Prayer Book was approved, and the communion service drew partly upon the Scottish rite for its text (actually it was a hybrid of 1662 and the Scottish liturgy). Thereafter it became a commonplace that there were *two* eucharistic traditions in the Anglican Communion – the one springing from 1662, the other – with the 'long canon' – from Scotland-America. In the twentieth century this latter tradition has spread into many other parts of the Anglican Communion, more particularly those of a 'high' or anglo-catholic tradition.

In England itself the *use* of the Prayer Book was radically affected by the rise of anglo-catholicism in the nineteenth century. The second generation of anglo-catholics from 1850 onwards produced a liturgical programme breath-taking in its scope and achievements. Church buildings were constructed in the Gothic Revival style with nave, chancel, and elevated sanctuary, choirboys in ruffs were imported into the chancel; communion became a weekly, even a daily, feature of church life; pre-Reformation eucharistic vestments were reintroduced; wafers, candles, frontals, images, stone altars, riddel curtains, baldachinos, sanctuary lamps, incense, and sacring bells appeared; priests took 'eastward' position in front of the communion table; Gospel processions became *de rigueur*; congregations learned to genuflect during the creed, and priests did so at intervals through the rite; fasting communion became the rule, in imitation of Rome; the confessional was reintroduced to prepare worshippers for communion; material from the Roman mass (whether in Latin or in translation) was added to the Prayer Book rite; and by the end of the century permanent reservation of the consecrated

elements was also being practised, with extra-liturgical devotions to the reserved elements accompanying such reservation. The strain upon the Prayer Book communion service, which had been devised in reaction *against* virtually every one of these features, was proving too much, and the possibility of the revision of the eucharistic rite began to surface. On the other hand, evangelical churchmen stood against this tide of innovation with their clergy in surplice, hood, and scarf, their communion tables unadorned, the celebrant at 'north' side (in accordance with the rubric), the service

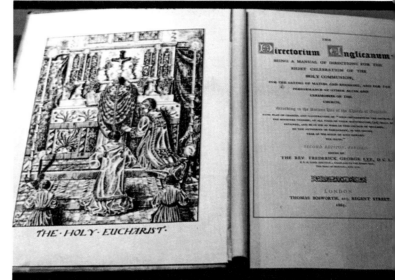

THE·HOLY·EUCHARIST·

A page from Directorium Anglicanum

read as straight as possible, and the bread '*such as is usual to be eaten*'.

In England anglo-catholic and evangelical parishes could often thrive next door to each other, each often apparently presenting a religion actually opposed to each other's, and yet both remaining Anglican, and claiming to be authentic Anglicanism (whilst the other was an aberration!). But in a larger context such parishes still had much in common with each other right through until the second world war. Both would administer communion at an eight o'clock service without music or sermon; both would make a sermon a centrepiece of an eleven o'clock service (catholics with a high mass,

evangelicals with a sung Morning Prayer); both would have a very formal and stiffly impersonal way of celebrating communion; and, of course, both would claim they were using the Prayer Book.

THE TWENTIETH CENTURY

The twentieth century in England has seen revision of eucharistic rites – in 1927-8, when parliament defeated the proposals, and in the years from 1966 to 1980, in which Series 1, Series 2, Series 3, and Rites A and B, were authorised. But the larger part of the century has seen only 1662 as the lawful eucharistic rite of the Church of England, and it is likely that, important as the new services are, some of the most important happen-

ings which concern the communion have not been the production of new texts for services at all.

The great sweeping change that has happened to the Church of England has been the coming of the parish communion. It was originally born as a '9.15' at St John's Newcastle-upon-Tyne in December 1927. (Being called the '9.15' – or the '10' o'clock, or whatever – is distinctive in England of either railway trains or church services.) That 9.15 brought together what had been a 'low' 8 o'clock communion, and a 10 o'clock 'Children's eucharist'. Thus, virtually for the first time, the Church of England had a service of communion at which hymns were sung, a sermon was preached, and communion was administered to the confirmed in the congregation. The sundered features of worship were being brought together, and familes could worship together at such a service, and perhaps join in a 'parish breakfast' afterwards – those were still days when the Roman Catholic practice of fasting before receiving communion was observed by large sections of the Church of England, and thus the worshippers at St John's would not have had breakfast before coming.

The parish communion concept grew steadily in the 1930s. Books were written about it, and it drew nourishment from the Roman Catholic 'liturgical movement' on the continent – a movement, almost unknown in those days to English Roman Catholics, which was seeking to make worship not just a priestly event, but a meaningful and edifying act of the whole congregation, building them up as the body of Christ. This thinking began to undergird the growing parish practice in the Church of England. It should, however, be noted that the appeal was almost exclusively to 'high churchmen'. Although the leaders of the parish communion movement said that their programme was unitive, bringing together 'high' and 'low' alike, in fact its effect upon the evangelical wing of the Church of England was minimal. Evangelicals were suspicious of treating communion as a panacea for all ills, suspicious that unbelievers were being herded into communion, suspicious of the fairly nominal preaching (e.g. 8-10 minutes), and suspicious of anglo-catholics generally, who had to be assumed to be trying to trap the innocent evangelicals into a sacramentalist stance!

In the 1940s and 1950s the rate of change to a parish communion grew considerably. Many went over to it because older patterns had run out of steam, rather than because they were deeply moved by doctrinal or doctrinaire reasons for it. But the simple appeal, 'The Lord's service for the Lord's people on the Lord's day', had its effect. And new parishes, if they were served by clergy schooled in this thinking, started off with the parish communion pattern.

Sometime in the late 1940s this began to have further effects on the *manner* of celebrating communion. Parishes began to pull their communion tables out from the east wall, so that the clergy could stand *behind* the table, and face the people across it – a practice used by Presbyterians and other Free Churchmen, and possibly desired by Cranmer (but with the whole arrangement turned 90° away from the usual church setting), but otherwise unknown in the Anglican Church since around the tenth century. More daring parishes started to bring the communion table further forward to stand on the chancel step – or on a platform built out into the nave from the chancel step. New church buildings were single-room chambers, built to express community *round* the table, not to focus vision along a long axis towards a distant east wall and mysterious sanctuary. The people were slowly given more of a part to play – though this often began not with obvious activities (like reading the Epistle and Gospel) but with the specially invented 'offertory procession' whereby laity carried the bread and wine from the back of the church to the front at the same time as bringing up the money collection. Children were made more

welcome by being invited to come to the communion rail with their parents (in any case, with *some* children it is unsafe for parents to leave them in a pew whilst going up to receive communion – the children get into mischief) and at the communion rail they received the laying on of a clerical hand with a brief blessing. They could not yet receive communion – when *will* this come? – but they could have some recognised part. First experiments were also made in the 1950s with house communions, perhaps initially in a fairly starchy and formal way – but the foot was in the kitchen-door.

In the 1960s evangelicals at last started to show interest in the parish communion, though they were slow to act on their convictions, and slower still to alter their church interiors. They tended to take a halfway step to recognising the centrality of communion in the life of the church, by changing Morning Prayer and Evening Prayer once a month each into a 'main service' communion. But it was still not an event at which children were welcome, nor one which actually exhibited the centrality of communion well. However, it did mean they gained experience of communion services at which

Moving the altar forward

hymns were sung, and sermons preached.

The 1960s also saw new styles of singing. Organs were losing their monopoly of the music, and other intruments were introduced. A readiness to experiment started to grow. The new texts arrived in 1967, and encouraged new thinking about presentation. Changes of a very unexpected sort appeared in the Roman Catholic Church from 1965 onwards. And a further new factor arose.

This last was the charismatic movement. It arose in the Church of England as a semi-underground society for private and individual holiness and piety. But its programme was overtly about the body of Christ and the use of the gifts of the Spirit in worship. Series 2 and Series 3, by encouraging flexibility, were a great help in bringing the joy and spontaneity of charismatics into Sunday church life in the 1970s. A new series of 'ceremonial' actions began – holding up hands in praise, laying on of hands as a special ministry of prayer, embracing warmly at the Peace, swaying bodies to the rhythm of music – and Anglicanism began to look freer than any other 'mainline' denomination, at least in some congregations. An ever-growing tide of simple – sometimes simplistic – choruses appeared, for guitar-playing, for singing as a round, for use during the administration at communion, and so on. Tongues, prophecy, and healings, all these became part of communion services.

But the 1970s were distinctive for a much wider part of the Church of England through the coming of Series 3 communion. Now God was to be addressed as 'you'; now an evolution to a sensible involvement of lay people throughout the service could move ahead; new media for communication were found – the overhead projector being not the least of these; and Rite A was designed in the years 1976-9 with a consciousness of the widespread evolutionary changes being made in the pattern, mood, and ethos, of eucharistic worship.

FROM THE EXPERIMENTAL SERIES TO RITE A

Series 1

Series 1 was a first attempt in 1966 to adapt the contents of the 1662 order to the 'shape' which had been emerging as the general consensus. It had large numbers of options, as it was merely making legal variants from 1662 which had already passed into use. But at heart it offered a long eucharistic prayer, making a single whole of the various parts which had been separated from each other in 1662. In Rite A the fourth eucharistic prayer is descended from this Series 1 prayer (and its wording can be compared with the 1662 Order), and in Rite B (which is still in 'thou' form) the first of the two eucharistic prayers is very similar to the original Series 1 text. Series 1 was still in Cranmer's style of language – its distinctive feature was the return (at least as an option) to this long eucharistic prayer. The whole fourfold 'shape' could also be obtained by preparing the elements just before the eucharistic prayer began, and by breaking the bread as a separate action after it was over.

Series 2

Series 2, first authorised in 1967, was the first service to be written deliberately to conform to this pattern. Now, in the ante-communion, the Gloria in Excelsis came at the beginning, there were three lessons, and the creed followed the sermon as a response to it. The new, rather 'open', pattern of intercessions was introduced for the first time, and the Peace was included at the end of the penitential section. The eucharistic prayer was a piece of new writing, much terser than Cranmer's work, but still addressing God as 'thou'. And this eucharistic prayer can be traced, somewhat changed, in the 'you' form as the second eucharistic prayer in Rite A – and as the second eucharistic prayer (in 'thou' form) in Rite B.

Series 3

Series 3, authorised from 1 February 1973, was the first service to address God as 'you', and became very popular (except for the ninth line of the Lord's Prayer, where 'Do not bring us to the time of trial' proved controversial). Its eucharistic prayer was novel in several ways for the Church of England, including the initial greeting 'The Lord is here. **His Spirit is with us**', the acclamations, the anamnesis, the doxology, and much of the seasonal material. In Rite A the first eucharistic prayer is clearly descended from it. Rite B by definition has nothing corresponding to it.

The making of Rite A

How did the service get into its present state? Well, it went through a process like this: firstly, in winter 1976-7 the Liturgical Commission put out questionnaires on Series 3, and concluded that users of it were in general very pleased with it (apart from that ninth line of the Lord's Prayer). Then the Commission itself went to work, and did some polishing up (including adding, in an appendix, forms of the eucharistic prayer from Series 1 and Series 2 translated into a 'you' form), got the text through the House of Bishops, and published it as a report to Synod on 18 May 1978. Synod debated it in July 1978, then remitted it to a 'Revision Committee'. The 'Revision Committee' had the task of sifting all the amendments members of Synod wished to make to the Commission's proposals, and producing a text revised in the light of all these amendments. There proved in fact to be over a thousand amendments sent in! So the Revision Committee produced a completely revised text – including, for instance, four eucharistic prayers in the main text of the service (sections 38-41), one of which was a newcomer. Even then, the task was not complete. There were still amendments to be moved in full Synod, and between the February and July sessions in 1979 the service took a total of 19 hours in full

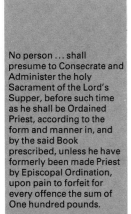

No person ... shall presume to Consecrate and Administer the holy Sacrament of the Lord's Supper, before such time as he shall be Ordained Priest, according to the form and manner in, and by the said Book prescribed, unless he have formerly been made Priest by Episcopal Ordination, upon pain to forfeit for every offence the sum of One hundred pounds.

1662 *Act of Uniformity.*

Synod. It was not much altered in the process, but small amendments were passed in Synod.

After all this, the service gained provisional approval on a show of hands in July 1979, then an overwhelming majority on the formal vote by houses in November 1979 to obtain final approval. Then, when the service had been approved, it was authorised for a ten-year period in order to ensure its place within the *ASB 1980*.

The service was originally called 'Series 3 Revised', but in the planning for the layout and contents of *ASB 1980* it was renamed Rite A. Its authorisation began on 1 May 1980, and 'Rite A' booklets were published from that date. They remain in use alongside the bound *ASBs*.

RITE A

The opening Notes

The opening 'Notes' are a series of permissions or directions which are grouped at the beginning of the service so as not to obtrude acres of 'small print' onto the pages of the service itself. The idea is that the service itself (with its blue rubrics) gives a 'mainstream' way of doing the liturgy, but variations are not penal (as they were in 1662!), and provision for them is made in the Notes.

One of the most important Notes is no. 2 concerning 'The President'. It has been a feature of the Church of England's worship since the time of the Reformation that only those ordained to the 'priesthood' – i.e. the 'presbyterate' or eldership – could officiate at communion. This is made clear in the Canons. In Rite A, as in Series 3, the officiating presbyter is called 'The President' – a term taken from Justin Martyr in his First Apology. The implication is that the president 'presides'. He does not do all the speaking, but acts like a chairman 'presiding' over the assembly so as to ensure that all participants do play their part. It is as 'chairman' that he opens and closes the assembly, with a greeting in the first place and a dismissal at the end.

Note 20 makes reference, as many of the rubrics do, to hymns. The Church of England has always been very careful about authorising the text of liturgical services – no one can just change the wording of the prayers at his own whim. But hymns are a different matter. Anyone may sing any hymn at his own choice, and the Church of England has no official hymn book and no control of what is sung. The 1662 service took virtually no account of singing – the new service encourages and promotes it. But this means that the theme of the Sunday eucharistic lessons should be taken seriously in choosing hymns – at least for the ante-communion. Sacramental hymns may be particularly appropriate if there is to be singing during the prepara-

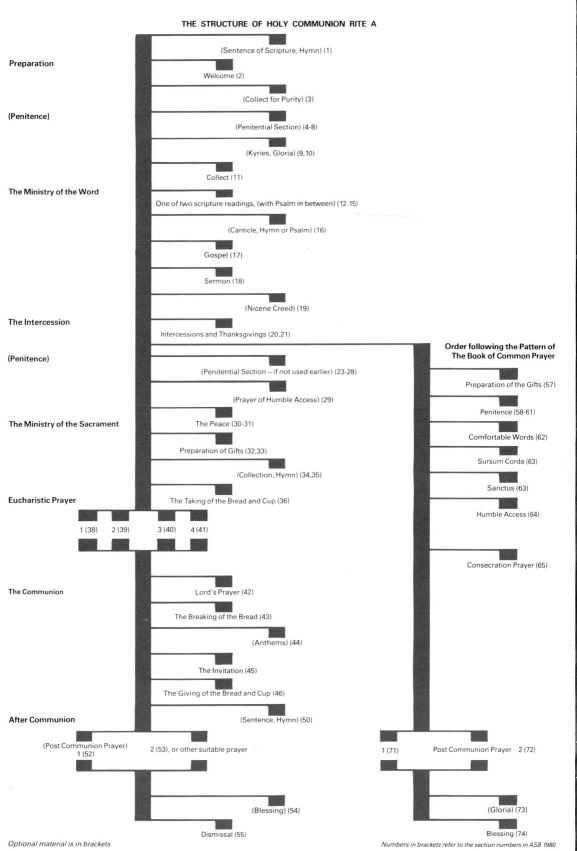

THE STRUCTURE OF HOLY COMMUNION RITE A

Preparation

(Sentence of Scripture, Hymn) (1)

Welcome (2)

(Penitence)

(Collect for Purity) (3)

(Penitential Section) (4-8)

(Kyries, Gloria) (9,10)

The Ministry of the Word

Collect (11)

One of two scripture readings, (with Psalm in between) (12-15)

(Canticle, Hymn or Psalm) (16)

Gospel (17)

Sermon (18)

(Nicene Creed) (19)

The Intercession

Intercessions and Thanksgivings (20,21)

Order following the Pattern of The Book of Common Prayer

(Penitence)

(Penitential Section – if not used earlier) (23-28)

Preparation of the Gifts (57)

(Prayer of Humble Access) (29)

Penitence (58-61)

The Ministry of the Sacrament

The Peace (30-31)

Comfortable Words (62)

Preparation of Gifts (32,33)

Sursum Corda (63)

(Collection, Hymn) (34,35)

Sanctus (63)

Eucharistic Prayer

The Taking of the Bread and Cup (36)

Humble Access (64)

1 (38)   2 (39)   3 (40)   4 (41)

Consecration Prayer (65)

The Communion

Lord's Prayer (42)

The Breaking of the Bread (43)

(Anthems) (44)

The Invitation (45)

The Giving of the Bread and Cup (46)

After Communion

(Sentence, Hymn) (50)

(Post Communion Prayer) 1 (52)   2 (53), or other suitable prayer

1 (71)   Post Communion Prayer   2 (72)

(Blessing) (54)

(Gloria) (73)

Dismissal (55)

Blessing (74)

Optional material is in brackets

Numbers in brackets refer to the section numbers in ASB 1980

LET'S HEAR IT FOR OUR VISITING PREACHER....!!!

tion of the gifts (section 35), or during the distribution (section 47).

Most of the other Notes are self-explanatory.

The Preparation (sections 1-3, 9-11)
The opening part of the service is an overture to the two main sections of the Rite: the ministry of the word (including the intercession), and the ministry of the sacrament. It is balanced by a conclusion, called 'After Communion'. The Preparation enables a relationship to be built up between president and people, it enables worship and praise to begin, and (where so desired) it enables penitence to be used as a preparation for the whole rite. The theme of the Sunday may emerge in the opening sentence (section 1) and in the collect (section 11), and may well be informally announced at section 2. An imaginative use of section 2 may also include the welcoming of a visiting preacher, the giving out of other notices, and the announcement of which eucharistic prayer will be used.

Prayers of Penitence (sections 6-8), see facing page (sections 23-28).

Reading the scriptures (sections 12-17)
The heart of the ministry of the word is the reading of the scripture passages. It is possible that the distinction between 'Epistle' and 'Gospel' goes back to the early second century, when not only were the books of the bible listed according to what was read at the eucharist, but the way of reading the New Testament in these two separate categories actually affected the way the books of the New Testament are bound together. So ancient and so powerful is the Epistle/Gospel way of seeing the New Testament.

The actual readings are controlled by a syllabus which follows the Old Testament sequence in the Sundays before Christmas; the Gospel sequence from Christmas to Pentecost; and the Epistle sequence from Pentecost till the ninth Sunday before Christmas. In each case the lessons from the other two lists are then chosen to match the theme in the

'controlling' lesson. And when only two lessons are read, then (as Note 10 provides) the controlling lesson cannot be omitted.

The responses at the end ('This is the word of the Lord' and 'This is the Gospel of Christ') are in the present tense to indicate that God not only spoke once through the writing of the books of the bible, but also that he *speaks* today through the reading of the word.

The sermon (section 18)
The sermon comes immediately after the reading of the Gospel, and is meant to be a climax of the declaring and applying of the word of the Lord. *ASB 1980* provides the readings set out in full (pages 397-982) so that a preacher may direct his hearers to *read* the passage from which he is preaching, and to follow his argument

in the actual scriptures. Equally, a congregation may, by opening their *ASB 1980s* at the right page, and looking up expectantly, force a reluctant preacher to preach from the scriptural passages.

Note 12 very slightly lightens the obligation to preach.

The Nicene Creed (section 19)

The creed is meant to be a response to the preaching of the word – and is a reminder to the preacher that a response of faith in God should be very appropriate following the sermon.

The creed is not exactly as it was when first declared at the Council of Nicaea (325 AD), but it defends the doctrine of the Trinity just as the Council of Nicaea did, but in fuller terms. It begins '*We believe*' because that is how the ancient Councils stated the faith – it was a confession which '*we*' all hold in common.

The creed is paragraphed into four paragraphs, three for the persons of the Godhead, and the fourth for the Church – but 'belief in' the Church does not include the same kind of 'trust and discipleship' that 'belief in' the persons of the Trinity involves.

The intercession (sections 20-21)

After the bible class, the prayer meeting. It may be led by lay people; it may have free (or extempore) prayer in it; it may be done in one of several different ways (see the rubric at section 20); it may be general in its scope – or it may be very particular. If the form at section 21 is used, the paragraphs give a framework for specific topics:

1 'Let us pray for the Church ...'
   A bidding
2 'Almighty God, our heavenly Father ...' *A beginning to the prayer*
3 'Strengthen *N* our Bishop ...'
   Prayer for the universal Church
4 'Bless and guide Elizabeth our Queen ...'
   Prayer for the nations of the world
5 'Give grace to us ...'
   Prayer for family, friends, and the local community

6 'Comfort and heal ...'
   Prayer for the sick and suffering
7 'Hear us as we remember ...'
   Thankful remembrance of the departed
8 'Rejoicing in the fellowship ...'
   An ending to the prayer

Whether the prayers are prepared, or are extemporary, it is helpful when using this form to keep the topics for which prayer is made related to the paragraphs as set out here.

Prayers of penitence (sections 23-28)

These prayers may have come in the Preparation at the beginning of the service. But if they come here they have a threefold purpose:

● As response to the ministry of the word
● As prayers grouped with the intercession
● As preparation for coming to the Lord's Table (which was certainly Cranmer's idea when introducing the section in 1549)

The Prayer of Humble Access (section 29)

may be used as part of the approach to the Lord's Table, whether or not the prayers of penitence are used at this point. A modern alternative to the traditional wording is included at section 82 – this was originally composed for Series 3, but was rejected by Synod, until it reappeared in Rite A.

The Peace (sections 30-31)

All is now ready for 'The ministry of the sacrament' to begin. But within this half of the service, there are two preliminaries to the sacramental meal – the 'Peace', and the laying of the table.

The 'Peace' derives from St Paul's words, but we do not know for certain that it was given at the eucharist in the New Testament. Soon after, it was. It is not just a merry back-slap, but is the Church's members recognising each other as in Christ before coming to the meal. It has extra meaning still when it follows a baptism or a confirmation or a marriage or an ordination – there is an

'I urge first of all that petitions, prayers, requests, and thanksgivings, be made on behalf of all men, for kings and all in authority ...'
1 Tim 2.1-2.

'Let a man examine himself, and so let him eat.'
1 Cor 11.28.

'Greet each other with a holy kiss.'
2 Cor 13.12.

'Greet all the brothers with a holy kiss.'
1 Thess 5.26.

But J.B. Phillips in *Letters to Young Churches* (1947, now in Fontana edition) coyly translates these as 'A handshake all round, please!' and 'Give a handshake all round among the brotherhood'.

137

extra welcome to be given in the 'Peace'.

The words at section 30 (and at section 83, which is well worth using) are about peace between believers *because they are in Christ*. The actions should show it. And when believers grasp each other by the hand, or embrace, then their words to each other should also be warm.

The people of God are now ready to feast together.

34). But it is *not* a good time for the jingle of coins (or even the rustling of notes) to intrude into the worship.

The eucharistic prayer (sections 36-41)
Now the 'shape' of the meal begins. The chief first part of it is the giving of thanks – *eucharist*. But before Jesus gave thanks, he 'took' the bread, and 'took' the cup. These actions were to designate the food

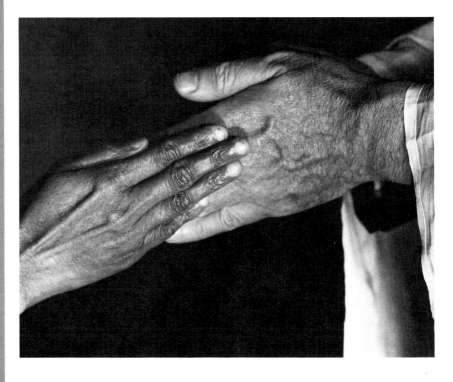

The Preparation of the Gifts (sections 32-35)
This is the other preliminary before the meal starts. The table has to be laid (section 32). Very often a hymn is sung (section 35), and then the preliminary job can be done unobtrusively. In some churches they like lay people to carry the bread and wine from the back of the church to the holy table (though this is unnecessary), and this has led to the collecting of money and the bringing of it to the holy table at the same time (section

and drink over which he was giving thanks. And so we do the same. Section 36 says: '*The President takes the bread and cup into his hands . . .*'. Because we give thanks over both bread and cup at once (and the president has to turn the pages of the service book whilst giving thanks!), it is usually impossible for him to hold the bread and cup throughout the eucharistic prayer. But he has lifted them to designate them, '*. . . and replaces them on the holy table*'.

'He will show you a large upper room furnished; there make ready.'

Luke 22.12.

The great action is the thanksgiving (eucharistic) prayer. The president and people greet each other in an opening dialogue which cements the relationship. Their words are not only a greeting, but are also full of Christian teaching. An obvious – but delightful – feature is the assertion that we are in two places at once! For –

● 'The Lord is here'

   'His Spirit is with us'

   – the assembly is the place where God the Holy Spirit who came to earth at Pentecost makes his home, and stirs us to worship.

● 'Lift up your hearts'

   'We lift them to the Lord'

   – the people of God are to go into the heavenly places, to 'have confidence to enter the holy place' (Hebrews 10.19), to join 'with angels and archangels'.

So we are *both* the dwelling-place of God the Spirit here on earth *and* the royal priesthood which has its own true dwelling-place (through the work of our great high priest) in the heavenly places. Both are true at once.

Then the dialogue gives the sense of purpose to this understanding of ourselves as the people of God – there is a task to be done now:

'Let us give thanks to the Lord our God.'

'It is right to give him thanks and praise.'

Our task now is thanksgiving – thanksgiving for creation, for redemption, and for God's making us his people. So the prayer continues with praise and thanks till that section is summarised in the angels' song:

'Holy, holy, holy Lord ...'

After we have 'told out' what God has done for us, we then turn to saying that we acknowledge Jesus' command to keep the feast 'in remembrance of' him, and describe *how* we are so keeping it. Our prayer becomes a petition that we should grow in Christ through sharing in the feast. Finally, a weighty 'doxology' – an ascribing of praise to God – concludes the prayer.

This pattern can be traced out in all four eucharistic prayers (sections 38 to 41). Each of the four prayers differs from the others in emphasis a little, but each has this basic structure, and each has the same congregational responses at the same place as the other three have them (except that only prayer 1 has the full congregational doxology).

What of the distinctive features of the four prayers? The quotations in the panel on the next page give a kind of keynote to distinguish each from the others.

'... a people for God's own possession that we should tell out the merits of him who has called us out of darkness ...' *1 Peter 2.9.*

The Latin *Prae-fatio,* our 'Preface', is not a 'foreword', but a 'telling out'.

'Holy, holy, holy, is the Lord of hosts; the whole earth is full of his glory.' *Is. 6.3.*

'Holy, holy, holy, is the Lord God the Almighty.' *Rev. 4.8.*

'We celebrate his one perfect sacrifice'	*Prayer 1* This is an immediate descendant of the eucharistic prayer in Series 3.
'We make with this bread and this cup the memorial of Christ ...'	*Prayer 2* This is descended from the eucharistic prayer in Series 2, but with an interesting addition near the end.
'We celebrate this memorial of our redemption'	*Prayer 3* This is the new prayer with a very strong echo of Hippolytus.
'We offer you through him this sacrifice of praise and thanksgiving'	*Prayer 4* This is descended from Series 1, and thus has strong echoes of Cranmer.

It seems best to stand throughout the eucharistic prayer. If we are to 'lift up our hearts' then we will probably do it better if we lift up our bodies at the same time – and we shall certainly lift up our voices better in 'thanks and praise'. The service drops a big hint (in Note 3) that dropping to our knees halfway through the prayer obscures its unity as a single prayer (and suggests we still have the 1662 Order in our minds). It does not take longer to say this prayer than to sing a longish hymn, and no one minds standing for hymns. Each prayer suggests silence at the end, and it is the opportunity for a hushed corporate stillness with the congregation standing.

The Lord's Prayer (section 42)
If congregations want to kneel (and there is no necessity!) perhaps now is a good chance. The Lord's Prayer has followed the eucharistic prayer in the Roman Catholic Church ever since the time of Gregory the Great (the Pope who sent Augustine to Canterbury in 597), and this position is well-established in other Anglican Provinces. Having the Lord's Prayer shortly before communion may have started because the worshippers saw Jesus, in the words he himself used, as 'the bread of life' – and they were asking to be nourished by *that* bread when they prayed 'Give us today our daily bread' and went on to receive communion.

The breaking of the bread (section 43)
We are now in the part of the service called 'The communion' (see the cross-heading). Just as the 'taking' looked forward to the thanksgiving in the part entitled 'The eucharistic prayer', so here all the sections look forward to the receiving of the bread and wine.

Breaking the bread is preliminary to sharing it. It is, quite strictly speaking, related to sharing together. It is not meant to be a sort of drama, representing the crucifixion, although it has been natural for people's minds to run beyond the words of the bible and think it meant this. ('Broken for you' is only found in poor manuscripts of the bible, and does

THE LORD'S PRAYER

The text of the Lord's Prayer is very little changed from the traditional form (which is explicitly allowed in the rubric at section 42). But once we do not say 'thou' to God we cannot say 'who art', and the alternative 'who are' is awful. So we adapt with 'Our Father in heaven'. 'Sins' is an easier word than 'trespasses' (though the Scottish worshippers who use 'debts' are nearer to the New Testament!). 'Temptation' has been much disputed – for it may refer to a fiery 'trial', rather than common or garden 'temptation'. And 'evil' might be 'the evil one', but the same word would be used for either in Greek.

The doxology at the end of the Lord's Prayer is not in the scriptural accounts, but is included partly because it is traditional, partly because it is ecumenical. A very small space before the doxology is meant to suggest that this is *not* part of what the introduction says 'our Saviour taught us'. He did not – we added it.

'Our Father in heaven,
your name be hallowed,
your kingdom come,
your will be done
as in heaven so also on earth.
Our bread for the coming day
give us today;
and forgive us our debts,
we also have forgiven our debtors;

and do not bring us into temptation,
but deliver us from the evil one.'
    (Matthew 6.9-13)

'Father,
your name be hallowed,
your kingdom come;

our bread for the coming day
give us each day;
and forgive us our sins,for we ourselves
also forgive
everyone who is in our debt;
and do not bring us into temptation.
    (Luke 11.2-4)

not seem to be what Jesus said). So the words used are taken from St Paul, where he (with his liking for puns or double meanings) says that sharing the body of Christ will build up the body of Christ! To 'break bread' together is, in middle eastern cultures, to pledge ourselves to each other in love and service.

The distribution (sections 45-47)
There are words of invitation (section 45) drawn from the old words used at the distribution in the 1662 service. They are meant to give all the teaching that they once gave at the distribution, but before that point in this service, so that the actual distribution can be done with shorter words. Then the communicants can say 'amen' and be more clearly responding to the grace of God.

The words 'Draw near with faith' are taken from the famous passage of the

Epistle to the Hebrews quoted earlier. They do not necessarily mean that we have to arise from our seats and 'draw near' to the ministers or the communion rails. Rather they mean that we are to draw near to the throne of God and receive from him (whether we walk to the table or the elements are brought to us).

Short forms of words are used at the distribution. The longer alternative is a prayer for the person receiving, and may well have the person's name included: 'Peter, the body of Christ keep you in eternal life.' The 'eternal life' which Christ gives we already have – we are to be kept *in* it, not preserved 'unto' it as the old words said.

The distribution may be done in many different ways. The Church of England now allows lay people of either sex (with the bishop's permission) to distribute either element, so that parishes should

'Let us draw near with a true heart in full assurance of faith.'

Heb 10.22.

never have difficulty in giving communion to even a large congregation. There is a long tradition of kneeling to receive, but Rite A never mentions that, and standing often allows a better use of space.

Meanwhile it is entirely appropriate to sing, at least after receiving communion, and section 47 provides for that. But the anthem at section 44 may also be used.

After communion
The end of the service is brief. Communion is meant to be a blessing and a strengthening for service. The only thing to do is say 'Thank you' to God and go.

The seasonal theme may be picked up again in a sentence or hymn (section 50), and sometimes the singing of a hymn may be used whilst the remaining consecrated bread and wine is either covered, with a view to its being consumed at the end of the service, or is consumed at the

HOW TO RECEIVE COMMUNION
What thoughts should the communicant keep in mind as he approaches the table and receives the elements? The possibilities are endless, but here are some suggestions:

● Reflect on the themes of the eucharistic prayer: creation, redemption in Christ, the priestly body of Christ, the Church.
● Reflect on the themes of the Peace and the fraction: we who share the bread are to share with each other. Look at your neighbours in the service in that light.
● Reflect on the lordship of Christ: you receive the bread and cup in obedience to him, but is obedience a hall mark of your relationship with your Lord the rest of the time?
● Reflect on 'in remembrance that he died for you': recall that it *actually happened* – there at Calvary on a specific date at a specific time of day – it *happened*, and the world is changed.
● Reflect on his presence: it is *his* table, where he meets us. He lives.
● Reflect on your own need: '... keep you, Bill, in eternal life' – he provides for *you*, the individual here and in need. What are your needs? – his feeding you is a symbol of his meeting your every need.
● Reflect on the world's needs: remember Jesus' words to his disciples 'you give them food to eat' – he gave them food that they should feed the multitude. So he feeds you in order that ... what?
● Reflect on his coming again – or on your own death: recall his words 'If anyone eats this bread he will live forever and I will raise him up at the last day.'

time (section 49). (But consuming at the time is unhelpful where the people are near the table, and the president has his face towards them – guests should not have to watch the washing up.)

The closing prayers (sections 51-53)
These are full of both thankfulness and aspiration – they look back to the communion and forward into service of God in the world. The second half of the second prayer ('Send us out . . .') has wound its way deeply into the devotional lives of Anglican worshippers in the few years since it was first written for Series 2. (And at section 86 a prayer based on this prayer is provided for occasions when there has been no communion, but only an ante-communion).

The dismissal (sections 54-56)
A blessing (section 54) is optional. The service is not moving to a great verbal climax with a solemn blessing but, if anything, is moving away from the high point of communion to a simple departure into the everyday world. So a blessing may slightly distort this movement, and it has been made optional. On the other hand, at high seasons of the year the alternative blessings in section 77 may be used to mark the season, and Note 18 allows the president to add a wider choice still.

On the other hand, the dismissal is mandatory. It marks the true end of the liturgical event, and enjoins the departure (section 56).

The first prayer provides a fascinating and enriching quest for those who will search the scriptures. Thus:

1 Cor 8.6 'Father of all'
Heb 13.15 'Thanks and praise'
Lk 15.20 'Still far off'

and let the reader pursue his own quest.

THE ORDER FOLLOWING THE PATTERN OF THE BOOK OF COMMON PRAYER

57 Preparation of the elements (not *quite* in the 1662 position)
58-61 Prayers of penitence
62 Comfortable words
63 Dialogue (Sursum Corda etc.), Preface, and Sanctus
64 Prayer of Humble Access
65 Prayer of Consecration (with five 'manual acts' ordered in 'indented rubrics')
66 Communion
69 Lord's Prayer
70-72 Post-communion prayers
73 Gloria in Excelsis (optional)
74 Blessing
75 Departure

THE ORDER FOLLOWING THE PATTERN OF THE BOOK OF COMMON PRAYER (Sections 57-75)
This 'order' branches off from the mainstream rite at section 22 in the main rite, and then provides the 1662 order.

The presence of this 'order' in the rite is a reminder of how the 'shape' of the service has been changed in the main provision. It looks as though when Cranmer restructured the rite in 1552 he

wanted the following principles to be employed:
● The distribution had to come immediately after the recitation of Jesus' command 'Do this in remembrance of me'.
● The penitential material had therefore to come earlier in the rite, and the obvious place was after the intercession, and before the 'Lift up your hearts'.

- However, there was a happy sequence of thought from the fourth comfortable word 'we have an advocate with the Father' to the call 'Lift up your hearts'. Thus the prayer of humble access had to be removed from after the comfortable words (which it had followed in 1549), and the greeting 'The Lord be with you/ and with thy Spirit' had to be dropped from the beginning of the dialogue.

'Then I said: "Woe is me! For I am undone, for I am a man of unclean lips ..."'

Is 6.5.

- A home was found for 'humble access', following the Sanctus. When Isaiah saw the vision of the angels singing 'Holy, holy, holy' in the temple, his next thought was 'I am unworthy'. So the 'Blessed is he who comes in the name of the Lord' was dropped from the end of the Sanctus, and 'We do not presume . . .' was inserted.
- The Lord's Prayer, and part of the end of the eucharistic prayer were moved to the post-communion. These can be found at sections 69 and 71 in Rite A.
- Cranmer brought the Gloria in Excelsis from the beginning of the service to the end, perhaps because he wanted to follow the biblical pattern 'When they had sung a hymn, they went out . . .' (Matthew 26.30).

So here this pattern is preserved for the future, with a modern language expression to enable it to fit into the new Rite. It remains very closely centred upon the work of Christ on the cross, and for this reason may be especially appropriate in Lent and at Passiontide.

APPENDICES

Sections 76 to 86 provide variants for special seasons of the year, or optional alternatives for any occasion, in a way which should enrich the overall provision in the rite. Most features of the appendices are self-explanatory, and mention has been made of them above.

OTHER SERVICES IN THE CONTEXT OF HOLY COMMUNION

ASB 1980 provides that baptism, confirmation, and ordination, should be ministered at communion, and permits that marriage and burial should, though without making it a norm in these cases. The usual place for such ministries to occur is after the sermon in place of the creed and the intercession. They often have their own special readings of scripture to come in the ministry of the word, and they are very suitably concluded by the Peace, by which the newly baptised, confirmed, married, or ordained, are greeted warmly in Christ by the supporting congregation who will now share with them in the eucharist.

The same pattern may well be used when some other event, not covered in the *ASB 1980*, is being incorporated into the eucharist. Good instances would be the anointing of the sick, the institution of a new minister, the commissioning of parish visitors (or other officers), and so on. The structure naturally brings these events into the very heart of the eucharistic worship whilst still allowing the flow of the ministry of the word and the ministry of the sacrament to continue unimpeded.

SUPPLEMENTARY CONSECRATION – CONSUMPTION OF THE REMAINS

Section 48 (and, in 1662's own way, section 67) provides for a supplementary consecration when that is needed. It is not a *new* consecration as though a new meal were being provided for anyone left out at the beginning! Rather it is the making up, within the context of a meal already started, of a lack which has occurred with either the bread or the wine. So the words of the prayer provided are not a full thanksgiving, but a brief form designed to bring the further supply into the full eucharistic context.

DRESS. GESTURE. POSTURE. CEREMONIAL

The Rite does not give detailed instructions for these. The Church of England allows in its Canons for great variety of dress for ministers who preside at communion, but says nothing about others who assist. So lay people in ordinary clothes may read the lessons, preach or teach, lead the prayers, and distribute the elements. Or they may be dressed up, according to local custom.

Similarly, the Rite allows (Note 3) that posture will be settled locally (though a few rubrics are provided for guidance as to the 'appropriate' postures for the confession, the readings from scripture, the sermon, the creed, and the Peace). The omissions from this list are worth considering.

Ceremonial is imposed even less than posture. It is usually related to the devotional traditions of particular parishes, the local understanding of Rite A, and the resources and setting within which the Rite is celebrated.

'At the holy communion the celebrant ... shall wear with the cassock either a surplice with scarf or stole or a surplice or alb with stole and cope, or an alb with the customary vestments.'

Canon B8, 2.

Section 49 (and section 68) provides for the consumption of remains. The 1662 Prayer Book always provided for this, lest any superstition on the one hand, or irreverence on the other, should attach to such consecrated elements. The practice is here continued, though the 'washing up' can now be done at the end of the distribution if desired. Usually it is a distraction to a congregation and should be left until all have gone. If the proposals of the Liturgical Commission for the communion of the sick are accepted, then the rubric will also allow some bread and wine to be kept 'for purposes of communion' to be distributed later by extended communion to those unable to be present.

HOW ELASTIC CAN RITE A BE?

What possibilities does the Rite then provide? What can the worshipper on holiday expect from a parish advertising 'Rite A'? What variants might this include? A few quick glimpses may give an answer.

A 'low' 8 o'clock

The clergyman alone takes the service. There is a minimum of activity or movement. There is no sermon, no hymn, no greeting of each other at the Peace. The congregation kneels for the eucharistic prayer, and responds by muttering into hands devoutly covering faces. They sit at far corners of the building from each other, and scurry away after the service without actually meeting each other. The Rite lasts twenty-five minutes.

A traditional parish communion

A choir processes in to a processional hymn, and is seated in sidestalls to the north and south of a 'nave altar'. A traditional setting of some parts of the service means that the ancient wording is used for these parts. Lay people read the lessons, except the Gospel which the president, clad in a chasuble, reads from the pulpit before he preaches. All still turn east for the Nicene Creed. A lay reader reads the intercession with the people responding between paragraphs. At the Peace, the churchwardens walk down the aisles shaking hands fairly formally with the end occupant of each pew. In some pews this is passed along, in others not. A housewife and a sidesman bring up the elements with the collecting plate, during the 'offertory hymn' (this service does not use the word 'offertory'), and they are received by a server and handed on to the president. In the eucharistic prayer, the congregation remains standing till after the Sanctus, then flops to its knees or posteriors. The president communicates himself before issuing the invitation to communion, and there is then a delay while the choir receives communion on its own, before the congregation at large is urged to come up. Some children are brought to the communion rail by their parents, and the priest lays a hand upon them and blesses them. Others are brought in a clump by Sunday school teachers. During communion the choir sings a sacramental hymn from *Hymns Ancient and Modern Revised*. At the end of the distribution the president cleanses the vessels with slightly elaborate care whilst the congregation sings a hymn. Then the congregation joins in 'Send us out ...', he gives a solemn blessing from in front of the communion table, and processes out behind the choir. He says the dismissal from the west end of the church, and a server returns to extinguish the two candles on the table. Coffee is served in an adjoining hall. It all feels rather like a Series 2, and that is exactly where the choir and organist would have liked it to have stopped.

A more self-consciously 'catholic' high mass

The choir sings an introit psalm as they are led in by a crucifer, with thurifer, acolytes, servers, visiting preacher, subdeacon, deacon, and priest swelling the procession. A modern setting is in use, though Martin Shaw was only abandoned recently. A Grail psalm is sung between Old Testament and Epistle. A Gospel procession, with candles – and *ASB 1980!* – forms up at the end of the Gradual hymn, and processes to the chancel step. The Book is censed before and after the reading. The preacher is escorted to the pulpit with great correctness. He himself makes much of the season in which the Sunday falls, expounding the choice of colour for the liturgical vesture and ornaments to show its teaching value. The creed is sung (but no one turns east). The intercession is led from an ambo facing the people, and makes special mention of the pope. At the Peace, the president uses the optional 'Let us offer one another a sign of peace' and the servers are greeted by him first, then take the greeting to the congregation. The thurifer censes priest and peo-

ple, and the president, flanked by two servers marches round the communion table censing it. He may also kiss it. As he places the ciborium and chalice on the table he says the Roman Catholic offertory prayers, and the congregation responds 'Blessed be God for ever' (section 33). There is then a ceremonial commingling of wine and water, and an

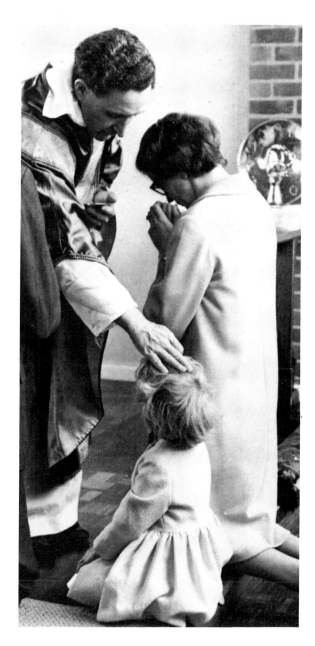

elaborate ritual washing of his own fingers. For the eucharistic prayer the congregation remains standing, and responds well. The acolytes hold high candles on either side of the table, whilst the president goes through a series of gestures towards the bread and cup, picking them up and genuflecting during the Narrative of Institution, and raising the priest's wafer aloft during the doxology. All bow low after the doxology. The acolytes restore their candles to candlesticks either side of the holy table. The congregation remains standing. The breaking of the priest's wafer is accompanied by the Agnus Dei from the choir. The servers, choir, and people come up

to receive communion – a separate wafer (with a stamped pattern of the crucifixion on it) is placed on the recipient's tongue, followed by a sip from a cup which is not given to him, but held firmly by the administrant. Many receive standing. After receiving, some genuflect before returning to their seats. The choir sing a medieval hymn of devotion to the sacrament from *The English Hymnal*. Then there is a meticulous cleansing of the vessels and a quick ending, with a lengthy procession out during the post-communion hymn, and the corporate prayer and the dismissal being led from the choir-vestry door.

An evangelical 'main service communion' (e.g. at a once-a-month evening service, where it replaces Evening Prayer).

For this there are no children present. There are no servers or assistants other than a lay reader. The penitential section comes at the beginning, and includes the Summary of the Law (section 5). No musical setting of the Rite is used, but the Gloria in Excelsis is said congregationally. Lay people come up to read the lessons, though the Epistle has been changed to suit a series of sermons being preached. There are bibles in the pews, so page numbers are announced with the readings. The sermon lasts for twenty minutes and concludes with an extempore prayer by the preacher 'praying in the message'. The intercessions are led by five different people, but there is no mention of the departed. At the Peace there is a swift turning to neighbours and shaking hands. Money is collected very ostensibly, whilst a sacramental hymn from *The Anglican Hymn Book* is sung. The money is then presented, and the 1 Chronicles 29 passage is said congregationally. Meanwhile some slices of white bread, and a cup of wine have been prepared on the communion table. The table itself is still in the chancel, pulled a little away from the east wall so that the president can just get behind it. During the eucharistic prayer the people stand.

They do not use 'Blessed is he who comes in the name of the Lord'. At the Lord's Prayer the congregation sinks thankfully to its knees. At the distribution (at which the lay reader assists) the cup is given to the people, and the cup lags well behind the bread. The people kneel to receive. After the distribution the seasonal sentence is not used, but the blessing is. A very low-key cleansing of the vessels is done in the vestry after the service.

A charismatic eucharist

A guitar group is leading the congregation in singing choruses before the service starts. A choir enters whilst this is happening, and the president has a word with the leader of the singing, and takes over the leadership from him. Thus the service starts. Very joyful singing (for they are warmed up) marks the service from the start. The choruses of hymns are often sung twice after the last verse. A setting for guitars is used for the sung parts of the service – the *King of Glory* setting. Members of the congregation praise God with their arms lifted up palms upwards to heaven. A look of joy comes onto their faces. Between the Epistle and Gospel a dance drama presentation is made, partly to the accompaniment of a chorus tune which the congregation picks up and sings, clapping to add to the rhythm. The sermon, though biblical, lays great emphasis upon expecting God to work miracles today.

After the creed the intercessions are entirely open, and after some warm extempore prayer, there is then an utterance in a strange language, and an interpretation of it – which is that God claims all the glory for himself, and his glory must be foremost in our motives. The president asks if anyone wants special prayer, and anyone who does stands up and his neighbours lay hands upon him and pray for him. At one point a member of the congregation starts to sing a chorus, and another takes it up, the instruments begin to accompany it, and it becomes a gentle congregational song.

When the Peace is reached all embrace each other warmly, milling around freely to convey this warmth to as many as possible. The eucharistic prayer is taken in a 'straight' way, but the sung responses come robustly and movingly from the congregation. For the administration various lay people assist in the distribution, and address the recipients by name. The ministers themselves receive last. Meanwhile the guitar group is back in action so that those who have received are singing 'alleluias' and other choruses in their seats. Some who have come to receive communion have not returned to their seats, but have gone into a side-chapel where they are receiving a personal ministry (with laying on of hands and prayer) for illness or inner distress or, possibly, on behalf of someone else in need. A rousing hymn of praise, with every hand held high in the air, concludes a service which is valued in proportion to its length (perhaps two hours or more), and to its atmosphere. Yes, it is Rite A, but Rite A stretched far . . . .

TAKING IT FURTHER

The letter of the rules of the Church of England does not stretch beyond a charismatic eucharist, but many would claim that the *spirit* of a modern Rite would allow experiments (and established usage too) well beyond that. Two such uses are in regular practice.

The informal eucharist

This may be a group in a home, or in a church lounge, or in a holiday centre. The group sits in a circle and reads and studies the word, sharing their understanding of it. They interchange news and requests for prayer, and pray extemporarily for each other. They all greet each other at the Peace, moving round the room to ensure that no one has missed anyone. They sing a hymn, and remain standing round a card-table for the eucharistic prayer. This comes from Rite A, and therefore enables them to respond. The Lord's Prayer, breaking of bread and distribution follow. All pass the elements to each other round the circle, ending with the president. After communion the president uses various verses of scripture to reflect the season, or the lessons of the bible discussed earlier, or the meaning of the sacrament, then one or two lead in extempore prayer of thanks and dedication, they all say 'Send us out . . .' and the president dismisses them.

Sometimes it may go further, so that no material from *ASB 1980* is in use at all, but all is extemporised. At that point, it ceases to have any connection with the Church of England's official provision.

The Agape

'Agape' is the Greek word for love, but it was used from the first century AD for the 'love-feast'. It seems that at Corinth and elsewhere a full meal was held by the Church at which the distribution of the sacramental elements was only a small, albeit central, part of the proceedings. The habit ceased during the third century but is being slowly revived – particularly on Maundy Thursday, and sometimes on Ascension Day or other special midweek occasions. For this there are no rules, and few standard patterns. But an agape *might* go as follows:

1 A welcome, a hymn, and thanks for the ordinary food
2 Soup
3 Reading from Bible
4 Main course
5 Brief homily
6 Sweet
7 Extempore prayer
8 Cheese
9 Peace, eucharistic prayer, distribution
10 Hymn
11 Coffee

The whole context of sharing with each other provides a warmth and mutual response in the sacrament far beyond that of the ordinary church service.

Rite B

Rite B is the 'thou' form communion service. It was added to *ASB 1980* in order to continue a 'thou' form rite, but it does not have collects and readings to

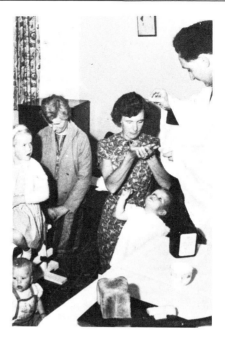

accompany it within the Book, and thus is unlike anything else in the Book. It is a combination of Series 1 and Series 2 communion services, which were united and slightly revised in 1975-6. But it never went through the detailed debate and revision which Rite A had in 1978-9 and is impoverished by comparison. It has less flexibility and fewer alternatives than Rite A.

However, virtually all the general articles about the eucharist are as relevant to Rite B as to Rite A. And the commentary upon Rite A is relevant to Rite B at most points, for Rite B follows a similar structure or 'shape' (though it is less clear about the distinction between the preparation of the gifts and the 'taking' of the bread and cup). It is very unlikely that congregations which use *ASB 1980* will be using Rite B from it.

Initiation Services

HOLY SPIRIT

'Jesus is Lord.'
> Original baptismal confession, see Rom 10.9

'If anyone is in Christ, there is a new creation.'
> 2 Cor 5.17.

'This is my covenant ... every male shall be circumcised'
> Gen 17.10

'To obey is better than sacrifice.'
> 1 Sam 15.22

'Circumcision is inward in the heart, kept in the spirit and not in the letter.'
> Rom 2.29.

'Peter said "Repent and each of you be baptised for the forgiveness of sins, and you will receive the gift of the Holy Spirit ..." ...and those who received his word were baptised, and there were added *that day* three thousand people ...'
> Acts 2.38,41

'Do you not know that we who have been baptised into Christ Jesus have been baptised into his death? We have therefore been buried together with him through baptism into death, in order that as Christ was raised from the dead through the glory of the Father, we also should walk in newness of life.'
> Rom 6.3-4

What is initiation?

'We christened our daughter Susan' one overhears a mother say in a queue at a bus-stop. What on earth has actually been happening to this baby who has been 'christened'?

One error is easily put right. Susan did not get her name at this 'christening' – she was given it by her parents soon after birth, and was registered as 'Susan', and would have been called 'Susan' even if she had never been 'christened'.

So what was the 'christening'? Literally it was a 'Christ-ing' of her – usually called (and in the bible always called) a 'baptism'. But the meaning of it is 'becoming Christ's'. It is a ceremony of becoming or beginning or of being adopted. Events which begin some new phase in a life are said to 'initiate' them. And services which initiate people – particularly baptism – are 'initiation services'. Susan has been put through the waters of baptism to begin a life of belonging to Christ. She is to be no longer her own but his. And her mother merely thinks she has got a 'name' – which she had already anyway!

INITIATION IN THE SCRIPTURES

Abraham was 'initiated' into the covenant of God when he received circumcision (Genesis 17), and he and his descendants were thereafter marked out as the people of God by this sign in their flesh. Abraham believed God before he was circumcised (Romans 4.12), and plenty of his descendants were circumcised but did not believe God. God made it clear that faith and obedience are more important than all ritual acts in his eyes. *But* he did insist upon the ritual acts too. That is part of the origin of Christian worship.

In the New Testament John the Baptist preached a baptism of repentance – not just repentance but repentance symbolised and expressed in baptism. It is quite likely (though we cannot be sure) that he got the rite from a Jewish practice of giving baptism to Gentiles to make them proselytes – women in particular needing some symbol and not being able to be circumcised. The scandal of John's baptism was that it proclaimed that *Jews* needed repentance and cleansing. It was an unthinkable new use for the rite.

Jesus apparently took over baptism from John, and made it clear to his disciples that he wished them to continue it. This they did from the day of Pentecost onwards. They taught both that men's hearts must be turned to God and that the outward rite would be both the means and the expression of this turning. Baptism was part of the proclamation of the good news – to submit to the gospel was to submit to baptism, and to submit to baptism was to submit to the gospel. The two went together – the inward and the outward.

Baptism was administered to adults the moment they began to express faith; there was no delay, no course of instruction, no sifting of candidates. The Christian Church was formed in Jerusalem on the day of Pentecost (and elsewhere later on in the Acts of the Apostles) by the baptism of new converts. Thus the bap-

Baptism in the River Congo

tised *were* the Church, and the Church *was* the baptised. The initiation provided a boundary or frontier to the Church, and gave it its identity. The baptised were the 'holy ones' (or 'saints'), and Paul, when writing letters to the Churches around the Mediterranean could always make his appeal 'You who have been baptised have been baptised into Christ's death in order that . . .'. It looks as though the waters of baptism were the point of no return, the burning of the boats, the actual conversion. It was as once-for-all-for-life as circumcision, even though it left no outward mark. If you were baptised you were treated as a believer; if not, not. And thus young children were brought up baptised from the outset, and treated as believers from the outset. (See below.)

Baptism of infants

But *were* infants baptised in New Testament days? Or, should they have been? Books and books have been written about this, and only a summary can be given here. The Church of England says 'Yes, infants were baptised and should be baptised for the following broad reasons':

- The practice of infant circumcision in the Old Testament points in this direction. No one could guarantee

'The Baptism of young Children is in any wise to be retained in the Church, as most agreeable with the institution of Christ.'

Article XXVII of the XXXIX Articles, 1571

153

'He was baptised immediately, he and all his, ... and he rejoiced with his whole house as he believed in the Lord' (*Acts 16.33-4*).

'The eunuch said "See, here is water; what is to hinder me from being baptised?" '

Acts 8.36 – and see the Day of Pentecost account earlier.

'Children, obey your parents.'

Eph 6.1, Col 3.20.

'Children, obey your parents in all things, for this is pleasing *to the Lord.*'

Col 3.20

Note that earlier in the same letter Paul wrote 'You have been buried with him in baptism, and you have been raised with him ...' (2.11) – the 'children' addressed in chapter 3 are included in the 'you have been buried with him in baptism' in chapter 2.

how the infants would turn out later: look at Esau – 'Jacob have I loved, but Esau have I hated' (Malachi 1.2-3). But Isaac was not to distinguish between them at birth, but *treat* them both as 'children of promise' – even though in the eyes of God only one of them was in fact such. Baptism replaced circumcision in the New Testament, partly because this included women more visibly into God's covenant, partly because the circumcised themselves needed the challenge of the Gospel and initiation into Christ – but *not* because Christian initiation is not applicable to infants.

● In the New Testament, we learn of households being baptised (Acts 16.15, 16.33, 1 Corinthians 1.16). The natural understanding of this is that the children of a household were baptised when the head of a household was baptised. In that case, children born after the conversion of parents would surely be baptised immediately after birth?

● The principle of baptising adults the moment they expressed the desire to be Christian, without having a long preparation, means that children could not be brought up unbaptised and still be treated as Christian. The only way to treat them as Christian is to baptise them from the start – just as with the adults who wish to be converted.

● In point of fact, in the Epistles all the recipients of the letters (of, say, Paul) were reckoned to be baptised, and these included 'young children'. Children were in the assembly, part of the body of Christ, from the start.

● There seems to be *some* evidence that infant baptism can be traced back to the first century AD in post-apostolic authors, and this confirms the early Church's understanding of the practice of the apostles.

It is easy, of course, to say 'But there are no instances of the baptising of infants mentioned in the New Testament.' It is

Baptism of the Emperor Constantine by St Silves[...]

also worth noting that there are no instances of Christian parents *not* baptising their infants mentioned in the New Testament. Whichever happened, it is taken entirely for granted by the New Testament writers – and that does not mean that silence on this point means that Christian parents did not baptise their infants!

People who have had an adult experience of conversion are liable to think that an infant baptism is misleading, and that baptism should be withheld until the growing child makes a real profession of his or her own faith. But *within the Christian family* the baptism of infants is a sign that they will be brought up *as believers*, at one with their parents in their faith in the living God. And this is in fact how believers do bring up their

Church in this task of realism.

Baptism expresses the Church's mission – bringing newcomers into the body of Christ. The Church of England sees missionary baptism as household baptism, and therefore provides for the baptism of parents and children together in the main service. This means that as far as possible baptism remains the same in its meaning whether given to adults or to infants. And, when needed, a special service for baptising infants is provided – and it derives from the main service.

Baptism and the laying on of hands

In the New Testament there are three occasions where baptism in water is followed by the laying on of hands. The reasons for this may have varied, and it is likely that the laying on of hands was a special sign of blessing, and of praying for those on whom hands were laid. But the great majority of references to baptisms, whether in the Gospels, the Acts, or the Epistles, are silent about any post-baptismal laying on of hands, and it is difficult to assert that the practice was the universal accompaniment of water-baptism – indeed in Acts 8 it looks like an emergency action, quite the reverse of a norm. In Acts 2.38 the gift of the Spirit seems to be as closely associated with water-baptism as is repentance, and the water-baptism therefore seems to have been full initiation.

However, by around 200 AD in the west, and 400 AD in the east, there arose a practice of always following baptism with either the laying on of hands or anointing with oil. This varying ceremony was related to the gift of the Spirit, but was given at the same service as the water-baptism – to infant candidates as well as adults. However, after 500 AD in the west the water-baptism of infants tended to get separated from the laying on of hands. The Church taught that a child who died without baptism could not be saved, so that (in days of high rates of infant mortality) midwives and other lay people gave baptism to infants within minutes of birth. No bishop could

children – to call God their 'Father' right from the start. There is no point where consciousness begins, or faith 'starts' – so the only point for initiation by baptism is immediately after birth.

This case (which is greatly abbreviated) is only a case for the baptism of children of believing, worshipping families. One of the great problems facing the Church of England today is the transition from the 'Christendom' assumption of the Reformation period that every English family is in fact a believing worshipping family, to a more realistic recognition that many families asking for baptism today for their children are in no sense believing or worshipping. The interrogation of the parents and godparents (section 42 – and it can also be used at section 11) is designed to help the local

'Children who are too young to profess the Christian faith are baptised on the understanding that they are brought up *as Christians* within the family of the Church'
    ASB 1980, Initiation, Section 42.

[The Samaritans] 'had only been baptised in the name of the Lord Jesus. Then they laid hands on them, and they received the Holy Spirit.'
    Acts 8.14-17.

'And the bishop shall lay his hands upon them and invoke, saying: "Lord God, you have made them worthy to receive remission of sins through the laver of regeneration of the Holy Spirit: send upon them your grace …"'
    Hippolytus, *Apostolic Tradition* 21 (c. 215 AD).

Anointing with oil as a subsidiary ceremony is permitted in the new service for both baptism and confirmation (see the Notes).

possibly be present to give what was now being called 'confirmation', and this had to follow at some later date. In northern Europe, including Britain, in the middle ages, dioceses were so large, and travel so difficult, that many grew up without ever being confirmed, and showed no desire to have it even when the opportunity offered. The idea that the initial giving of the Spirit took place at this service disappeared, and it was seen as a 'strengthening' – 'con-*firm*-ing' the candidates. So the emphasis in sacramental initiation fell squarely upon water-baptism, and 'confirmation' was a kind of sacrament of growth. (None of these changes happened in the east, where the presbyter to this day anoints the infant within the baptismal service, and the presence of a bishop is not required.)

A medieval confirmation

At the Reformation, the Church of England made confirmation into an occasion for teenagers to ratify for themselves the faith they had professed by proxy in infant baptism. It was preceded by catechising, and it admitted the candidates into communion. The service lost all reference to the coming of the Spirit (which had survived in the medieval Latin text, even when it was not generally believed) and became a simple catechising, followed by a laying on of hands with a simple prayer for God's blessing – a prayer which could be used on any occasion, very unlike a sacramental formula. (In the *ASB 1980* services this prayer is now a congregational prayer for the candidates after confirmation (see sections 26 and 81).

In 1662 the Prayer Book included for the first time a service for baptising 'those of riper years' (probably teenagers, who had missed infant baptism during the Commonwealth period). A rubric at the end required those baptised at this age to present themselves swiftly for confirmation, which meant that confirmation was being seen not only as a certificate of having learned the catechism, but also as admitting to communion in a way that seemed to make it a necessary part of initiation. On the other hand, the actual service of confirmation in the 1662 Prayer Book still assumed that it was to be used for those who had been baptised as infants and now needed to 'renew the solemn promise and vow' made in their name at baptism, 'ratifying and confirming the same in your own persons' – which fitted very badly with an adult baptism where the candidates had made their vows in their own persons only a few days before. It looks rather as though the bishops of the restored Church of England were ensuring that dissenters should have to kneel before them – the bishops – in order to belong to the Church of England at all, and this was seen as a temporary provision to tidy up the problems remaining from the Commonwealth period.

On the other hand, they *did* require

such confirmation, and the discipline has remained to this day. It is not surprising that the Liturgical Commission, which first began drafting new initiation services in the 1950s, should have decided that for adults baptism and confirmation should be put together in one service, over which the bishop should preside – and that this should be a communion service. It is very like the pattern found in Hippolytus in 215 AD. But it still leaves questions as to how *biblical* the pattern is, and what the point of confirmation is for those who have been baptised as adults. The debate continues in the Church, whilst the new services also continue – admittedly somewhat imprecise at an important point, but allowing the debate to go on within the Church of England without excluding any party. That is why the main service of initiation is 'Baptism, Confirmation, and Holy Communion', and the separate baptism of infants and confirmation of adults are printed later in *ASB 1980*, and are derived from the main service.

BAPTISM – DOES IT REALLY MAKE THEM CHRISTIAN?

If baptism 'initiates', are all baptised English people Christian? If baptism brings the gift of the Holy Spirit, are all baptised English people filled with the Spirit? Or, if the vast proportion of English people have been baptised, why has it apparently done them little good?

The answer is that baptism is not magic. God gives his Spirit before, or at the time of, or after, baptism, or not at all, or without baptism at all. He is free to do this as he himself sees fit. And he has given to us basic rules for baptising. The New Testament gives the Church the warrant to baptise when:

> *either* an adult is expressing faith in Christ,
> *or* an infant is born into a believing family.

If we do not keep the basic rules, we must not be surprised that baptism has

... in July 1976 the General Synod voted ... to keep the present practice in regard to confirmation. The Commission clearly accepts this decision; although some of its members regret it and would prefer to see baptism itself to be the liturgical climax of initiation – particularly in the case of adults. As far as confirmation for those baptised in infancy is concerned, a case can certainly be made for keeping it. But problems do arise when attempting to justify the confirmation of adults who have just been baptised: and the number of such people is increasing. Some members of the Commission feel that the time has come when this issue must be faced.'

Liturgical Commission's introduction to the Report *Alternative Services Series 3 Initiation Services*, GS 343, 1977, p. 7

'This Synod ... desires that there should be a re-examination of the conditions upon which infants are accepted for baptism.'

Motion passed in the General Synod in November 1976

apparently done little good in such cases. And as England, with so many other countries, moves slowly from the 'Christendom' position of the Reformers (where every citizen is presumed to be a believer), to a true 'missionary' situation (where every citizen is better presumed to be an unbeliever – at least until he professes faith), so the anomalies of baptising many without faith may well remain.

'We judge that Baptism is a sacrament generally necessary to salvation, but that the grace of regeneration does not so necessarily accompany the act of Baptism that regeneration invariably takes place in Baptism ... in no case is regeneration in Baptism unconditional.'

Judgement of the Ecclesiastical Committee of the Privy Council on the appeal of George Gorham from the Court of Arches in 1850

Of course, it does not have to be so. Parishes might become stricter about the qualifications for infant baptism – and some parishes have already done so. And the more baptism is restricted to those who qualify (see the '*either* ... *or* ...' above), the more it will truly represent the boundaries of true faith.

But a great difficulty is that, since the time of Augustine of Hippo (356-430), parents have believed that a child must be baptised to be saved. The rate of infant mortality was high till thirty years ago, and so for 1500 years in western Europe parents have clamoured for baptism for their infants, in order to save them from terrors beyond the grave. The reasons are deep in the folk-lore of the community ('He'll never do well till he's been christened'), and Augustine's theology is not usually in mind directly – rather the grandmother is asking when the child will be 'done' ...!

Parents are not to think their child needs to be baptised to receive a name. Names are fixed other ways! And equally parents are not to think their child needs to be baptised to go to heaven if he or she dies. This is a superstitious belief going back to St Augustine, and haunting parents who have enough grief with the loss of a child in any case. Baptism is not magic – and the love of God is not switched on suddenly for a dying child by the use of baptism just before death. It is there anyway. The services specifically cover this point, and do so to help get rid of the magical view which has so often been around.

The use of infant baptism *is* scriptural. But the practice of baptising every child brought for baptism has confused the boundaries of the Church, confused the parents themselves – and persuaded many good Christians that infant baptism itself is wrong. The Church has to be wary about letting these unhelpful impressions linger on.

But surely we should not reject children brought for baptism?

The difficulty with being cautious about giving baptism to all and sundry is that parents who have no other experience of the Church feel very rejected if they cannot have baptism on demand. But being cautious about baptism need not mean being rejecting of the family. And one provision the services now have is for a 'post-natal' service of thanksgiving which is not baptism.

These services (after birth and after adoption) are not meant to be about joining the Church, or becoming part of the body of Christ. They do not actually 'initiate' at all (and this must always be made clear). But they do mark the beginning of life with a 'thank you' to God – and, in the case of adoption, they mark the beginning of life in a new family. In both cases the new life is changing the family itself, and so there too there is a new beginning.

There are no demands made upon parents or children by these services. There is no commitment to discipleship, no opportunity for hypocrisy or misunderstanding. The services simply say 'thank you' to God for his particular gift of a child – a gift in the order of creation, not that of redemption. This can exactly meet the needs of those who do not belong to the Christian fellowship.

However, there are those within the fellowship who will also want to use these services. Many a believing couple who are going to bring their child to baptism still want to give thanks to God for the child's birth as a previous separate event. And other parents who are not persuaded that infants should be baptised, but still themselves belong to the Church of England, can mark the gift of a child from God by giving thanks to him in this way.

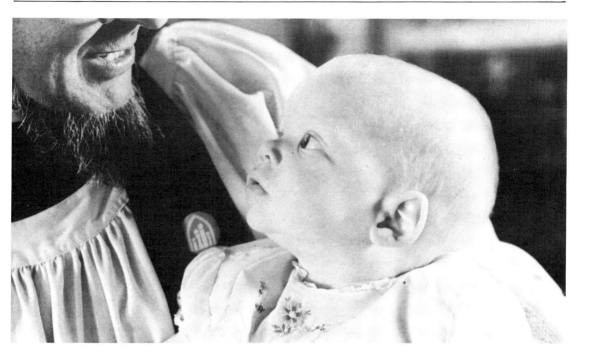

ADMISSION TO COMMUNION

On the day of Pentecost those who were baptised and 'added' to the church immediately began to 'break bread' from house to house. St Paul also makes it clear that not only does baptism make people members of the body of Christ, but also that they continue in the body by sharing the bread of the eucharist. In other words, to be initiated by baptism is to be initiated into sharing the eucharist. The accounts of baptism in the second century AD bear this out – the candidates were baptised in a separate place (a baptistery?), and then brought into the eucharist, to be greeted by the kiss of peace and welcomed to share at the Lord's table. The services in *ASB 1980* are constructed on the same principle – that baptism and confirmation are given at a communion service, and those who are candidates themselves receive communion for the first time at this service. If there is no communion at the time of confirmation, then a 'first communion' follows soon after.

But what about infants? It seems that in the early Church infant baptism led naturally into infant communion, and this is still done in the eastern Orthodox Churches to this day. The child is fully included in the fellowship from the start, and the logic of including him or her in the Church from the outset by giving baptism is properly continued by also giving communion to those baptised.

But we do not do it. Why not? Probably because in the middle ages the idea arose that children should be able to answer simple questions about their faith before being admitted to communion at around the age of seven. The reformers then took the idea further, insisting on an adult understanding of the faith – fearing lest children should otherwise lapse into the superstitious beliefs about the sacrament in which they viewed themselves as having been brought up. So they laid great emphasis upon understanding, and made confirmation the climax of the teaching of the catechism and other instruction. In this way, they delayed the admission to communion to around 13 to 16 years of age.

'Our fathers were all ... baptised into Moses ... and all ate the same spiritual food and drank the same spiritual drink ... And all these things have become examples to us ...

1 Cor 10.1,2,6 – those who were baptised also ate and drank

'We break the bread to share in the body of Christ **Though we are many, we are one body, because we all share in one bread.'**

Rite A, based on 1 Cor. 10.17 - continuance in the body springs from sharing in the one bread.

SHOULD YOUNG CHILDREN RECEIVE COMMUNION?

If parents leave their children in a creche or Sunday School when they go to a communion service, they may not feel the force of this question. Their own children are not *at* communion – why should they feel the need to *receive* communion? But where the children are present the need is felt very strongly – and, above all, it is a need which is not just a concession to 'equality for children', but is a true recognition of their place with adults in the one body of Christ where the one bread of the eucharist is shared. At the moment we seem to say 'yes, you belong to Christ by baptism, but you are not to join at his table'. A child might well reply 'You expect me to show the marks of grace in my life, by a pattern of discipleship, but you deny me the means of grace which you claim is so important.'

In the last hundred years there has been slowly growing pressure within the Church of England to bring down the age of admission to communion – and the pressure has grown considerably in the last thirty years, particularly when children have been in communion services with their parents at the Parish Communion – often kneeling at a communion rail beside them and receiving a laying on of a hand with à prayer of blessing but without receiving the bread and wine they see given to their parents.

The short-term way to bring down the age of admission to communion is to lower the age of confirmation. This has been happening slowly, and nowadays confirmation is often given to children of 10 or even under. But this is an inherently unsatisfactory solution, as confirmation includes not only admission to communion, but also an adult ratification of baptismal vows. The more the age for confirmation is pushed downwards the less meaningful will that ratification be. If that is to continue as a central part of confirmation then the age ought to be kept up at around 13 to 16 rather than let drop.

The more radical solution is to admit to communion prior to confirmation. This has been greatly debated in the Church of England, and has been the subject of some unofficial experiments. It has become canonical in overseas parts of the Anglican Communion. And the question will not go away, but recurs every time a child at the Parish Communion says (whether to parent or minister) 'May I have some too please?' One day we shall all have to answer 'yes'.

PROGRESS TO 1980

In the 1549 and 1552 Prayer Books there was provision for infant baptism (including 'private' baptism for emergencies), and for confirmation which included the catechism. In 1662 there was added 'The Ministration of Baptism to such as are of Riper Years'. The term 'Riper Years' suggests not so much adults as teenagers – those up to the age of 17 who had been allowed to miss infant baptism through the tolerance of 'anabaptists' during the Commonwealth period. Now there was to be a once-for-all catching up on them! And they were to be confirmed also, in order that they should not escape any feature of the Anglican system. At the Restoration the Catechism was split off and became a separate service in the book. The 1662 book does not give any indication of how adult and infant baptism might be combined in one service, or how adult baptism and confirmation might be combined in one. These possibilities were not even considered until very recently.

In the 1927-8 proposals one or two phrases in the baptismal services were softened, and a first use of the Acts 8 passage about the Spirit coming upon the Samaritans through the laying on of the apostles' hands was added to the confirmation service. These services tended to supersede the 1662 ones in the years following 1928, except in parishes where 1928 was viewed as erroneous.

When the experimental era began in 1966, the 1928 baptismal services were authorised as Series 1 services, but the 1928 confirmation service was defeated in the House of Laity and became clearly illegal. It has not been used since then, and that Acts 8 passage (which *must* be describing something of an emergency, not something standard and usual in the Church) has not reappeared in liturgy – not even as a proposed lesson in the list of possible 'Epistle' passages.

The Liturgical Commission had a first chance to try uniting adult baptism with confirmation in services put out (for discussion only) in 1960. These were then revised in 1966 (when 'The Decision' became a separate section and divided the vows into two distinct groups), and were authorised in 1967 and 1968 as Series 2 services. They are still authorised to this day, and would naturally accompany a use of Rite B eucharist in 'thou' form of address to God.

From 1971 to 1976 the Church of England debated the 'Ely' report on Christian initiation. This not only said that water-baptism *is* complete sacra-

mental initiation (which would make confirmation redundant for those baptised as adults), but also recommended the admission of young children to the eucharist. During this period the Liturgical Commission had to delay publishing Series 3 rites, lest they should be out of step with the policy of the Church of England. Finally, in 1976, the General Synod decided to make no changes in the pattern of initiation at all, except to ask the Commission to add a service for the Thanksgiving for the Birth of a Child. The Commission was then able to complete its drafts and publish them. The report came out in 1977.

The main new features of the Commission's work were the Thanksgiving service which the Synod had requested (actually, it became two services, as Thanksgiving for Adoption was added also), and the inclusion of infant baptism (on the principle of 'family baptism') within the baptism-plus-confirmation rite. So all the parts which were separate in 1662 could now be used together.

The progress of the services through Synod took from November 1977 to February 1979. In that period various changes were made. The main obvious ones are that a new position was offered as an optional place for the signing with the sign of the cross in baptism, the Welcome was moved in the main rite to come after confirmation, and opening Notes provided for the use of oil in both baptism and confirmation, though no new wording was included to accompany the use of oil.

The services were authorised from Pentecost 1979, and the booklets containing them were the first Series 3 services to show the *ASB 1980* page format and layout. Offprints of the service for infant baptism on its own, and of the service for adult confirmation on its own, were also published. The services were then marginally 'adapted' to take their place in the *ASB 1980* itself.

'The Curates of every Parish shall often admonish the people, that they defer not the Baptism of their children longer than the first or second Sunday next after their birth ....'

Opening rubric in the Private Baptism of Infants in 1662

12th century font at Long Wittenham, Berkshire

The Services

THANKSGIVING FOR THE BIRTH OF A CHILD

What it is **not**:
A baptism
A 'Churching'
A naming
A blessing
What it **is**:
A 'thank you' to God
A look forward in hope
Jesus said:
'Let the children come to me; do not try to stop them; for the kingdom of God belongs to such as these ...'
And the Church says:
'Jesus' words are *not* about giving baptism to children, so we have put them into *this* service, not the baptism one.'
Perhaps the Church should issue a certificate to say what this service was – lest anyone think it was a baptism.
'We receive this child into our family ...'

Because this is a 'post-natal' service, two distinctions have to be made clear at the outset:

- It is *not* an infant baptism (see Note 1), and must not allow any possibility that it should be thought to be a baptism. In particular it should not take place at a font, and the service never even suggests that the minister should take the child in his arms, lest that much of a ceremony be interpreted as a baptism! Children who have been through this service remain strictly unbaptised!

- It is *not* the 'Churching of Women'. It may well replace the old 'Thanksgiving of Women after Childbirth' in use, but its contents are different. 'Churching' was thanksgiving for the mother's recovery (which would be possible even if the child had died), whilst the new service is a thanksgiving for the birth of the child. It is appropriate that the child should be present, and should be brought by both parents for a family thanksgiving.

The structure of the Thanksgiving Service
Prayers of thanksgiving

Versicles and responses *or* Psalm 100

Reading of Mark 10.13-16
Giving of a Gospel to the parents (optional)

Lord's Prayer

Prayers for the home and the future of the child

Blessing

The intention is that a simple 'thank you' to God for the birth of a child should lead into a forward-looking hope for the child's future life.

THANKSGIVING AFTER ADOPTION

This service is very similar to the previous one, though the need it meets is in some ways different. And the service has two distinctive features:

- Prayer for the natural parents of the child (section 24)
- A prayer of 'Welcome' for the adopted child (section 25)

In days when there is a shortage of children for adoption the prayer of thanksgiving from parents, who have usually waited at least five years before being allowed to adopt, comes from the heart.

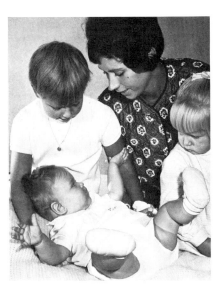

BAPTISM, CONFIRMATION, AND HOLY COMMUNION ALL AT ONE SERVICE

A family is coming to baptism, just as apparently happened in New Testament times. They are going to be initiated at a Parish Communion on a Sunday morning. How then shall it be done?

For hundreds of years – indeed until 1979 – the Church of England did not allow for this event. But now we have this inclusive service for them all. Indeed, as the subtitle shows, other adults can be baptised and confirmed (or just confirmed), and other infants or children can be baptised, in addition to the family initiation at the heart of the service.

'Doing' all the family at once is a help to our understanding of baptism. All the way through the baptism the service is the same for them all, with the very smallest adaptation for those unable to answer for themselves. The Church of England does not now have two different things – 'baptism' and 'infant baptism' – it has just one, which is simply baptism. The service is the same, the vows are the same, the theology is the same, the obligation of discipleship is the same.

It is only in the last thirty years that the practice of giving baptism and confirmation to adults at a single service has arisen. The Prayer Book made no provision for this, and confirmation used to be given on its own, with the rare candidate for adult baptism being baptised not at the confirmation service, but on his own, perhaps a few days before the bishop's visit for the confirmation. Furthermore, such confirmations would rarely be at a communion service – once again the Prayer Book made no such provision.

Now that baptism, confirmation and communion are brought together into one service a more satisfying pattern of initiation has resulted, and one in many ways more like the pattern in the third century AD. The vows are only said once, the welcome is only said once, the 'first communion' happens on the same occasion, and the kiss of Peace is a true acceptance into the Church and into communion with others. The bishop presides over the whole rite, and by his own role in the Church not only adds solemnity to a very significant occasion, not only brings the word of God for that occasion, (though he does do both these), but also reminds the whole congregation that initiation is not a matter of entry into the local congregation only, but into the wider, indeed the worldwide, Church.

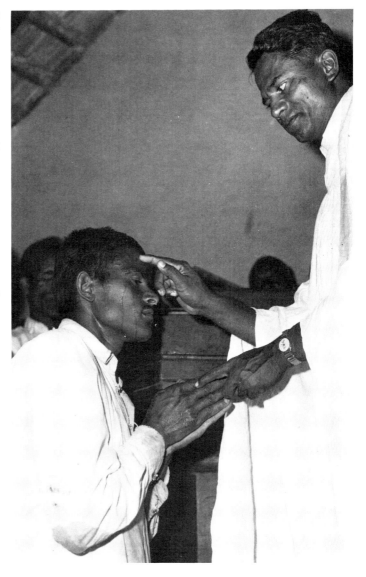

STRUCTURE

The service is set out as the diagram shows, with a very clear progression.

Why this structure?

There is a natural progression about this order, which has been improved and refined over various stages. The following features are important and have helped to shape the structure:

- In a communion service, it is now usual for 'extra' events to come after the sermon and in place of the creed and intercessions. If penitence is used at all (and it does not have to be) then it should come at the earlier position in Rite A, during the Preparation (section 3).
- The interrogation during 'The Decision' corresponds to the ancient 'Renunciations', which often came in the early Church at a point separate from the affirmations of faith as a preliminary to the baptism.
- The blessing of the water (section 17) provides a theological rationale for baptism, and appropriately divides the 'Decision' from the affirmations of faith.
- The affirmations themselves belong closely with the actual baptism. In the ancient western rites it seems that the candidates were actually standing in the water when they made these affirmations, so closely did the declaration of faith and the submission to baptism belong to each other.
- Because the intention is to bring baptism and confirmation as close to each other as possible, there is now no need for any 'ceremonies after baptism'. The signing with the sign of the cross can come earlier (at Section 14) and the candle can be dropped. Similarly the Welcome, which in Series 2 infant baptism came after the baptism, is now delayed to follow the confirmation.

Although the Liturgical Commission, which worked hard over the years to achieve this sort of order, would now defend it equally hard, yet it is possible in use for there to be problems. Imagine a church building where an ancient font at the west door is to be used for baptism, and a chancel step for the confirmation. What does the bishop do, when he has one adult candidate for baptism (and perhaps no infants), but thirty or so candidates for confirmation? What he apparently has to do is to take 'The Decision' from the chancel step (perhaps with the candidates all in a front pew), and then take *all* the candidates, not just the one, down the aisle to the font. There he blesses the water, interrogates *all* the candidates for their affirmation of faith, and baptises the one baptismal candidate. Then he shepherds them all back again to the chancel step for the confirmation. And this seems absurd.

Font in Saintbury church, Gloucester, with a dove, a symbol of the Holy Spirit, on top

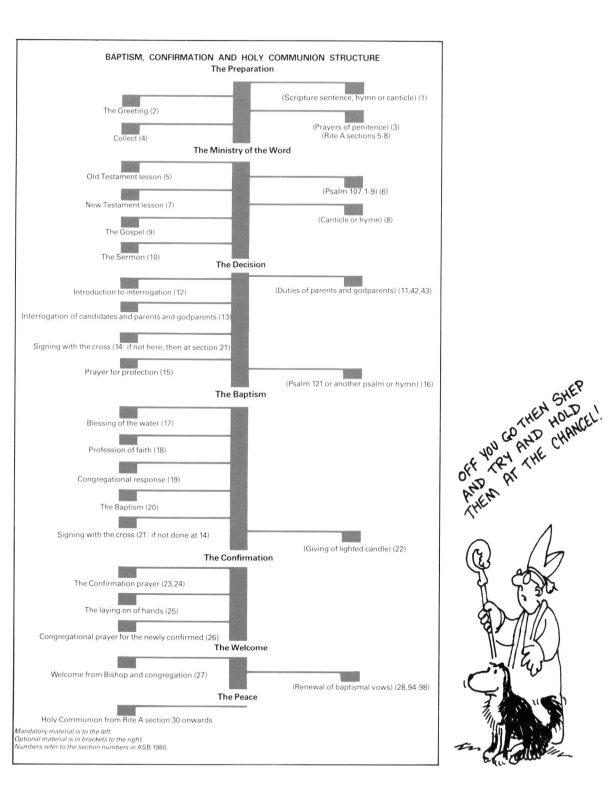

BAPTISM, CONFIRMATION AND HOLY COMMUNION STRUCTURE

The Preparation

(Scripture sentence, hymn or canticle) (1)

The Greeting (2)

(Prayers of penitence) (3)
(Rite A sections 5-8)

Collect (4)

The Ministry of the Word

Old Testament lesson (5)

(Psalm 107.1-9) (6)

New Testament lesson (7)

(Canticle or hymn) (8)

The Gospel (9)

The Sermon (10)

The Decision

Introduction to interrogation (12)

(Duties of parents and godparents) (11,42,43)

Interrogation of candidates and parents and godparents (13)

Signing with the cross (14: if not here, then at section 21)

Prayer for protection (15)

(Psalm 121 or another psalm or hymn) (16)

The Baptism

Blessing of the water (17)

Profession of faith (18)

Congregational response (19)

The Baptism (20)

Signing with the cross (21: if not done at 14)

(Giving of lighted candle) (22)

The Confirmation

The Confirmation prayer (23,24)

The laying on of hands (25)

Congregational prayer for the newly confirmed (26)

The Welcome

Welcome from Bishop and congregation (27)

(Renewal of baptismal vows) (28,94-98)

The Peace

Holy Communion from Rite A section 30 onwards

Mandatory material is to the left.
Optional material is in brackets to the right.
Numbers refer to the section numbers in ASB 1980.

OFF YOU GO THEN SHEP AND TRY AND HOLD THEM AT THE CHANCEL!

The Commission stuck to their guns when the bishops put this sort of case to them. They allowed an opening Note 10 which gives the bishop discretion to vary the order slightly.

However, what this problem reveals is that the use of architecture and furnishings has not yet caught up with new orders of baptism and confirmation. A case like the one described cries out for some provision for baptism to occur at the chancel step, or very near it. Then all would be clear and simple. Fonts came at the west end of churches for symbolic reasons – to represent 'entry' into the Church, hence the location of them by the west door. But the medieval *use* of such fonts had the candidates *outside* the door, until they were let in to be baptised! Once the candidates are sitting in a front pew from the beginning of the service that sort of symbolism is vanishing, and the rite ought to ensure that the whole administration of both water and the laying on of hands is visible to all the people.

The Ministry of the Word

The main teaching of the readings is about initiation, or, with the Old Testament, the making of a covenant (which is the background to the initiation of particular people into it). The Acts 16 reading is about household baptism (the jailer at Philippi), and the Epistle passages set out the meaning of baptism, or the 'fruit of the Spirit' (Galatians 5), or the significance of 'being the people of God' (1 Peter 2). The Gospel readings include one about Jesus' baptism by John (Mark 1.1-11), one about rebirth (John 3), one about the cost of discipleship (Matthew 16), and one about the 'Great Commission' (Matthew 28). But other readings may be used (opening Note 9), and bishops who find themselves preaching frequently at initiation services may well want to observe the themes of the various Sundays rather than going round the small circle of the same passages again and again.

The Decision

This whole section is about the turning from evil. In order that it should not appear as a mere turning *away*, there is also included the strong reminder of the one *towards* whom we turn;

> 'Do you turn to Christ?'
> **'I turn to Christ.'**

But overall the section has three distinct emphases on separation from sin:
- The renunciations
- The signing with the cross, with the instruction to 'fight valiantly under the banner of Christ'
- The prayer for protection from any attack or invasion by 'the powers of darkness'.

The signing with the sign of the cross does not have to come here. Until 1979 all the Church of England services since 1552 had had it after the actual baptism: and it can still come there. But its theme goes very closely with the theme of the Decision, and if it is given here then it avoids any confusion later on – where large numbers not only of lay people, but even of clergy, seem to have thought that the sign of the cross *was* itself the outward sign of baptism, and not a subsidiary explanatory ceremony. Now, if the sign of the cross is given here, its subsidiary role is very clear, and the actual baptism follows well separated from it.

The signing with the sign of the cross is the only use of it mentioned in the whole range of new services. This corresponds to the provision in the baptism services of the Prayer Book, where the post-baptismal 'signing' was the only occurrence of the sign of the cross in the whole book. It seems that Cranmer kept it in 1552 because it was not what he would have called 'dark and dumb', but was explained as it was used. One of the most consistent attacks upon the Prayer Book by the puritans concentrated upon this 'popish' ceremony – their objection being that it was without any mention in the bible. The churchmen resisted these attacks stoutly.

A family baptism in East Africa

The Vows

The declarations of repentance (in 'The Decision') and of faith (in 'The Baptism') are together usually called the baptismal 'Vows' or 'Profession'. The two sets of interrogations cover *three* sets of candidates each:

- Those who are being baptised and confirmed as adults and thus make their own baptismal vows for themselves for the first time.

- Those who have been baptised earlier (probably as infants), and, whilst bound by the vows taken earlier in their name, have never made those vows before with their own mouths. They thus come to confirmation and 'ratify' their baptismal vows.

- Those who are being baptised in infancy and therefore cannot speak for themselves. Others are to answer for them. But, to make absolutely sure, the service insists that god-parents and parents

'. . . must answer both for themselves and for *these children*!'

They must answer

for themselves, as true believers who qualify the children for baptism and must themselves be committed to new life in Christ

for the children, because it is the *candidates* who are to be committed to the new life, or their baptism would be without meaning. So sponsors speak as *proxies*, making aloud the profession which the candidates are committed to (yes, to belong to Christ) even though they are too young to say it themselves.

The previous services did not make it absolutely clear whether the interrogation was directed at the sponsors or at the candidates. Now it is absolutely clear it is directed at BOTH!

The way in which each of the three sets of candidates is covered by the interrogation is set out very clearly in the service.

This 13th century font is large enough to immerse a baby, like all ancient fonts

The 'Blessing of the Water'

The prayer at section 17 was in previous services called 'The Blessing of the Water'. This is a shorthand title for a long prayer which is meant to include a large amount of scriptural teaching about baptism, and to pray for the benefits of baptism to be given by God to the candidates.

The teaching is built round various uses and meanings of water, including a passing allusion to 'baptism' as meaning 'death', as Jesus used it about his own death. The prayer for the effectiveness of the baptism takes the form 'Bless this water' – but the prayer is *not* a prayer for the water, but for the *use* of the water on the candidates. It is not self-contained as merely 'Bless this water' would be, but is rather 'Bless this water, that . . .'.

Although this prayer gives a structure and a deepened meaning to the service, in baptism a 'blessing of the water' has never been viewed as having the same significance as the consecration of the eucharistic bread and wine. In an emergency (see sections 106-11), water can be used for baptism without any 'blessing' of it at all. Equally, no one has to worry what happens to baptismal water *after* the baptism (although at communion there is care taken about finishing up what is left after the distribution). And, to cap it all, if baptisms are done – as they well may be done – in a river or the sea, then the water may get 'blessed' every week or so! Every now and again a family produces a bottle of Jordan water (yes, from the river Jordan itself) and asks that it should be used – but as the emphasis is upon the *use* of the water, not upon its *nature* (let alone its origins!), such a practice is at best harmless sentiment, and at worst sheer superstition.

The prayer, having started with the provision of water by God, and having continued with Christ's death and resurrection, then asks that the candidates may not only be united with Christ in his death and resurrection but also may receive the Holy Spirit. Baptism is seen as the point of full conversion, full commitment, full initiation. The prayer should be heartfelt for our children as well as for adults – though we should also remember that the commitment of a growing child is that which is proper for his or her own age.

The affirmations of faith

The affirmations (sections 18, 19) have been saved up to be put closely beside the actual baptism. Of course, there may be large numbers of candidates for confirmation who are already baptised. But the baptismal candidates should be standing by the place where they will be baptised, so that the connection with the baptism is very clear (remember how in Hippolytus' account they stood *in* the water to make the affirmations). It is obviously helpful if the confirmation candidates are near at hand, and are equally being addressed directly, but they must not obscure what is happening at the baptism by crowding the scene.

The affirmations are 'Trinitarian' in

form. The creed we call the 'Apostles' Creed' is developed from the most ancient baptismal affirmations of faith, and the three-fold structure is clear in that also. The candidates declare that they 'believe and trust' – a very clear way of expressing their total commitment to the one God, Father, Son and Holy Spirit. The Trinitarian nature of the affirmations leads into baptism 'in the name of the Father, and of the Son, and of the Holy Spirit'. The Trinitarian nature of the God whom we worship is not seen as an optional extra which well-educated Christians can let their minds work on when they have first grasped the fundamentals of the faith. Many Christians – indeed many clergy – would appear to think this way. But the baptismal service is a very strong witness against that way of thinking. Here, at the very dividing-line between the Church and the world, the primary confession of faith needed and the primary formula used at the actual baptism are above all else Trinitarian. The doctrine of the Trinity is *not* an intellectual balancing-act for the highly skilled and slightly bored or donnish Christian philosopher – no, it is the first statement of the nature of the God with whom we *all* have to do, and it stands there at baptism at the gateway into the Church for *all* to accept at the point of entry. The doctrine of the Trinity is a fundamental of the faith – it is *this* God in whom we believe and trust.

The point is reinforced by the congregation's part (section 19). Those already baptised, presumably standing at this point, make their affirmation of faith in the Holy Trinity also, reassuring the newcomers that this *is* fundamental, and reassuring themselves that they have not drifted from their baptismal faith.

The baptism

The meaning of the formula of baptism is now clear (section 20). To be baptised 'in the name of' someone is to be placed under his headship. Baptism is the assertion of the headship of the triune God over the candidate. But it is more than an a verbal claim – it is a sacrament with an outward administration of water which God has ordained as a means of asserting his claims upon human beings.

This in turn means that, although the candidate has actively affirmed his faith, at the point of baptism he is passive. The baptism is given to him, done to him, and he submits to it. The minister, on God's behalf, administers this sacrament of the lordship of the triune God, and the candidate humbly receives it.

The first method of baptising which the Church of England acknowledges (and this has always been true) is submersion. It stands there in the rubric, and has a continuous witness from the days of Anglo-Saxon baptisms in rivers to Norman fonts which can still be seen today and are large enough to dip a baby,

Mali, East Africa: a river baptism

SOME HYMNS SUITABLE FOR A BAPTISM SERVICE
And can it be that I should gain: Charles Wesley
Awake, awake, fling off the night: John Raphael Peacey
I bind unto myself today: attributed to St Patrick
Jesu, lover of my soul: Charles Wesley
Just as I am without one plea: Charlotte Elliott
Lift high the cross: Michael Newbolt and George Kitchen
My faith looks up to thee: Ray Palmer
Now, in the name of him, who sent: Fred Kaan
Rock of ages, cleft for me: Augustus Montague Toplady
Thine for ever, God of love: Mary Fawler Maude

and from the days of Cranmer's Prayer Books which explicitly required submersion (though there could be exceptions!) right through to *ASB 1980* which makes it the first choice still. This is worth emphasising because so many Christians think that the Church of England's method is 'sprinkling', which is not even mentioned as a possible method.

Dipping infants may have problems, though even then determination to do it will triumph over such problems. Dipping adults has only the problem that church buildings are rarely equipped with the necessary tank and plumbing. But, again, the Church of England ought to be ready to do what it says it does. Candidates ought to be given the opportunity of being submersed, and if they desire it the Church of England should provide it. This does *not* mean borrowing the local Baptist building (which would be a sure way of admitting that 'we' do not really do that sort of thing) but it means that either provision is made (possibly of a temporary sort) in the Anglican building, or that a secular pool (or river) is borrowed for the occasion – perhaps with a procession back to the church building for the eucharist.

Submersion has an element of dramatic enactment of death and burial about it, and may therefore be a powerful symbol. But it has to be remembered that baptism has many other meanings (including being transplanted as a limb into a body), and submersion will not necessarily dramatise them – and also that a sacrament gains its power essentially from God's institution, and from his declaration of its meaning, and *not* from our power to make the symbol look like what is symbolised. There is no way of showing that all New Testament baptisms involved submersion – the likelihood is that many did not – and it is perhaps not surprising that the first decades of missionary work among the Eskimos of Northern Canada never involved total submersion ... Desirable submersion may be – and the Church of England gives it to those who desire it: necessary it cannot be – and baptisms are fully baptism where only 'pouring' (the other option) is given. Even pouring can have great dramatic effect, if that is what is wanted. But the essential task is to fulfil what Christ has instituted – baptism with water 'in the name'.

Once or three times? The Liturgical Commission in their report said 'three times'. This gives some force to the Trinitarian formula, as the minister *does* what he is saying. But there were objections in General Synod that the old Prayer Book allowed a single administration of water and that liberty should not now be restricted. So in the present text there is simply an opening Note (no 11) which urges the threefold administration whilst allowing the single one.

The ceremonies after baptism

The signing with the sign of the cross (section 21) was put here by Cranmer in 1552, and remained immovable until the new service was authorised with the alternative position at section 14. As the text is printed out at section 14, the signing may well more frequently come there. However, sentiment may still expect it here, and the moral charge to resist evil also comes well here. If so, the sign should *not* be made with the baptismal water (which helps confuse people as to what is the actual sacramental sign of baptism). All should be baptised before any are signed – it is a separate event. And no one should think that this is 'reception into the Church' (which the old book seemed to teach). Baptism itself is that reception. This minor ceremony is by way of explanation of the meaning of the baptism already given.

The other ceremony is the giving of a candle. It gives opportunity for servers to stand by with lighted candles from which smaller baptismal candles may be lighted and handed over to adult candidates and the sponsors of infant candidates. This can be very dramatic. But the ceremony is entirely optional, and may be viewed as adding further minor ceremonies which obscure rather than explain the major ones.

The rubric here says that any person may give the candle to the recipient. This means that, when several persons are baptised at one service, the giving of the candle to each might be done simultaneously rather than in a long sequence. And, if the bishop chose to delegate his functions (see opening Note 8) a similar method of administering the signing with the sign of the cross (whether at section 14 or section 21) might also be used to good effect.

The confirmation prayer

The confirmation prayer (sections 23, 24) is very ancient, and has remained almost unchanged by succeeding alterations to the service. When the post-baptismal

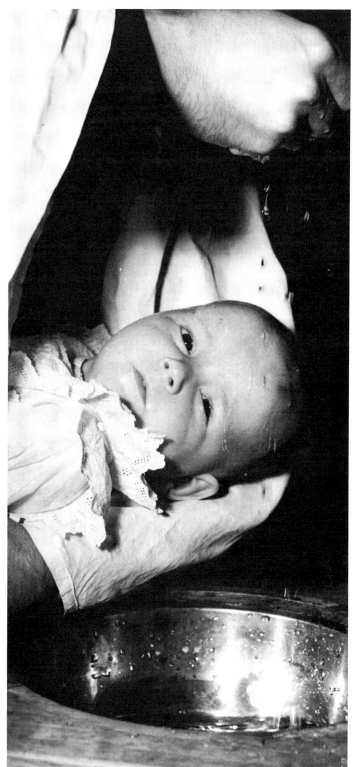

laying on of hands came in the western Church (possibly in the latter part of the second century AD), it was associated with the initial gift of the Spirit, as in the 'emergency' passage in Acts 8.14-17 which has so often been a proof text for confirmation. Thus the prayer which became settled usage was based upon Isaiah 11, a prophecy of the Messiah and the messianic spirit. This raised the problem that it suggested that water-baptism was not a sacrament of the initial gift of the Spirit, and confirmation was. Cranmer, who believed that water-baptism was complete sacramental initiation, changed the crucial line in the prayer, from the Latin

'Send down upon them from heaven the Holy Spirit the Comforter'

to the non-initiatory

'Strengthen them ... with the Holy Ghost the Comforter.'

The rite was about growing strong within the Christian life – not about receiving the Spirit in order to begin it.

Today when the Church of England contains people who would prefer the Sarum text to the Cranmerian one, a way through has been found by going back to the actual text of Isaiah 11. There the prophet says of the Messiah:

'The Spirit of the Lord shall rest upon him'

and so the bishop now prays for the candidates

'Let your Holy Spirit rest upon them' which conveys hints of *both* beginning *and* continuing!

As the bishop is stretching out his hands towards them, the candidates are all kneeling (or possibly standing) before him. Adults who have been baptised a few minutes earlier have now rejoined those who have come for confirmation only. They are to be ready, at the conclusion of the prayer, either to kneel before him in turn as he sits in a central chair or stands at one place, or to kneel in a row that he may pass along the row to lay hands on each in turn.

MEMBERSHIP OF THE CHURCH OF ENGLAND

Baptised people who are not confirmed may declare themselves 'members' of the Church of England when joining the Electoral Roll, and become 'members' by their own declaration. Thus confirmation is not to be equated with 'membership', though, under the present discipline, worshippers should be confirmed in order to receive communion or to hold any office in church government.

Members of other Churches who wish to become members of the Church of England may join the Electoral Roll without ceasing to be members of the other Church. But if they seek confirmation, they may well be viewed as belonging more exclusively to the Church of England.

Baptised and communicant members of other Churches are welcomed to communion in the Church of England as guests, without any requirement of confirmation. But if they declare themselves members of the Church of England, they cease to be guests, and should be confirmed in order to receive communion.

Roman Catholic and, probably, eastern Orthodox Christians who wish to become members of the Church of England are not confirmed for a second time, but instead are 'received' into membership of the Church of England after a brief question and answer. Such reception does not require the presence of a bishop, but should be done on the bishop's authority.

The laying on of hands

Then comes the laying on of hands (section 25). The great common factor of all uses of laying on of hands is that they all are eminently personal ways of praying for a person especially designated by this touch. Touch involves affirmation, affection, identification, and love. In the New Testament it is used for healing, for commissioning, and for special prayer (in Acts 8.14-17 special prayer for the Spirit!). Our use of it here does not pretend to be an exact repetition of any of these New Testament uses, but it does claim to be a following of the New Testament 'example' – that is, the example of using the laying on of hands at all – probably (in Cranmer's mind) to distinguish it from confirmation by anointing with oil, which the Roman Catholic Church practised, but which he could not see was 'after the example of the apostles'.

As solemn prayer, it designates the recipient not only by the laying on of hands, but also by naming him. The prayer itself asks God to 'confirm' the candidate. The word 'confirm' in this prayer is as wide in its meaning as 'confirmation' itself is: the bishop prays in this shorthand way that everything which the candidate has professed for himself, and everything contained in the Gospel of Christ, may be and continue to be true for him from that time onwards. Thus the prayer is for life in the Spirit – God is asked to confirm the candidate 'with your Holy Spirit'. The candidate says 'Amen'.

The congregational prayer

The prayer which Cranmer wrote to express this continuing in the Christian life follows (section 26). He wrote it for the bishop to use at the laying on of hands, but it is lengthy and has now been postponed from that point to be used by the congregation, to gather up every worshipper's prayers for each candidate into one joint, weighty intercession for them all. It is the sort of prayer which godparents, who have duly seen their godchil-

'Upon whom (after the example of thy holy apostles) we have now laid our hands, to certify them (by this sign) of thy favour and gracious goodness towards them.'

Book of Common Prayer 1662, Post-confirmation prayer

'God has received you ... We welcome you'

ASB 1980, section 27. Note the tenses.

dren confirmed, may want to make a regular prayer for them thereafter. It well expresses the forward-looking nature of confirmation.

The welcome

The welcome (section 27) is a distinctly post-baptismal provision, and is not even found in the later service of confirmation on its own. But it comes after confirmation in order that the flow of the service earlier may not be broken, and because those who have been confirmed may well *be* welcomed, even if they are not central to the wording of the welcome. In this main rite those baptised as infants, and not confirmed, are in view as well as those who have been baptised and confirmed. The wording is designed to refer back to baptism – God has formally made people members of the Church in baptism: the Church now gets a chance to

speak, recognises what God has done and welcomes the newcomers as one with them. There may be some way in which the bishop can present them for the welcome.

The Peace

The communion service then begins with the Peace (section 29; Rite A section 30). This is no change of direction, but a powerful continuation in the same direction. Those who have just been welcomed by the congregation's words can now be welcomed by their embraces! The Peace is the place where the Church identifies itself on approaching the Lord's table, and the newcomers are now fully incorporated into the life of Church, to be brought into the feast by the existing members. The Peace has a special joy to it on baptismal occasions.

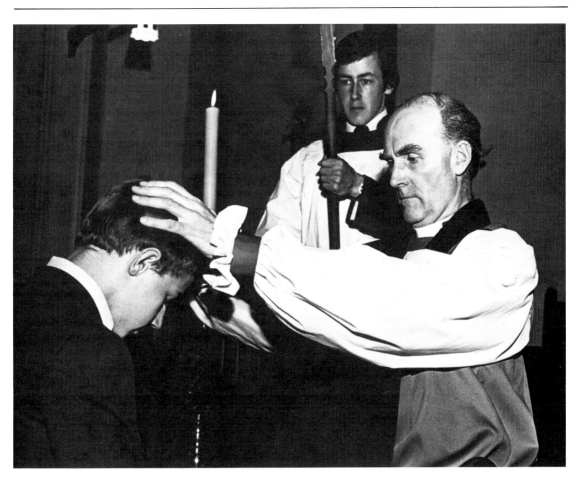

The communion

The service of communion continues (sections 30 and 31). The great loss from an ordinary eucharist is the intercession. It may well be that not only the 'propers' mentioned in section 30 should be used, but also that some (brief) intercession for the newly baptised and/or confirmed should be added after communion. The rubric at section 51 of Rite A permits other prayers, and here in the initiation services there are prayers for the candidates provided at sections 32 (for those baptised), 33 (for those confirmed – following Cranmer's old post-confirmation prayer), 34 (for families baptised), and so on. But informal or extempore prayer might also be used.

The bishop as president concludes the service (section 31).

Derivative Rites

BAPTISM AND CONFIRMATION WITHOUT COMMUNION

This service is a footnote to the main rite (sections 32-41), or a reconstruction from the main rite. At the centre of the rite it is exactly the same as the main rite. But its setting is slightly different in each case. Practice since the 1960s has been moving fast towards having initiation in the context of communion. That is why the main rite involves communion. But baptism and confirmation can be administered without communion, and there is then a need for more prayers. These are set out – section 33 is Cranmer's old post-confirmation prayer duly modernised – and may be useful even when there is communion.

After section 41 provision is made to put baptism and confirmation in the context of Morning or Evening Prayer.

BAPTISM OF CHILDREN

In England today, despite the hesitations of many in the Church about 'indiscriminate' infant baptism, the baptism of infants is far and away the most frequently used of the initiation services. The Canons require that infant baptism should 'normally' be given at a main service of a Sunday, so the service should not have to stand on its own. It has been a sad feature of the last hundred years or more that the Prayer Book rite for infant baptism, despite its own insistence that it comes after the second lesson in Morning or Evening Prayer, has been moved to a separate time of its own – often 4 pm. This has meant both that the parents bringing children for baptism did not have to attend a main service of the Sunday, and the regular worshippers were not only not 'put in mind' of their own baptism, but also were unable to know the size of the problem of 'indiscriminate' baptism with which the clergy were struggling. This infant baptism rite therefore insists that it should 'normally' (Notes 1 and 7) come within public worship on Sunday, and immediately after the rite there are two orders of service set out to show how infant baptism should be included within either Holy Communion or Morning or Evening Prayer.

The infant baptism rite itself derives almost entirely from the main rite for household baptism and confirmation discussed above. However, at a few points it has distinctive provision of its own. The most important of these follow.

Godparents

Godparents are not mentioned in the bible. When families are baptised at the formation of a local Church (as happened in Philippi, Acts 16) then there is no emphasis on the liturgical arrangements,

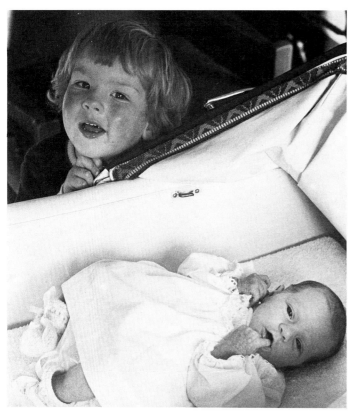

let alone on the role of minor participants. But as soon as we get descriptions in the post-apostolic writers of how infant baptism was given, we find godparents. They may be the parents themselves – the point is that they articulate as proxies what the infants cannot say for themselves. And the rubrics speak of 'parents and godparents' together. If they are separate people, then there will

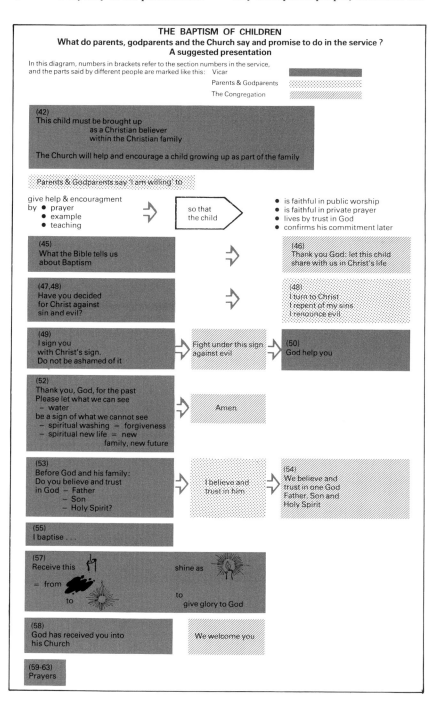

THE BAPTISM OF CHILDREN
What do parents, godparents and the Church say and promise to do in the service ?
A suggested presentation

In this diagram, numbers in brackets refer to the section numbers in the service, and the parts said by different people are marked like this:

Vicar

Parents & Godparents

The Congregation

(42)
This child must be brought up
          as a Christian believer
          within the Christian family

The Church will help and encourage a child growing up as part of the family

Parents & Godparents say 'I am willing' to

give help & encouragment
by • prayer
   • example
   • teaching

so that the child

• is faithful in public worship
• is faithful in private prayer
• lives by trust in God
• confirms his commitment later

(45)
What the Bible tells us
about Baptism

(46)
Thank you God: let this child
share with us in Christ's life

(47,48)
Have you decided
for Christ against
sin and evil?

(48)
I turn to Christ
I repent of my sins
I renounce evil

(49)
I sign you
with Christ's sign.
Do not be ashamed of it

Fight under this sign against evil

(50)
God help you

(52)
Thank you, God, for the past
Please let what we can see
   – water
be a sign of what we cannot see
   – spiritual washing = forgiveness
   – spiritual new life = new
                   family, new future

Amen

(53)
Before God and his family:
Do you believe and trust
in God – Father
        – Son
        – Holy Spirit?

I believe and trust in him

(54)
We believe and
trust in one God
Father, Son and
Holy Spirit

(55)
I baptise . . .

(57)
Receive this
= from
   to
shine as
to
give glory to God

(58)
God has received you into
his Church

We welcome you

(59-63)
Prayers

their parents and learn their Christianity from the patterns of life of their parents. Only when this is understood can the Church proceed to baptism.

The address to the child (section 43) is an attempt to cater for those too young to take lifelong commitment upon themselves in their own persons, but old enough to hear and understand what is said.

The ministry of the word

Section 45 is a special 'catena' (or chain of scriptural passages) which replaces the normal scripture reading, in order to bring the particular character of infant baptism to light. But it can be replaced by a normal reading (Note 10). It is in any case often omitted if baptism is given at another service (see the rubric).

A sermon is not mentioned, but gains its place from the service in which baptism comes. If the baptism takes place on its own – and it should not (opening Note 7) – then an address might well precede the whole rite, or come after section 43.

The 'catena' leads into a congregational prayer (section 46), which

looks back to God's love for those present, known in the past
looks forward to God's love to be shown to the candidates in the future.

The rest of the service

The rest of the service (sections 47-63) contains virtually nothing distinctive at all – it has all been found in the main rite and its subsidiary provision.

The 'propers'

The suggested psalms and readings to be used with the service in which baptism comes are set out after the rite. It is worth noting that the Gospel passage about Jesus welcoming and blessing the children (Matthew 19.13-15 or Mark 10.13-16) is not provided at all. It now clearly belongs with the Thanksgiving services.

The readings cover several different themes, but they do not attempt to be arguments for infant baptism (which is

usually be five in all – two parents and three godparents, of whom two will be the same sex as the infant. In this book they are often jointly called 'sponsors'. All together say the affirmations of faith for the infants, and all together are held responsible for the upbringing of the infants. But both commonsense and the bible tell us that the great responsibility falls upon the parents. They are to bring their children up *as* believers, *as* under the headship of Christ, from the start. And baptism is the start.

The preliminary interrogation

The preliminary questioning (section 42) is the 'screening' of the sponsors. Only believing parents, as far as we can see in the scriptures, qualify their children for baptism. Are these parents then believing? The questioning here (which it may be very useful for anyone considering bringing a child to baptism to reflect upon) is designed to draw out whether or not the parents and godparents are committed to Christ and to life in the Church. They are not to 'send' their children to Sunday School (as an older view would have seen their responsibilities) – no, they are to be an 'example' to their children, who pick up the ways of why the Mark 10.13-16 passage was in the old Prayer Book). As the argument is lengthy, and not dependent upon one single passage, it could hardly be made by putting in a special reading anyway. The nearest approach to the theme would be the story of the baptising of the Philippian jailer with his household in Acts 16.25-34. This is one of the readings suggested for the Epistle in the main rite, where household baptism is in view, and so it is not in the list of readings for children. Rather, the passage from the New Testament, both Epistles and Gospels, point to the general nature of baptism, whether for adults or infants. This helps to keep infant baptism from drifting away from adult baptism.

CONFIRMATION OF THOSE ALREADY BAPTISED

The heading of this derivative service places confirmation within a communion service, just as the main rite of initiation was in a communion service. The service could in fact be conducted simply by using the main rite, and leaving out the parts that apply to giving baptism. But as confirmation is often given without baptism, it makes a cleaner-looking service to set out just the confirmation parts of the service on their own, which can then be followed without omissions.

What then is confirmation, when it comes without baptism? Largely, it is a retelling of the meaning of baptism for those already baptised. This can be seen in the collect (section 67), the lessons (and particularly the Old Testament lesson from Ezekiel 36 and the three passages provided for the Epistle), and the renewal of baptismal vows. The service is meant to draw out this meaning and to recall the candidates to living the baptismal life. This in turn raises the emphasis seen in the main rite that the baptismal life is life in the Spirit. Life in the Spirit is the theme of the collect, of many of the lessons, and of the prayers before, at, and after, the laying on of hands.

At the end of the service the lessons are set out in full, to enable the service to be offprinted and used on its own, so that the lessons can be followed by all the congregation.

Finally, there is provision for 'Confirmation without Holy Communion'. It can come on its own (sections 86 to 93), or within Morning or Evening Prayer. These orders allow for the use of the extra post-confirmation prayers which are set out, and may also be used after communion when comfirmation is given at a communion service. The general intention is that only exceptionally should confirmation be given without communion.

RENEWAL OF BAPTISM VOWS

Confirmation includes a 'renewal of baptismal vows'. They are no new vows, they are a reaffirmation and ratification of that to which baptism – and the baptismal vows – have already committed the people of God. But there may be many other occasions when Christian people should renew their once-for-all baptismal commitment. Just as in the confirmation service (sections 75-7) the vows from the 'Decision' in the baptism service are united with baptismal affirmations themselves (sections 96-8), and the prayers provided for use after confirmation when there is no communion are also set out (sections 99-104).

When is it appropriate to renew baptismal vows? The earlier rites provide for it whenever there is confirmation (sections 28 and 82) to come immediately after the confirmation. Note 1 here suggests an alternative earlier place (after sections 10 or 74). But there are many other suitable occasions. In one sense, every time Christians receive communion, or (in the words of the communion service) offer themselves to God 'to be a living sacrifice', they are renewing their baptismal discipleship. So it is unnecessary and misleading to have this more solemn and special 'renewal' too often in public worship. It should be used to mark occasions of very special commitment. Such occasions might be:

For the whole congregation at once:
- At confirmations (some bishops like to lead the whole congregation in such a commitment, and of course there will often be present parents and friends who have no clear Christian commitment themselves and may respond to this challenge.)
- At Easter (see Note 1 and section 94: Easter is the highest point of the Christian year, and the ancient time for baptisms. The renewal enables the Church to respond with as full a commitment as possible to the cry 'Christ is risen', and thus link the joy of Easter and of Easter communion with the meaning of baptism.)

- At New Year (see Note 1: this matches the secular concept of 'New Year Resolutions', and outbids them with the greatest resolution of all. In Christian terms it echoes the Methodist 'Covenant Service'.)
- In preparation for a parish mission or some other special parish turning-point.

For particular members of a congregation:
- At confirmation (especially when there are those who, although they have been confirmed earlier, now reckon that they have been converted and wish to make public acknowledgment of it before the Church.)
- At the conclusion of a parish mission or similar occasion (when the lapsed have been restored and are formally to confess this before God and the Church.)

CONDITIONAL BAPTISM

Section 105 is an odd section. It reflects an odd problem. Baptism is given once-for-all for life – it initiates, and so cannot be repeated. It is just like a marriage service – when two people have been married once, they are married for life. If they quarrel, they do not need another marriage ceremony, they need to get back to the meaning of the original marriage ceremony. So, once a person has been baptised he or she is baptised for life. The Church cannot repeat the ceremony without calling in doubt whether any baptism really initiates. Usually at a baptism a certificate is issued, and a record is kept in the church's baptismal register, and thereafter the record is clear – the person concerned is a baptised person, and there should be no question about it from either himself or herself or from anybody else at all.

Just sometimes the record is not quite clear. Perhaps all records were lost in wartime bombing, or perhaps the denomination which gave baptism did not keep or issue records at all. A candidate comes for confirmation, the question about date and place of baptism is asked (and it should be), and there is no clear answer. What then should be done?

- Firstly, there should be every effort made to trace the records.
- Secondly, some eye-witness (perhaps a parent) may be found to sign a statement that the person *was* bap-

tised in such-and-such a church around such-and-such a date. (Where the candidate was an adult his or her own recollection and statement should suffice).

- Thirdly, only if and when no evidence can be gained at all should 'conditional baptism' be used.

Very occasionally there is doubt as to whether what was given *was* Christian baptism at all. We have seen that an infant baptism *is* a baptism, and that should not be doubted (even by those who would prefer not to have infants baptised). We have seen that baptism by pouring is just as much baptism as baptism by submersion. So when could there be doubt?

- Firstly, if there is uncertainty whether water was used at all.
- Secondly, if there is uncertainty whether it was baptism into the Trinity (see the rubric in section 105). It would not disqualify it from being Christian baptism if the formula 'in the name of Jesus Christ' were used rather than 'in the name of the Father and of the Son and of the Holy Spirit', provided that it was within a Trinitarian Church that the baptism was given – for its *meaning* then would be Trinitarian.

It is likely that baptism by Unitarians, Mormons, Jehovah's Witnesses, and non-Trinitarian bodies should not be counted as baptism at all, and if such people are converted to become Trinitarian Christians they should be given unconditional baptism, even if a Trinitarian formula was used at the baptism.

The actual form given here simply ensures that the candidate *has* now been baptised, without judging whether that baptism was given at the original doubtful occasion, or is given now. The important thing is to *be* a baptised Christian – and it is more important to be it than to be absolutely sure when the baptism was given.

EMERGENCY BAPTISM

The 'emergency' is the danger of death. Believing parents wish their children to be united with them in the body of Christ outwardly in baptism as well as inwardly in God's love, and from very early times have expressed this by having infants baptised when in danger of death, rather than risk them dying without baptism. Occasionally it can happen also that an adult who was expecting to be baptised shortly finds himself on his death-bed wanting an 'emergency' baptism – or, if he is unconscious, those who knew his desire for baptism may give it to him.

Such baptism is a statement by the Church (and by the parents of infants) that candidates for baptism will be given baptism whether they are about to die or not – baptism has a reference to the resurrection of Christ, and expresses our hope in Christ beyond the grave. It would be absurd not to give it to a person who would have received it if he or she had lived.

But such baptism should not be treated as magic or be allowed to become a focus for superstition. So parents distressed because a baby is dying need not be further distressed by agonies about whether God will receive the baby or not.

This is set out in section 106. Ever since Augustine (354-430) taught that salvation depends absolutely and without exception upon being baptised there has been a strong strand of superstition about this, and section 106 is the first denial of that superstition. It is difficult to know what infant salvation means (we know so little of what person an infant was who dies within minutes of birth). The bible has little to say, and we are caught in a mystery here in which we simply bow before God and entrust all to him. But we *can* say (as we can say of an adult believer) that baptism is not, in the last analysis, *the* great determining factor which divides the saved from the others in God's sight. We say simply that the people of God should be baptised, and therefore we baptise when we can those who would have been candidates for baptism anyway.

Because it *is* an emergency, there is no congregation, and there may be very little of a service apart from the actual baptism. Often nowadays one hand with a few drops of water on it is inserted into an incubator in order to do the baptism. And there need not even be an ordained minister. A lay person (section 107) will suffice, and nurses and midwives are often trained to know how to baptise. The provision of the Lord's Prayer and a blessing (section 108) is a minimum to pray for the newly baptised – and these prayers come *after* the baptism, that is, when the emergency action is over! Then a certificate should be issued, and a record kept (e.g. in the hospital chapel records).

Another new provision is the very clear statement (section 109) that baptism is *not* the way a child gets a name. Usually a name is given by parents and registered with the Registrar of Births *before* baptism. But if baptism is given within minutes of birth, then the naming can come later.

Finally, if the candidate baptised in an emergency lives, then it is appropriate to ask for the public profession of faith which would have accompanied the baptism in the first place if it had been done in public (sections 110-1).

The Marriage Service

WHAT IS MARRIAGE?

In the bible the story of creation includes the story of the gift of Adam and Eve to each other to become husband and wife. The biblical pattern is of two partners 'cleaving' to each other, and thus becoming – for the rest of their lives – 'one flesh'. The physical union through sexual intercourse is contained within a pledge of mutual faithfulness to each other, and the oneness with each other which that union gives is seen as lifelong oneness. Similarly, the secure social framework which such pledging gives provides the right context for the birth of children. Children know their parents from other adults, property can be securely handed on and bequeathed to kith and kin, and both natural instincts and deep social needs are simultaneously satisfied. Monogamy, or the 'cleaving' of one man to one woman for life, is found in many other religions and ethnic groups apart from Judaism and Christianity, witnessing to the deeply implanted instinct which arises from God's creation ordinance, an instinct which rejoices in both the differences between men and women ('vive la différence') and their resultant complementarity. If the joy and satisfaction of happy marriage comes from the grace of God, then it is no exaggeration to see his 'common grace' as having overflowed to many many different peoples of the earth.

Because the lifelong commitment to each other is so serious, and the sexual initiation so profound and symbolic (and, we hope, joyful also), all societies have made public rituals for the bringing together of the man and woman. It is a social event – no slipping away in elopement, no casual coupling in a corner, no private arrangement without witnesses – and to believers it is a religious event. Just as the daily papers list 'marriages' with 'births' and 'deaths', so no other event between the beginning and ending of life is so full of significance, so demanding of celebration in the presence of God with vows taken in *his* sight, and blessing sought for the years ahead from *his* hand. So Jewish and Christian society have in turn seen it, and so we inherit it. There is not just a marriage – there is a marriage *service*. There are not just vows – there are vows *in the name of God*. And the social customs (white dresses and bridesmaids and confetti and exchange of rings) have woven themselves into the Christian ceremony for which we meet. Such is the event for which any service book must provide. The weight of centuries of tradition is upon it – that is what makes it solemn – whilst the joy of the actual participants runs through it – and the service must allow for that. What then is the rite's history? How does it provide for the joy of bride and groom?

History

A formal and public ceremony allowing two people to live together as husband and wife existed from the earliest times. By it the couple have always made their promises and society given its approval. Friends and neighbours have joined in the festivities of the occasion sharing the joy of the bride and groom.

In England the distinctive options of a church or a Register Office wedding illustrate the historically diverse approaches to marriage in the eastern and western Churches. In the east a marriage ceremony had to be a religious one with a priest present to give the blessing. If not, the marriage was not viewed as valid. In the west, however, church law did not demand a blessing and the marriage was seen as quite independent of the religious ceremony. In the east the priest was said to do the marrying, whilst the west viewed the couple themselves as marrying.

From pre-Christian times there was an exchange of gifts, the vestige of which is seen today in the giving and receiving of a ring. It is no longer meant to suggest

material security, instead a token of love and the symbol of marriage. Traditionally the ring has been made of precious metal in an unbroken circle, symbolising sterling value and unending love.

MARRIAGE IN THE OLD TESTAMENT

The Jewish customs included betrothal and the wedding itself. Betrothal was the first stage (Deuteronomy 22.23) when there was the settlement of a present. It was the ransom paid to the father of the bride which, in the case of Jacob (Genesis 29) was not money but years of service. In the course of time this gift came to provide security for the bride and when it was settled betrothal was complete.

After the betrothal the woman was under the same restrictions as a wife, and if unfaithful was ranked as an adulteress. The man, too, was under equal obligation, as is illustrated in the story of Mary and Joseph. Joseph saw himself betrothed in such a way as could only be ended by divorce – the course of action he contemplated when he learned of Mary's pregnancy.

After a shorter or longer period the marriage followed and there were two parts to the wedding procession. The bridegroom and friends marched to collect the bride from her home and then, on return, the celebrating company escorted the bride and groom to their future home. (See the glimpses in Isaiah 61.10 and Psalm 45.14,15.)

There would then take place the wedding supper (Matthew 24.1-14) and it would be lavish or simple according to social status. At the close of the feast the bride, in splendid garments (Psalm 45.13-14; Jeremiah 2.32) and attended by friends, would be escorted to the nuptial chamber (Judges 15.1). She would remain veiled: that was how Jacob could be deceived into having intercourse with Leah instead of the beautiful Rachel in Genesis 29.23. Hence the duty to preserve the evidence of virginity and consummation (Deuteronomy 23.13) to safeguard against the slander of a malicious husband.

CHRISTIAN MARRIAGE: THE NEW TESTAMENT BEGINNINGS

The parable of the wise and foolish virgins and the fact that Jesus attended a wedding at Cana in Galilee serve to underline the Jewish customs which are the context of the New Testament.

Jesus himself emphasises the Genesis teaching about a man leaving his father and mother and the two becoming one flesh (Matthew 19.5). St Paul teaches that Christian marriage is to be 'in the Lord' (1 Corinthians 7.39). Jesus also spoke about divorce (Matthew 5.31-32) and did so against a specific situation where there was danger of complete marital breakdown.

To the Jew, marriage was a duty and divorce abhorrent. The problem was that

the woman was viewed as a possession at the mercy of the father or husband. The woman had no legal rights and could not divorce her husband for any reason. Yet the man could divorce his wife for any reason and, what is more, the process was simple. All he had to do was to hand the bill of divorcement to the wife in the presence of two witnesses and she stood divorced. The Jewish ideal was under threat and divorce had become easier and easier.

The Greeks likewise had divorce – the man could merely dismiss his wife in the presence of two witnesses, though he did have to return the dowry. The Greeks also accepted a social system of extra-marital relationships where the husband could go with any woman but the wife was kept in secluded purity. Thus the Christian teaching of fidelity and chastity was a source of amazement to the Gentile world. But it was more than that – to Jew and Gentile alike it was a clarion call to return to the pattern of God's creation ordinance.

Naturally the Christian commitment caused strain and even divisions in family relationships; nonetheless the Christian ideal stood in stark contrast to both Jewish and Greek ways of life.

THROUGH THE CENTURIES

As Christianity severed from Judaism, so the various crisis points of life came to have distinctive Christian ceremonies. Just as the sacraments of baptism and the eucharist developed their own particular forms of words, so the same happened with marriage.

Hints as to the early understanding of marriage come in various of the Church Fathers. Ignatius (c. 107 AD) insists on the sanctity of the relationship by encouraging the ceremony to be with the permission and the blessing of the bishop. Tertullian is excited by the relationship between a man and a woman as God-given, and desires the ceremony to be within the eucharist with the blessing of the Church. And because it is God-given, he is opposed to remarriage.

Later hints come from Gregory Nazianzus (c. 390 AD) who mentions the joining of the right hands (Ep 193) and again in Ambrose (339-97 AD) who speaks of the veil and the benediction (Ep 19). However, it is not until 866 AD, in a reply by Pope Nicolas to the Bulgarians that we get a full description of marriage. He mentions three distinctive elements – the espousal; the giving of a ring in the presence of witnesses; and the mass following the ceremony, with the

> 'It is right for men and women who marry to be united with the consent of the Bishop and not according to lust.'
>
> Ignatius, *Ad Polycarp* 5

'How shall we describe the happiness of a marriage which is cemented by church, ratified by the oblation, and sealed with the benediction?'

Tertullian,
Ad Uxorem 28

Tertullian (c.150-220 AD)

blessing as they leave the church.

We noted earlier that the western interpretation of the validity of the marriage differed from that of the eastern Church. Here in the west both a religious and a secular rite developed. For the religious rite, associated with the eucharist, there were the promises, the prayers, exchange of rings, and the drinking from a common cup by the bride and groom. These western characteristics were enshrined in the Roman sacramentaries and placed in the eucharistic setting. Clearly, as far as the western Church was concerned, marriage was a ceremony for convinced Christians.

Marriage in England

Because at the Reformation the whole country was viewed as Christian, the only form of marriage allowed was with the use of the Prayer Book rite, and divorce was unknown (except for Henry VIII and the very occasional aggrieved nobleman who got a Private Act of Parliament through the Lords and Commons). When, in the nineteenth century, parliament permitted secular marriage in a registry office, and also permitted divorce, then the Church of England became only one agency amongst others which could solemnise a valid marriage.

The Church of England also had to decide, over against the state, whether it was prepared to treat divorced persons as able to marry in church. Thus a divided situation arose – the Convocations of the clergy passed resolutions calling upon the clergy not to officiate at the marriage of divorced persons, whilst the state protected any clergyman who wished to perform such a ceremony, and the Church was not able to inflict penalties upon him.

It would be difficult to see any one mind behind the Convocation resolutions. Probably three different sets of people were acting together:

- Those who thought that the first marriage established an unbreakable link (Latin *vinculum*) between a couple, such that they not only *should* not get divorced, they in fact *could* not, whatever the law might say. Thus a remarriage would be a spurious, misleading event, as one partner would still be 'bound' to the previous spouse. This is the *indissolubilist* position. (It is held to this day by the Roman Catholic Church, though it is much alleviated by the ever wider grounds on which that Church will grant (not divorce but) nullity – a declaration that, whatever the appearances, no original marriage took place.)

- Those who thought that divorce and remarriage might be possible in theory, but that the scandal of having one of the partners taking a second set of vows of lifelong fidelity whilst in clear breach of his/her first such vows (which might even have been taken in the same church and in front of the same congregation!) was too much for the Church to take into its system.

- Those who thought divorce and remarriage, whilst not necessarily desirable, to be the best course forward for at least some people, and a course which God could and should bless, and which the Church could therefore hallow by its rite – but yet recognised the extreme difficulty of identifying which couples were so qualified in the sight of God, and the impossibility of observing a selective principle in identifying such couples.

These views have sufficiently held the field right up until the time of writing for there to be as yet no change in the Church's public front. But a report lies before the Church of England at this moment which could lead to a change in the discipline. Certainly an ever-growing number of clergy have been taking advantage of the protection afforded by the law of the land to give marriage to couples of whom one or both partners have been previously divorced.

At the same time, the Church of England has moved a long way in recent years in its treatment of the remarried. On the assumption that they have been married in a Registry Office, many clergy have still been prepared to offer services of 'blessing' of the marriage, not greatly different in some cases from the marriage service itself. Others have directed couples to Methodist churches round the corner! And others again, whilst they have stuck to the letter of not assisting such couples to marry, have nevertheless given them a warm welcome, and used them as leaders in the local Church, once they were married. And the very acceptability – for so acceptance is read – of such couples within the life of the Church *once they are married* has led to a growing cry that the Church of England is hypocritical in refusing to give such couples the actual ceremony of marriage.

Overseas, various Anglican Provinces have passed Canons which in differing ways, do give a more straightforward set of powers to the clergy to perform such marriages. In one case, the Church of the Province of South Africa, a special preface has to be read at the beginning of such a church marriage indicating the fact that this is not a first marriage for both partners, and expressing the view of the Province which admits such a marriage without commending it over-warmly.

Martin Luther, whose 'Little Marriage Book' of 1529 had a great influence on services after the Reformation

One further restriction still exists in England. No one who has been divorced and remarried or who has married a person who has been divorced can be ordained. This regulation is being reviewed at the time of writing along with the broader regulations about divorce and remarriage in church.

In a secularising society the ideal of monogamy is slowly disappearing around the Church of England. Premarital sexual relationships, casual sexual relationships, various forms of 'group marriage', and forms of homosexual pairings: all these both witness to the slow disappearance of the ideal, and also help it to disappear. The marriage service stands like a beacon, setting the light of the ideal before many who not only do not keep it, but perhaps hardly even know it exists. The question for the Church itself is how far it can adapt its own practice to show compassionate understanding for those for whom the ideal has seemed impossible or has not worked out – and still retain credibility for the ideal itself. It is a question which the 1980s have to resolve.

THE CHURCH OF ENGLAND CEREMONY

The theology of marriage has always been expressed in the Church's rites, and the Church of England is no exception to this. The services in the 1549, 1552, and 1662 Prayer Books naturally expressed lifelong fidelity ('till death us do part'), but also expressed some emphases which have been severely questioned in the twentieth century:

● The assumption of male supremacy – whereby the bride is 'given away' by one male (her father) into the possession of another (her groom). This assumption was of course underpinned by the law of the land until recent years, and without the law's support it might be viewed as a harmless, dated ceremony, without real meaning, or even the power to mislead. However, even in 1928 the word 'obey' was removed from the bride's marriage vows – and it is actually surprising to find that the opportunity for her to choose to say 'obey' still exists today. What she actually *does* after the marriage is a different question ...

The assumption of a curious ranking order of the 'reasons why matrimony was ordained' – first, for the procreation of children; secondly for sexual union; and, thirdly, for the 'mutual society, help, and comfort that the one ought to have of the other'. As these 'reasons' were stated in this order, it was hard to avoid the conclusion that this was God's order of priorities – which is contrary not only to instinct, but also to rational theology.

The assumption that sexual union itself was a kind of concession allowed to the weakness of human nature, rather than an integral and joyful feature of the two becoming one. All the language used about sexual union in the old Prayer Books had this *grudging* character to it.

The proposed 1928 service did something about the first, nothing about the second, and staged a slightly coy retreat from the third. With the addition of an optional blessing of the ring and a few other changes, it was then authorised as Series 1 marriage service and remained in use from 1966 right through to the present day. The Liturgical Commission was too busy in the 1960s to produce a Series 2 marriage service, and the next rite was Series 3, which in essence is the rite in *ASB 1980*.

The Commission's report was published in May 1975. It was, as a Series 3 service, in a 'you' form of address to God. But the Commission was striving to correct the imbalance of teaching conveyed by the earlier services (whilst also striving not to overwork the word 'love' ...). In its introduction to the service the Commission drew attention to the following features of the rite:

The self-giving of the couple to each other is fully mutual – and this is particularly dramatised in an exchange of rings, or at least a mutuality of words, where before the giving of the ring was a unilateral act.

The ranking order of the 'reasons why matrimony was ordained' was reversed. The living together for the sake of each other came first, the sexual union second, and the having children third.

The references to sex were positive and accepting and even slightly alluring. They were neither coy nor grudging.

The service went through the usual procedure in Synod, and emerged with some changes made:

The 'eucharistic structure', whereby the ministry of the word preceded the marriage, was permitted even when there was no celebration of the eucharist in view.

The Preface was rewritten from beginning to end, which lengthened it, and arguably strengthened it also. The reference to sexual union dropped 'acts of love' and replaced it with 'the joy of their bodily union'.

The opportunity for the bride to say 'obey', which had been relegated to a Note in the Commission's report, was restored by the provision of a full set of options in the text of the rite.

The Sarum Manual had the bride say she would be 'buxom in bed ...'

'[matrimony] is not by any to be enterprised, nor taken in hand, unadvisedly, lightly, or wantonly, to satisfy men's carnal lusts and appetites, like brute beasts that have no understanding ...'

'[matrimony] was ordained for a remedy against sin, and to avoid fornication; that such persons as have not the gift of continency might marry and keep themselves undefiled members of Christ's body.'

Book of Common Prayer, 1662 Solemnisation of Matrimony, Preface

---

A NOTE ON CELIBACY

The new services do not provide for any 'consecration' of celibacy, and in most cases celibacy is simply the condition of not having found the right marriage partner – yet. The ancient and medieval theologians seem often to have treated celibacy as a 'higher gift' (indeed a higher calling) and to have allowed marriage as only a second-class or inferior form of discipleship. Now that we are well delivered from this mistake, we have no business to fall into the opposite one. Those who are single are to be honoured in their loyalty to Christ and their self-control whilst they are single, and they are entitled to sympathetic recognition that they might actually prefer it otherwise but are living as loyal disciples whilst God so calls them to live. The life of the Church ought not to be so family-orientated that the single are not only shut up in their singleness but shut out of the heart of Christian fellowship also.

> 'We have come together in the presence of God, to witness the marriage of N and N, to ask his blessing on them and to share in their joy. Our Lord Jesus Christ was himself a guest at a wedding in Cana of Galilee, and through his Spirit he is with us now.
>
> The Scriptures teach us that marriage is a gift of God in creation and a means of his grace, a holy mystery in which man and woman became one flesh. It is God's purpose that, as husband and wife give themselves to each other in love throughout their lives, they shall be united in that love as Christ is united with his Church.

THE MARRIAGE SERVICE PREFACE

Mrs Jean Mayland, a member of the Liturgical Commission, and a vicar's wife, writes about the writing and revising of the preface as follows:

Before the Liturgical Commission began work on the first draft of the marriage service a discussion was held as to whether a preface to be read out in church was suitable for the modern service. We decided that it is still appropriate even in the twentieth century to remind the congregation in this way of the nature of Christian marriage and also to provide a source of teaching and marriage preparation for the couple.

Once we began work on the preface we soon agreed to reverse the order of the reasons for which marriage is given. This reversal is partly for sociological reasons. In the past many parents died as soon as (or before) their children were through adolescence and it was natural to see children as the primary purpose of marriage. Now couples live much longer and need loving support and companionship from each other long after the children have grown up and left home. There is however also good scriptural warrant for this new order of priorities.

We also agreed that the preface needed to express a more positive Christian attitude towards sex. The great difficulty proved to be just how to put this into words. One early draft contained the words 'Marriage is also the one true channel for sexual fulfilment.' We express the most complete exchange of love in sexual union, so deep that a lifelong commitment is the best declaration of it! Such direct reference to sex, however, proved too strong for weaker stomachs, and the preface went to the Synod with the words 'Marriage is given . . . that they may know each other with delight and tenderness in acts of love.' When the

matter was first debated in Synod one speaker said that the Liturgical Commission obviously never read women's magazines and if we did we should understand the double meaning of the words we had used. We understood well enough! The double meaning was the very reason why the words were used.

These words became the centre of the storm in the Revision Committee, where after lengthy discussions the present words about the second purpose of marriage were substituted. The present words are, I think, an improvement and recover the earlier idea about marriage as the true place for sexual union. Similarly, the recovery of the image of Cana in Galilee and the increased role of joy in the preface were from the Revision Committee.

Other results were not so good. Too many amendments were probably accepted and although the preface was written and rewritten dozens of times to accommodate them as smoothly as possible its length increased in the process.

More battles ensued when the service was returned to the Synod. The preface withstood the attacks reasonably well. The one sad loss was the mention of the bride and bridegroom belonging to one another's families. This seemed a very important idea to the Liturgical Commission but the Marriage Commission was obviously very worried by it. I never understood why. In this day and age the extended family is so much needed by the young people, and old people need their children's affection instead of being forgotten in old people's homes.

For all its chequered history, however, the preface does, to some extent at least, succeed in emphasising the self-giving love that is the hall-mark of a Christian marriage: in presenting marriage as a relationship to be entered into seriously and responsibly and also in proclaiming it as a means of grace and a source of joy.

Marriage is given, that husband and wife may comfort and help each other, living faithfully together in need and in plenty, in sorrow and in joy. It is given, that with delight and tenderness they may know each other in love, and, through the joy of their bodily union, may strengthen the union of their hearts and lives. It is given, that they may have children and be blessed in caring for them and bringing them up in accordance with God's will, to his praise and glory.

In marriage husband and wife belong to one another, and they begin a new life together in the community. It is a way of life that all should honour; and it must not be undertaken carelessly, lightly, or selfishly, but reverently, responsibly, and after serious thought.

This is the way of life, created and hallowed by God, that N and N are now to begin. They will each give their consent to the other; they will join hands and exchange solemn vows, and in token of this they will give and receive a ring.

Therefore, on this their wedding day we pray with them, that, strengthened and guided by God, they may fulfil his purpose for the whole of their earthly life together.'

ASB 1980, The Marriage Service, Preface

BIRTH CONTROL

The expectation of the marriage service is that a married couple will 'have children' (the wording was chosen to allow of adoption), though this fruit of a marriage is not placed as the first and central purpose of a marriage by *ASB 1980's* rite. But birth control gives most couples the opportunity to plan the number and spacing of their children, and in principle separates sexual union from conception. Thus there is now possible not only the limitation of the numbers of children (which would generally be viewed as responsible parenthood), but also a complete refusal to have them at all. And, because that refusal is possible, the barren couple who would dearly love to have children can often be thoughtlessly represented as not wanting them. It is difficult to say that Christian couples who marry should all reckon to have children (and certainly the arguments cannot all be set out here), but it is certain at the very least that both partners in a marriage which is to have no children should be equally committed to that policy.

The Church of England has consistently refused to give any synodical approval to induced abortion as a way of limiting families.

THE MARRIAGE SERVICE

With the optional introduction (1-5) the concern for God in his creation is given clear expression. He is the source of all love (1) and the marriage relationship as a gift in creation is implied. Marriage is marriage be it entered into in the Church or the Register Office, and the prayer (3), that those who are to marry will love one another and continue in that love throughout life, gives expression to the Christian ideal of a life-long union.

Bible Reading and Sermon

There is provision for one or more readings from the bible and a sermon to be preached, either after the opening prayer or after the conclusion of the marriage ceremony. Given here, at the beginning, it helps the preface in setting the right tone to the service. In its later position it gives both the couple and the congregation something to think about, both as they pray and as they go out after the service. In the old 1662 Prayer Book, there was provision for a sermon right at the end of the service with an address on the duties of man and wife to be read if the minister did not wish to preach. The lack of a proper place for readings and sermon in the old prayer book was because it was based on the assumption from the middle ages that the marriage service would take place within a communion service which would, of course, contain readings and sermon. There is now a provision for this to happen with the new marriage service, and the details of two alternative ways of mixing together the communion service and the marriage service are contained at the end of the service.

The Preface

We are given a helpful introduction spoken by the priest which combines the natural causes for marriage with the Christian interpretation and commitment. The bible, though originating in a culture very different from ours, makes it clear that for the proper structures of society a man and a woman on marriage comprise a new family unit. The primary function of marriage is not childbearing, but a sharing in companionship, part of which is the sexual and physical relationship, through which a family is created. But the Church has never said a childless marriage is not a real marriage, and the growth in contraceptive efficiency makes the planning of a family or of not having a family a greater certainty.

Besides the doctrinal emphasis on companionship and love there is the second affirmation that God's plan in sexuality is for man and woman, male and female. It is important to affirm this as not only the norm but as God's norm.

That is not to deny that there may well be men or women whose sexual orientation may be such that they will only find *companionship* with someone of their own gender, but it is to affirm that marriage and the sexual relationship is for a man and a woman in a life-long commitment.

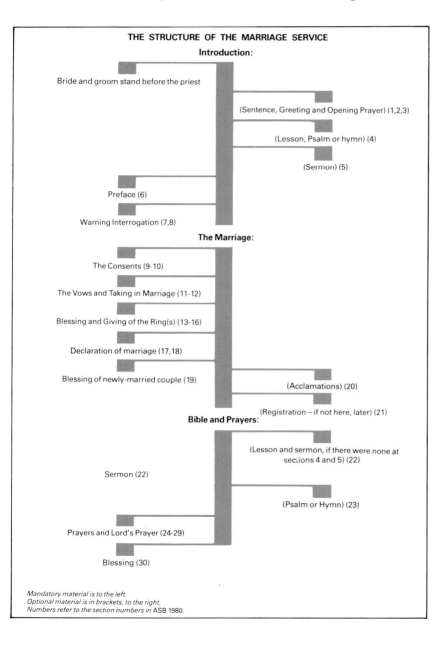

THE STRUCTURE OF THE MARRIAGE SERVICE

Introduction:

Bride and groom stand before the priest

(Sentence, Greeting and Opening Prayer) (1,2,3)

(Lesson, Psalm or hymn) (4)

(Sermon) (5)

Preface (6)

Warning Interrogation (7,8)

The Marriage:

The Consents (9-10)

The Vows and Taking in Marriage (11-12)

Blessing and Giving of the Ring(s) (13-16)

Declaration of marriage (17,18)

Blessing of newly-married couple (19)

(Acclamations) (20)

(Registration – if not here, later) (21)

Bible and Prayers:

(Lesson and sermon, if there were none at sections 4 and 5) (22)

Sermon (22)

(Psalm or Hymn) (23)

Prayers and Lord's Prayer (24-29)

Blessing (30)

Mandatory material is to the left.
Optional material is in brackets, to the right.
Numbers refer to the section numbers in ASB 1980.

It is to be an exclusive and privileged union between one man and one woman, consummated by intercourse. It is the view which Jesus upheld (Matthew 19. 4-6, Mark 10.6-9) and the ideal to which the Church is committed. Behind the human union Jesus insists there is a divine yoke and that 'what God has joined together let no man put asunder'.

The marriage

Marriage is meant to be wedlock and not padlock, a relationship of love in which a man and a woman are able to grow and develop their potential. Such is the relationship that there is joy and happiness, not only with the couple but for the couple by the assembled guests. Hence the priest says:

'We have come together in the presence of God, to witness the marriage of N and N, to ask his blessing on them, and to share in their joy.'

Central to this joy is that they are the 'ministers of the sacrament'. The priest presides, guides the proceedings, leads the prayers, blesses and performs the legalities for which he is authorised, but he does not marry. The couple marry one another, as has been happening since creation.

'Marriage is a gift of God in creation and a means of his grace, a holy mystery in which man and woman become one flesh.'

The way in which they marry is stated by the priest at the conclusion of the preface:

'They will give their consent to the other; they will join hands and exchange solemn vows, and in token of this they will give and receive a ring.'

Marriage is something they do – they marry. To do this implies the observance of the legalities through banns or licence, and then the willing consent of each to the other. Hence each has to answer the question posed by the priest,

'N, will you take N to be your wife/husband? Will you love her/him, comfort her/him, honour and protect her/him, and forsaking all others, be faithful to her/him as long as you both shall live?'

with 'I will'. In other words it is a willing commitment to a complex relationship in which each is to remain a person and yet be a part of a different unit of 'one flesh'. Unity and separateness are essential and human suffering occurs when humans wish to attempt to possess each other and cause destruction.

The next step is the vow they make to each other which is a reminder of the comprehensive nature of the marriage relationship. It is a life-long commitment and because of this serious step being taken, they have been reminded in the preface that

'It is a way of life that all should honour; and it must not be undertaken carelessly, lightly or selfishly, but reverently, responsibly and after serious thought.'

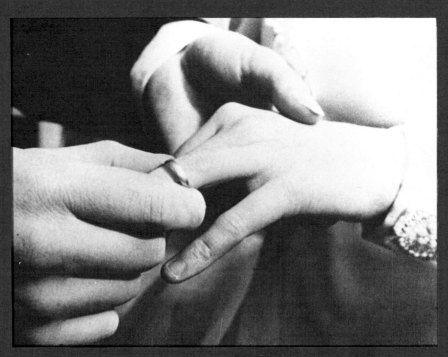

THE BLESSING OF THE RING

In the medieval marriage service, there was a very complicated ceremony for blessing the ring during which it was sprinkled with holy water, signed with the sign of the cross and the man was instructed to place the ring on the bride's thumb saying 'In the name of the Father', then on the second finger saying 'and of the Son', and on the third finger saying 'and of the Holy Spirit', and on the fourth finger saying 'Amen'. He had to leave it there because medieval tradition said there was a vein that ran direct from the fourth finger to the heart, the seat of the affections. There are echoes of the two latin prayers that accompanied this ceremony in section 19 of our new service where they are now applied to the bride and groom rather than to the ring. The prayer of blessing for the ring at section 13 is now a simple and direct prayer that God will use the ring as a symbol to remind the couple of the promises they have made to one another. When you pray for a married couple, you can pray that God will use their ring like this in times of temptation, distress, agony, tension and joy.

That being said, the man and woman separately make a vow to their partner:

'I, N take you, N,
to be my wife/husband,
to have and to hold
from this day forward;
for better, for worse,
for richer, for poorer,
in sickness and in health,
to love and to cherish (or to love,
    cherish and worship/obey)
till death us do part,
accordingly to God's holy law;
and this is my solemn vow.'

The ring is then the sign of this relationship into which they have entered wholeheartedly with life-commitment.

The mutuality of the service is strengthened by the fact that not only does the man make a statement in giving the ring (14) but so does the woman, either in receiving the ring (15) or in the giving of a ring to the husband (16).

'I give you this ring/I receive this ring
as a sign of our marriage.
With my body I honour you,
    all that I am I give to you,
and all that I have I share with you,
within the love of God,
Father, Son and Holy Spirit.'

'I, N take you, N, to be my husband/wife, to have and to hold from this day forward: for better, for worse, for richer, for poorer, in sickness and health, to love and to cherish, till death us do part, according to God's holy law; and this is my solemn vow.'

Living together

Following the giving of the ring the priest addresses the congregation and declares not only their marriage (17) but also the warning against any person dividing up what God has joined (18).

The relationship is of complete self-giving of person, possessions and failings, and in this new marital status they have the opportunity of developing their life together. Sometimes specialised counselling is necessary because of personality adjustment or sexual problems, and that aid is available to strengthen, not to mark 'failure'.

Married life starts at the wedding. So the concluding part of the service is prayer for their life together, an opportunity for the congregation to begin praying for the newly-married couple. There are two prayers set to be followed by additional prayers, which the couple may choose or write themselves. The first prayer (24) acknowledges that it is God's Holy Spirit who is going to give love and joy and peace to the couple so long as

their hearts are open to receive his riches. The second prayer (26) is a prayer which can clearly only be used for those looking forward to having children, while the third prayer (27) looks forward to them setting up home together, sees Jesus as the one who is their Lord and King and sees the Christian possibilities for the use of their home. The man and woman need not only the blessing of God but also the strength of God for their union.

The marriage is finalised, consummated by intercourse, lack of which traditionally has given sufficient ground for annulment; once intercourse has occurred, the marriage can only be dissolved by divorce. It is the total union that completes the liturgical action and the blessing incorporates not only the man-God relationship, but also this man-woman dimension when the priest says (19):

'that you may please him both in body and soul
and living together in faith and love, may receive the blessing of eternal life.'

This theme returns in the final blessing (30):

'God the Holy Trinity make you
   strong in faith and love,
defend you on every side,
and guide you in truth and peace.'

The Prayers

The direction of freedom written into the rubrics is an innovation which, if used, should be done with care. The use of silence and written or extempore (made up at the time) prayer, is an expression of what has happened in the service, and an expression of the desire of the couple for the future.

Written prayer   Many great Christian men and women of the past wrote down what had happened to them and it led them on into new insight with God. Such a course of action could well lead to similar results for couples if they were to write their own prayers to be used in the service.

Such a prayer needs to be shown to the priest for his comments so that he can make use of it during the ceremony. Normally it would be he who said the prayer, but some other person chosen by the couple and acceptable to the priest could say it, or some couples may want to pray it themselves. Consultation with the person taking the ceremony will ensure that the service is personal, and well done.

Extempore prayer   In the right situation this can be very helpful. Such a situation is where there is a gathering of people well known to one another, and where this is the case extempore prayer often knits the people together in a remarkably meaningful way.

● Such prayers, spoken out loud and spontaneous, should not be too wide in scope, for they need to be very personal, or they lose their real contribution at this point of the service.
● Some real thought needs to be given as to who might be asked to pray such prayers. In order to avoid anxiety in the service it needs to be people with experience of this way of praying.
● It needs to be stressed that the prayer should not be too long – extempore prayer is often spoiled by its length.

Silence, if used properly can deepen the meaning and purpose of the service, but if used wrongly, can create tension and anxiety. When a congregation has been trained to use silence, it can really enhance any service of worship. Usually, the problem at a wedding is that it is rare that the people present form any one particular congregation.

● Warning must be given of a period of silence, or people will be wondering what should be happening, and miss the value of the experience.
● If some people are present who have no experience of Christian worship, a few words of explanation can be helpful as well as necessary.
● The silence must not be too long or too short. Experience teaches the right length of time, and the priest is the best person to direct.

Instead of the additional prayers (Sections 31-38) prayers which they could have written or selected in co-operation with the priest may be used. Silence may be kept: or free prayer may be offered.'
ASB 1980, The Marriage Service, Note 11

GOING TO A WEDDING SOON?

The services in *ASB 1980* can be used at other times than when you happen to be listening to them in church. If you are going to a wedding soon, or getting married yourself, or wanting to review how your married life is going, you could do worse than to sit down and read through together the preface to the new wedding service. Have a look at the promises the man and the wife make to one another and ask yourself what do these mean, or what would these mean to me? Do I and my partner or future partner mean exactly the same thing when we talk about 'having and holding, cherishing' for instance, or what does 'forsaking all others' mean to me?

THE CHURCH WEDDING

A clergyman writes:

People making use of a church for their wedding do so out of a variety of motives:

- It is the custom and all members of the family have got married at that particular church.
- They desire a nice setting for their photographs.
- They desire a religious ceremony.
- They are committed Christians and wish to celebrate their marriage with the members of their congregation as a witness to Christ.

Dress will be varied, from brides in plain costumes to white and cream bridal gowns; guests in topper and tails to casual wear.

The ceremony is accompanied by organ music, and usually two hymns are sung. The bride accompanied by her father or relative will enter the church to the bridal march and stand next to the bridegroom at the front of the church with the priest facing them.

He will say a prayer, read the preface which states clearly the Christian ideal of marriage and then invite the guests and the couple themselves, to declare any impediment to the proposed marriage. The bride and groom are then asked separately whether they are prepared each to take the other to be their partner in a commitment of a certain quality. When they have affirmed that they are, they hold each other by the right hand, make their vows in turn, and give and receive a ring or rings. Then the priest declares their marriage and blesses their union.

The registers are then signed (though sometimes this is delayed till after the service) by the bride and groom and the witnesses, and the priest gives the bride the wedding certificate.

There then follow the prayers said by the priest, or some other person or persons in which prayer is offered to God for the life of the newlyweds. At some stage during the ceremony the priest will have given a short address about marriage: some do so at the start, some before the prayers, some at the end of the ceremony.

THE REGISTER OFFICE WEDDING

A Registrar writes:

People making use of a Register Office for their wedding ceremony can be put into three main groupings:

- Those who do not wish to have any religious ceremony.
- Those who find themselves unable to have a religious ceremony because of divorce, mixed religion etc.
- Those who will also be having a religious ceremony but because the place of marriage is not registered in law for marriages, must first conform to state law.

The variety is endless: from a full dress wedding as in a church, to a couple who bring witnesses in off the street . . . and every situation in between. Variety is also apparent in the quality of accommodation provided by the local authority, and this will affect procedure, as does the number of ceremonies performed each year.

The description which follows is an outline of a typical ceremony in a Register Office dealing with a thousand ceremonies each year.

The Ceremony

The couple will assemble in the waiting area with their guests, normally the bride arriving last. At the appointed time the couple are taken into the Marriage Room by the Registrar of Marriages who makes a final check on the particulars to be entered in the register, collects the fee, ascertains whether rings are to be used and who the witnesses are. Then he will lead the guests into the room.

The Superintendent Registrar then conducts the ceremony and informs everyone that the place in which they are assembled has been registered for the celebration of marriage and gives them an opportunity to declare any impediment to the proposed marriage. The couple are asked to stand and give their full names.

They are reminded of the solemn and binding character of the vows they are required to make and each then repeats a declaration that they are not aware of any legal impediment to their marriage. After the giving or exchange of rings the couple make the marriage contract with each other. They are pronounced husband and wife and proceed to sign the register.

It is customary to hand the bride the marriage certificate before they leave the room, sometimes before, sometimes after their guests.

The whole ceremony will take approximately fifteen minutes and can aptly be described as brief, simple and painless.

Before you are joined together in matrimony however, it is my duty to remind you of the solemn and binding character of the vows you are about to make.

Marriage, according to the law of this country, is the union of one man with one woman, voluntarily entered into, to the exclusion of all others.

Register Office Ceremony

PRACTICAL MATTERS

Who can get married? Where? When?
Those over the age of sixteen can get married with their parents' consent (or without consent at the age of eighteen). They can be married in their parish church, providing they live within the parish, have not been married before to anyone still living and have had banns called or obtained a licence. If neither party lives in the parish of the church where the ceremony is to take place, one or other must be on the electoral roll of that church. Such qualification demands regular worship for a six-month period before application.

The wedding can take place on any day between the hours of 8.00 am and 6.00 pm. The couple must approve which service is to be used. If it is to be from *ASB 1980* they choose not only which of two sets of vows they use but can also, if they desire, write their own prayers for inclusion in the service.

Historically, since it was assumed the newlyweds would take holy communion as soon as possible after the ceremony, it has sometimes been thought that both partners should have been confirmed. Because confirmation numbers have declined it has become the custom to ask whether both bride and groom have been baptised. However, Church law does not demand baptism, and normally a clergyman will conduct the ceremony if only one has been baptised.

Making the arrangements

Legally, if the marriage is to be after banns, since banns have to be called in church on three Sundays, the minimum notice required is three weeks. By licence that time can be cut to three days. However, normally much longer notice is required because of the numbers of weddings taking place, or holiday periods when clergy, organists etc. are away. In popular places where there is a larger number of couples preparing for marriage, as long as six months or even a year may be necessary to secure a particular date and time.

The service on the day would last about forty minutes and the arrangements for the hymns and music would normally be made with the clergyman.

Preparation and help

Getting ready for the wedding, and after the marriage as well, help is often needed and is available. The priest who is to take the service will want to see the couple beforehand, not only to ensure that the legalities are observed, but also to go through the service in practical detail,

and to explain the meaning of the service. He will be able to draw out the Christian virtues and offer guidelines in the art of living together.

Sometimes, beforehand or after the wedding, specialised help may be needed because of sexual problems or personality clashes. The clergyman may be unable to give direct help, but will be able to suggest the best agency to help in that particular problem. Help is at hand, and that is comforting in such an all-embracing relationship as marriage.

Dress

Marriage is a very special event in a woman's life. Traditionally the bride has worn a long white dress, but there is no law to say that this must be so. White has been the colour of purity and a special dress for a special day has great appeal. The important thing is that it should be decent, and suitable for the occasion. It might be a short dress, a suit, or an off-white long dress.

The man likewise dresses for the occasion: formal dress like topper and tails, or a lounge suit.

HOW TO ORGANISE A WEDDING

1 Find a willing partner!
2 Agree a date in consultation with friends and relatives.
3 Make enquiries about receptions.
4 When you have a provisional reception place and time, book the wedding, if in the Church, with the vicar; if in the Register Office, at the Register Office.
5 Arrange for sharing of responsibilities like the cake, the flowers, booking the cars, arranging for a photographer.
6 If going away for a honeymoon make arrangements for stay and travel, making sure, if you are going by public transport, that there is ample time for the reception and getting to the station.
7 If going overseas, arrange for passports.
8 If it is a church wedding, and one of you lives outside the parish where you are getting married, arrange for the banns to be read in your home church as well.
9 Arrive on time on the arranged day.

CHRISTIAN MARRIAGE FROM THE INSIDE
Ian and Ellie Benstead write:

Looking back to our marriage some twelve years ago, we see it as a step into which we are both as convinced as ever that God led us, and as an event of the greatest significance in our lives. First and foremost it was a commitment to each other, blessed by the Lord and witnessed by an assembly of our individual and mutual friends and relatives such as can never again be mustered. We look back on our marriage service as a truly memorable and meaningful foundation for life together.

We think that we realised at the time, and certainly we are convinced now, that Christian marriage, a lifelong covenant, must never be entered into 'carelessly, lightly or selfishly', and that humanly speaking such a commitment may honestly be difficult to make. It is only with God's help that we are able to make our marriage work or last, and there are certain aspects which we see as part of his generosity and guidance which deserve special mention and which give us confidence for the future. The key words are **love; children; submission; communication.**

To acknowledge these aspects as part of God's provision and will for us gives

202

MUSIC FOR THE WEDDING
Traditional music

      Bridal March: from 'Löhengrin': Wagner
      Wedding March: from 'A Midsummer Night's Dream': Mendelssohn

Other music often used

      Trumpet Voluntary: Jeremiah Clark (often attributed to Purcell)
      Trumpet Tune: Purcell
      Toccata in F from 5th Organ Symphony: Widor
      Water Music (Finale): Handel
      'Nun danket alle Gott': Karg-Elert

Suitable hymns

      Love Divine, all loves excelling: Charles Wesley
      The Lord's my shepherd: *Scottish Psalter* 1650
      Praise my soul, the King of heaven: Henry F. Lyte
      May the mind of Christ our Saviour: Katie B. Wilkinson
      Now thank we all our God: M. Rinkart
      We rest on thee: Edith G. Cherry
      Great is thy faithfulness: T.O. Chisholm
      Then I saw a new heaven and earth: Christopher Idle
      or hymns from the marriage section of any hymn book.

them a special value and significance not applicable in a secular context.

Christian married love includes physical attraction, a high degree of mental compatibility, and spiritual unity in Christ. Its intensity fluctuates; on occasions we must work at it, but it is the underlying knowledge that the Lord will not withdraw his blessing that gives us security even when one of us is in the trough of a wave.

We see communication as one of the most vital aspects of keeping a marriage alive and growing. Sexual intercourse is perhaps the most joyful and fulfilling means of communication, and there is no greater delight than the mutual and simultaneous satisfaction of one another's desires within the security of the marriage relationship. We found it took time and patience to achieve this (no instant success here!), and we continue to work together for an ever-improving experience.

Equally important, and essential to the success of all other aspects of marriage, is verbal communication; the need to share experience and feelings both positive and negative. In a busy world, and particularly where there is a heavy commitment to church and other interests too, this can be hard to achieve. For us an important contribution to providing the requisite time and atmosphere for real communication has been to take baths together at the end of the day; a bit of a squash but ideal for airing our reactions to the day's events! Particularly in early marriage it is essential to establish a pattern of honest interchange; the willingness to admit – or accept from one's spouse – criticism or appreciation. These things need continually *saying*, not just thinking, if our relationship is to mature.

One of the greatest crisis points of a marriage can be the birth of the first child. Established roles have to be realigned. We certainly had to do some painful rethinking! But of course the delight of seeing God's creative hand in the whole glorious and majestic progression of conception, pregnancy, labour, and birth is an unrivalled experience for a couple to share together. Then the mutual task of caring for, stimulating and educating the little one is an exciting and absorbing task to be undertaken together.

In every marriage there are times of staleness, times of crisis and distress, just as there are high peaks of joy. At all times we need to submit ourselves continually to God and remind ourselves before him of our marriage commitment and our firm belief that he has given us to one another. The degree of balance of our

submission to one another falls quite naturally into place in the context of the Christian marriage as a permanent contract between two people, approved by God, rather than a temporary arrangement to be jettisoned if things do not go too well.

As time goes on our submission to God should be developing into a complete confidence that God's will is indeed the best for all of us. This is an assurance we would like to see developed in ourselves and passed on to and embraced by our children and others who may be influenced by our relationship. This we feel is a worthy aim for Christian marriage.

Funeral Services

Many today try to ignore death. If you don't look at it, it will go away. And so we pretend it won't come. We make no preparations for it. We fight against it with all the might of modern medicine. We refuse to talk straight about it, and use a special language with words like 'passed on', 'casket', 'floral tributes', 'if anything should happen to me'. We never know what to say when we meet someone recently bereaved, and avoid them in embarrassment in case it's catching. Comparatively few die at home, compared with earlier centuries, so many people have never seen someone dying, or a dead body. These are things we try to protect one another from, and death can perhaps appear more innocuous if wrapped up in a clinical atmosphere, unseen by most.

Our attitude to death results in all sorts of unhappiness, fear of the unknown, mental illness because of repression, neglect of the dying (masquerading sometimes as an attempt to make them look on the brighter side so that they get no chance to talk before they die about things which might upset us). Dishonesty between close relatives is one of the results of our failure to prepare openly for death, with some spending their last days in an unhappy charade, unable to admit the truth to each other.

But in fact, whatever we do, we can't escape it. However we wrap it up or try to ignore it when it happens to others, death will come for us. Christians should be among those who can look death in the face and talk openly about it. The funeral service should help us honestly and Christianly to do that. But it can only do that if it expresses what we ourselves believe.

WHAT DO CHRISTIANS BELIEVE ABOUT DEATH?

'It was her faith that kept her going.' 'Now, he was a real Christian; you could tell from the way he died.' When people say things like this, what do they really mean? Sometimes it is just a way of saying how much they thought of the person who has died. Sometimes, though, people are saying that there is something different about the death of a Christian – and about Christian mourners. Just what is it that Christians believe, that makes them different when it comes to death? Here are some of the main things Christians say they believe.

Death is natural

It is a fact of nature. Everyone has the human need to be able to face the fact that life is short and that death is final. Human – and spiritual – problems arise when people fail to face these facts, and try to pretend that death doesn't exist, either for themselves or for someone who has died. Sometimes people try to keep

the dead person's room exactly as it was when he or she was alive; sometimes they try to get in touch with the dead through a spiritualist medium.

The bible uses a number of ephemeral pictures for our life: a shadow, flower, grass, 'Man born of a woman is of few days, and full of trouble. He comes out like a flower and withers. He flies away like a shadow and continues not.' (Job 14.1,2). St Peter quotes Isaiah 40: 'All mankind is like grass, and all their glory like wild flowers; the grass withers and the flowers fall' (1 Peter 1.24). Life is short: 'You have made my days a few handbreadths, and my lifetime is as nothing in your sight' (Psalm 39.5). And death is final. There is a clear discontinuity between this life and the next: 'We brought nothing into the world, and we can take nothing out' (1 Timothy 6.7). This is one of the opening sentences of the Funeral Service (section 2), and one of the helpful purposes of the funeral service is to be a public and open recognition that a death has taken place. It is part of the mechanism of adjusting to the fact that someone we love has died. The theme is taken up in the service in Psalm 90 at section 4: 'The days of our life are threescore years and ten .... Teach us so to number our days ...', and in Psalm 103 at section 15: 'The days of man are but as grass ...', as well as in the traditional words of section 16 'In the midst of life we are in death ...'

Death is terrible

Our short life determines what happens after death. 'It is appointed for men to die once and after that comes judgement' (Hebrews 9.27). St Paul says of this life, 'Now is the hour to receive God's favour; today is the day to be saved!' (2 Corinthians 6.2). And Jesus himself speaks of a time when it will be too late: 'Many will seek to enter and will not be able ... you will begin to knock at the door saying, "Lord open to us." He will answer you, "I do not know where you come from." '

And it is Jesus who speaks of eternal fire and eternal punishment, of the division of all people into two classes on the day of judgement. St Paul speaks of those 'who do not obey the gospel of our Lord Jesus' suffering 'the punishment of eter-

nal destruction and exclusion from the presence of the Lord.' (2 Thessalonians 1.7-9). This is the death spoken of in Section 16 of the service: 'deliver us from the bitter pains of eternal death.' The second reading in the service (section 5, 1 Corinthians 15) shows us that the pain of this death comes from sin: 'The sting of death is sin, and sin gets its power from the law. But thanks be to God, who gives us the victory through our Lord Jesus Christ.' Death is terrible, awesome, because it marks the end of the opportunity to respond to the one who has taken away the sting of death and won the victory over it. The joy of the early Christians was evident because they were sure that for them death was no longer terrible, because of what Christ had done for them.

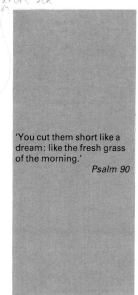

'You cut them short like a dream: like the fresh grass of the morning.'
Psalm 90

Jesus has won the victory over death
'Thanks be to God, who gives us the victory through our Lord Jesus Christ' (1 Corinthians 15.57). Because of this victory, a personal relationship can be established between the believer and Christ, which begins now and goes through death. Using terms from the law courts, St Paul shows that the guilty sinner is pronounced right with God, freed and forgiven for his sin, when he trusts Christ. This happens because of his union with Christ; the believer cannot grow more right with God: he is either right with God or not. It is as definite as death: 'When a person dies, he is set free from the power of sin . . . we have died with Christ' (Romans 6.7). So the death to the past, to sin and self, that a person dies when he becomes a Christian (symbolised by going under the waters of baptism), ensures that at his physical death he can be sure of this continuing union with the risen Christ: 'Since we have died with Christ, we believe that we will also live with him' (Romans 6.8). He is on the winning side, and nothing can separate him from the victory of Christ.

No wonder the funeral procession in the early Church was a triumphal procession.

'Hold thou thy cross before my closing eyes' is therefore good advice, so long as the reminder of the cross concentrates attention on the victory of Jesus on the cross, shared by the believer approaching death. This is the note of assurance struck early in the service by the prayer at section 3: 'You have given us a true faith and a sure hope . . . that we may live as those who believe in the communion of saints, the forgiveness of sins, and the resurrection to eternal life.' It is clearly there in all three readings and in the Te Deum (section 7): 'You overcame the sting of death and opened the kingdom of heaven to all believers.' It is there in the commendation (section 12: 'in the faith of Jesus Christ . . . who died and rose again to save us') and in the committal (section 17: 'in sure and certain hope of the resurrection to eternal life through our Lord Jesus Christ, who died, was buried, and rose again for us.' The victorious nature of a Christian funeral can also be emphasised by the hymns which are chosen and the dress of both

ministers and mourners: white, and not black, was the colour of the early Church.

We shall be raised from the dead

The resurrection was so much part of the Christian life and message that the Church in the Acts of the Apostles was said to preach 'Jesus and the resurrection'. Jesus calls believers 'children of the resurrection' and says of himself, 'I am the resurrection and I am the life; he who believes in me, though he die yet shall he live, and whoever lives and believes in me shall never die' (John 11.25-26, the sentence which opens the Funeral Service as it has done since 1549).

The *ASB 1980* Funeral Service contains one of the classic bits of New Testament teaching on the resurrection, 1 Corinthians 15 (section 5). From this we can see that

● the resurrection is going to be a spiritual thing: 'flesh and blood cannot inherit the kingdom of God'. This knocks the idea that we will just go on doing all the old earthly, bodily things on a slightly higher level, like playing football one division up.

● the resurrection is going to be a bodily thing, though: 'It is sown a physical body, it is raised a spiritual body' and 'God gives it the body he has chosen'. This knocks the idea that our disembodied souls drift away to live a happy life: to the Jewish mind (and Jesus, Paul and the first disciples were Jews) true bliss could only happen in some reunion of body and soul.

● the resurrection is going to see us changed, but with some possibility of recognition: 'With what kind of body? ... What you sow is not the body that shall be, but a naked grain, perhaps of wheat or of some other kind; and God gives it the body he has chosen, to each kind of seed its own particular body.' This knocks the idea of identikit Christians in heaven, and also any suggestion that we will lose our individual personality

in some group soul. There will be a vast difference between our earthly bodies and our heavenly ones, because God has prepared such tremendous things for us that we cannot understand now. But there will be continuity: when you sow wheat you expect to recognise the wheat when it comes up, and not everlasting flowers. Examine the Gospel accounts of the resurrection appearance of Jesus and you will find a similar sort of wonder, and recognition that is not always immediate.

God loves us all, and expresses this love in Christ

Sometimes the knowledge of this love is all that the mourners need to take from

'This is what love is: it is not that we have loved God but that he loved us and sent his Son so that we might be forgiven.'

1 John 4.

the Funeral Service. How do we know God's love? Because he reveals it to us in Jesus, sending him to earth to die on the cross for us and to live with us as his Holy Spirit pours his love into our hearts: incarnation, crucifixion, indwelling love – that is the pattern of God's dealings with us and of the way we should minister to one another in bereavement.

'God so loved the world that he gave his only Son, that whoever believes in him should not perish, but have eternal life' (John 3.16) is one verse that says this right at the beginning of the service. Surprisingly, it is a total newcomer to funeral services, appearing during the Synod revision; but it helps, together with verses from Deuteronomy, Lamentations, Matthew, Romans and 1 Corinthians, at the start of the service to set the sense of a loving God taking care of those who trust him, as his children. This is maintained in the use of Psalm 23 at section 4, reappears at section 15 (Psalm 103) and in some of the additional prayers (sections 56, 57). The theme of love is stronger in the provisions for the Funeral of a Child, both in the readings from Mark 10 and Ephesians 3, and in the addition of a phrase to the commendation (section 27): 'Heavenly Father, by your mighty power *you gave us life, and in your love* you have given us new life in Christ Jesus . . .'.

'Psalms were chanted and the ceilings of the temples were shaken with uplifted shouts of "Alleluia".'

Jerome, AD 345-420, on Fabiola's funeral.

FUNERALS IN THE PAST
In the Early Church
In ancient Rome five things made up the funeral:

- The ceremonies at home, including the last kiss (to catch the dying man's soul), the washing and anointing of the body and the placing of a coin in his mouth to pay Charon, the boatman who ferried the dead across the River Styx.
- The funeral procession, with everyone wearing black clothes. The name for these was *lugubria*, from which our word lugubrious comes. This happened at night, with torches and sometimes music, as the bier was carried to the place of burial or cremation.
- The actual burial or cremation.
- The ceremonies of purification for the relatives and the dead person's house.
- The funeral feast.

Clearly early Christian funerals took on some of the same elements. Simply because of what has to be done physically, the preparation of the body, the procession and the actual burial or cremation are still the things, together with the funeral feast, that give the Christian service its structure. But the whole atmosphere changes. Christian funerals are held in the daytime. The mourners are clothed in white, not in black. Instead of the pagan crying and wailing, psalms and hymns are sung. The bodies of the dead are treated with respect and not as dirt, and yet the other extreme of lavish clothing for the grave is avoided. Here are people for whom death is not the grim ending of life but an occasion for joy as Christians go to be with their Lord, sure of the resurrection. The cata-

Second century wall
painting (showing the wise
men) from the catacomb of
Domitilla, Rome

combs outside Rome bear witness to the care with which Christians treated their dead, and to their faith.

The joy and the faith of the early Church can be seen reflected in Augustine's account of the funeral of his mother Monica in 387 AD. He quotes a conversation she had with some friends who asked if she was not afraid to die so far from home, to which she says,

'Nothing is far off from God, neither is there any cause to fear that, at the day of judgement, he will not know well enough from what place he is to raise me up again.'

She wanted a simple funeral

'For she, when the day of her death drew near, did not crave that her body might be sumptuously adorned, or embalmed with spices, nor desired she any choice monument, nor cared she to be conveyed for burial to her native land.'

When she died, 'I closed her eyes' and repressed all feelings of sorrow:

'Nor did we think fit to celebrate that funeral with weeping and loud-voiced cries, because with such demonstrations of sorrow men are wont to

lament who think on death as a misery or even as utter destruction. But she died not miserably, nor indeed did she die utterly ... And behold, the corpse was carried forth, we both went and returned without tears ...'

One element in the Roman funerals which was taken up by Christians was the funeral feast. The pagan funeral feast at the graveside was connected with the idea that the dead man needed both food and also company to cheer him up, and was clearly open to abuse as relatives and friends drowned their sorrows in wine and tried to remove their hurt with pagan humour. The Christian funeral feast eventually succumbed to the same temptations. Originally the Christian feast said something in practice about the communion of saints and the joy of Christian fellowship, witnessing to the death and resurrection of Christ and providing an occasion for the distribution of food and money to the poor. The feasts happened not only immediately after the funeral but also on the commemoration days, three, seven and thirty days later, and annually after that. But soon we find Augustine speaking of

Augustine of Hippo
(354-430 AD)

Third century wall painting from the catacomb of Callistus in Rome, showing an agape or love feast.

'those debaucheries and lavish banquets in cemeteries' and Gregory writes, 'Let us also offer our bodies and souls a living sacrifice . . . so shall we keep the feast day as will give pleasure to Christ and honour the martyrs. If, however, we come together to satisfy the belly and to enjoy the changing and fleeting pleasures, and so turn this place of temperance into a place of gluttony and satiety . . . I do not see how our conduct corresponds with the occasion.' By the end of the fourth century the funeral feast was banned.

The replacement for the excesses of the funeral feast was the celebration of the eucharist, both at funerals and on the anniversary of the death. So the writer of the *Apostolic Constitutions* can ask in the fourth century, 'Do you according to the Gospel, and according to the power of the Holy Spirit, come together even in the cemeteries, and read the holy scriptures, and without demur perform your ministry and your supplication to God, and offer an acceptable eucharist . . .?'

Medieval developments

The five elements in early Church funerals – the preparation of the body, the triumphal funeral procession, the singing of psalms during it, the reading of the scriptures and prayer at the graveside, and the eucharist – are not only developed but transformed in atmosphere in the medieval period.

Gone are the joy and triumph, the waving of palm branches and shouts of alleluia. The mourners are dressed no longer in white but in black. Psalms are still sung, but they are penitential ones: we get our word 'dirge' from this period, from the opening word of the second part of the office of the dead, *dirige*. The early glad confidence of a Church sure of the resurrection has gone, and in its place has come a deep consciousness of sin and judgement which can only be dealt with by a period of purgation for the soul of the dead person. Prayer for the dead is no longer a joyful recognition of communion together in Christ, but a desperate pleading for release from punishment – as in the York Use in England: 'Loose him, and deliver him from the cruel fire of the boiling pit.' So the wealthy left money so that masses might be said for their souls, sometimes establishing chantry chapels in churches so that this might be done. Monasteries exchanged lists of their dead brethren so that they could be prayed for, and a custom grew of clothing laymen as monks on their deathbed so that they would benefit from these arrangements. Increasing payments had to be made to get onto the obituary lists of the monasteries. The tendency for the worship of the Church to get totally overwhelmed with the keeping of the anniversaries of the dead and praying for them led to the growth of the observance of All Souls' Day, widely kept by the early thirteenth century.

By the end of the medieval period the funeral service had changed from being a set of words to go with the necessary actions, to being a meditation on death and judgement. The early pattern became continuous (and impressive for that) but was capable of being followed only if death occurred in a monastery. Thus we find the dying man has the Passion from John's Gospel read to him, followed by psalm, prayer and the receiving of communion. More psalms follow once he has died, during the preparation of the body and the procession to the church. Continuous reading of the psalms, antiphons (sentences of scripture) and prayers for the dead man follow, until the mass for the dead and the burial.

But by the end of the middle ages we find a much shorter form, no longer continuous with the ministry to the dying man. It begins, on arrival at the dead man's house, with a psalm and a sentence of scripture; the body is carried to church with the intoning of the penitential Psalm 51 ('Miserere'). The office of the dead (readings and psalms) is then said, followed by the funeral mass, sprinkling the coffin with holy water, and the absolution of the dead. An anthem and psalms accompany the procession to the grave, which is blessed before the body is placed in it. Lord have mercy, the Lord's Prayer, responses and prayer for the dead person end the graveside service, with the seven penitential psalms again taking the mourners back to the church.

The Reformation

All the funeral services of the Reformation were a severe reaction against the elaborate, Purgatory-dominated medieval pattern. The extreme reaction can be seen in the reformed tradition of John Knox, which culminated in the directions of the Westminster *Directory*, published by Parliament in 1645 as a replacement for the Book of Common Prayer:

'When any person departeth this life, let the dead body upon the day of buriall, be decently attended from the house to the place appointed for publique buriall, and there immediately interred, without any Ceremony. And because the customes of kneeling down, and praying by, or towards the dead Corps, and other such usages, in the place where it lies before it is carried to buriall, are Superstitious: and for that, praying, reading, and singing both in going to, and at the grave, have been grossly abused, are in no way beneficial to the dead, and have proved many wayes hurtfull to the living, therefore let all such things be laid aside.'

Archbishop Cranmer, predictably, provides a much less radical revision of the provisions for funerals in the first Prayer Book of 1549. The procession is still there, to the church or to the grave, with scripture sentences to sing, two out of three of them from the medieval offices. The burial itself begins with the sentence 'Man born of a woman ...' and the anthem 'In the midst of life ...', and includes a commendation of the dead man's soul and prayer for him. But this

'Almighty God, we give thee hearty thanks for this thy servant, whom thou hast delivered from the miseries of this wretched world, from the body of death and all temptation. And, as we trust, hast brought his soul which he committed into thy holy hands, into sure consolation and rest.'

1549 Collect

Roman tomb showing figures of the Good Shepherd

The more radical revision came in 1552 when Cranmer omitted all the singing of psalms, the provision for the holy communion, and, meeting the objections of Martin Bucer and other reformers, all reference to prayer for the dead. The whole service, now very short, appears to take place at the graveside.

It was this 1552 service, restored by Elizabeth in 1559 and still being objected to by the Puritans in 1661 at the Savoy Conference which was re-issued in the 1662 Prayer Book with a few changes: two psalms were added after the opening sentences, to be followed by the reading, the burial and the prayers, which were slightly altered and rounded off with the saying of 'The grace of our Lord Jesus Christ . . .'. This is the service, regarded by some as one of extraordinary beauty, which has served the Church of England well for three hundred years. It is clearly directed at the living, not the dead, to provide both comfort and challenge in the awefulness of the presence of death. It speaks clearly of the resurrection and of hope, though its very solemnity inhibits it from expressing the joy and praise of the earliest Christian funerals. Its balanced structure, climaxing in the Lord's Prayer immediately after the moment of burial, worked well for a pattern of funerals where interment took place immediately in the graveyard outside the church. But that pattern no longer holds good today.

'Let these ... be sufficient to take away the gross error of purgatory out of our heads; neither let us dream any more, that the souls of the dead are any thing at all holpen by our prayers: but, as the Scripture teacheth us, let us think that the soul of man ... goeth straightways either to heaven, or else to hell, whereof the one needeth no prayer, and the other is without redemption.'

Homilies of the Church of England, 1562

prayer is altogether different from the medieval style, giving thanks for him and combining trust that his soul is at rest with prayer for all the elect to be made perfect at the resurrection. The service in church may come before or after the actual burial, and includes psalms from the medieval services, the reading of part of 1 Corinthians 15 on the resurrection, and prayer. The final section provides for the celebration of holy communion. The collect here is typical of the new stance of the service in not being centred on the dead, praying for him, but being centred on the living mourners, praying for them.

PROVIDING A NEW FUNERAL SERVICE

A number of clear needs and pressures could be seen when the Church of England Liturgical Commission came to work on a new funeral service in the 1960s:

● the need to have more positive joy in the service.

● the need to have a fuller provision to cope with the modern situation of cremation, and crematoria and cemeteries being often at some distance from the church.

WHERE ARE THE DEAD NOW?

Part of the problem of this question arises because we tend to look at everything from the angle of our human time scale, instead of from the angle of God, to whom a thousand years are as one day. It was a problem that bothered the Thessalonian Christians, and we have part of Paul's reply as one of the readings in section 5 of our Funeral Service. He reassures them that believers who have died have not missed out on the resurrection: 'Those who have died in Christ will be the first to rise, then those of us who are left alive shall join them ...' He describes them as asleep in Christ and when he speaks of his own death to the Philippians he talks of being 'with Christ'. In one of the alternative readings (Romans 8.39) we are assured that nothing can separate believers from the love of Christ. So one answer to our question is that dead believers are in some place of sleep, with Christ.

But one of the dangers of this is that it is bound by our time scale, and also it seems to invite us to think of the shadowy existence of the Old Testament Hades, even if it does not bring medieval pictures of purgatory into our minds. The age to come has already broken into our time with the resurrection of Jesus, and there seems some justification for speaking as Paul does in 2 Corinthians 5 (another of our alternative readings) of God having a heavenly body already prepared for us, in which we enter into a foretaste of heaven with Christ. The modern Roman Catholic funeral mass captures this with the preface of the dead:

> 'Lord, for your faithful people life is changed, not ended.
> When the body of our earthly dwelling lies in death
> we gain an everlasting place in heaven'

This is now found, suitably amended, as the second of the proper prefaces to be used in the eucharistic thanksgiving when there is a service of holy communion (section 49). The other echo of the same theme comes in the use of the sentence from Revelation 14.13 at the start of the committal (section 14).

- the need for alternatives for the funeral of a child (such an alternative had appeared in the 1928 Prayer Book which failed to get parliamentary approval).
- the growing pressure from anglo-catholics for prayers for the dead and for funeral eucharists.

The Commission's report of October 1964, published in 1965, was headed 'The Burial of the Dead and commemoration of the faithful departed', and its introduction contained a long defence of prayer for the dead. The joint Convocations of the clergy approved the service, but the House of Laity asked for a joint committee to be set up to explore whether agreement could be reached between anglo-catholics and evangelicals on a joint form of words which all could use. No one was against prayers of thanksgiving; few had problems over words commending the faithful departed to God at burial; but evangelicals, while willing to say something about the departed, would not accept prayers which implied doubt as to their blessedness, or suggested their dependence on the Church militant. The joint committee, under the chairmanship of the Bishop of St Edmundsbury and Ipswich, produced a unanimous report acceptable to both anglo-catholics and evangelicals. The Convocations refused to accept their recommendations and the House of Laity passed a motion explaining why they refused to reintroduce Series 2 Burial –

PETITION FOR THE DEAD

Is it right to pray for the dead? What sort of dead – just Christians or others too? What sort of prayer – thanksgiving or intercession too? These questions have divided the Church of England since the time of the Reformation and were the subject of an official report, *Prayer and the Departed*, in 1970. Though the whole Church is by no means divided into two camps, the traditional arguments for and against may be summarised as follows:

For petition for the dead

● Why should we stop praying for someone just because he's died? Prayer is an expression of love: we don't stop loving, so why should we stop praying? As well as expressing human emotional needs, prayer for the dead is an expression of the communion of the saints, of the solidarity we have with the Christian dead.

● Prayer for the dead expresses confidence in God's loving care for the Christian dead, and is in no sense pleading with God to change his mind about them.

● Knowing what human nature is like, there is considerable scope for growth in maturity before we are fit for God's presence. If there is any chance of growth in light, love and peace, we should pray for it – and praying for an increase of these things doesn't imply that the dead do not enjoy anything of them at present.

● We do not deny or undermine the doctrines of assurance and justification by faith when we pray for someone who is alive: why should we assume that praying for someone who is dead is a denial of these doctrines?

Against petition for the dead

● To pray for non-Christians to become Christians after death is wrong. This life is the time for making the irrevocable choice for or against God, and no change is possible after death. Prayer for Christians which might be interpreted as prayer for the dead in general, tends to blur the need to respond to Christ in this life, and to give the false (and unintended) impression that the decision can be put off until after death.

● It is doctrinally misleading and unnecessary to pray for peace and everlasting life for someone who already has it. To pray for rest and peace is to imply he does not already enjoy it. When someone becomes a Christian, the completeness of Christ's work is appropriated by him, he is 'in Christ'. This status, of being justified, forgiven, completely accepted by Christ and sure of eternal salvation, is something the Christian explores on earth, bound by an earthly body. At death, he is with Christ, already experiencing a foretaste of his eternal destiny which was settled while on earth, beyond the realm of our time-scale and the possibility of development.

● Praying for the dead undermines Christian assurance. For the believer, Jesus has promised that no one can snatch him out of the Father's hands, and nothing should be said which might detract from this certainty.

● Prayer should be based on God's promise, or command, or example. There is no promise, command or clear example in the bible relating to prayer for the dead. The only example ever quoted is 2 Timothy 1.17, where Paul prays for Onesiphorus, 'May the Lord grant him to find mercy on that Day!' But there is no indication that Onesiphorus is dead, and even if he is, the prayer is one of commendation to God's mercy on the day of judgement and not intercession about his present state.

with only seven members voting against.

The archbishops referred the question of prayer for the dead to the Church of England Doctrine Commission, which produced the unanimous report *Prayer and the Departed* in September 1970. Meanwhile, the Liturgical Commission began work on Series 3 Funerals in 1969, sending a unanimous report to the bishops in the spring of 1972. It was this service, amended to take account of the debates on the report *Prayer and the Departed* in 1972, and amended in its progress through the Synod, which was finally authorised in February 1975, and appears in the Alternative Service Book.

What is the funeral service for?

It is quite possible to have a funeral with no words at all. This is what the puritans wanted (and enforced in the Westminster *Directory*) in the sixteenth and seventeenth centuries. The traditional Church of England position was expressed by Richard Hooker in the mid-sixteenth century when he criticised the puritans: 'Let any man of reasonable judgement examine, whether it be more convenient for a company of men as it were in a dumb show to bring a corpse to the place of burial, there to leave it covered with earth, and so end ...' or to have a service with readings, 'psalms, and prayers, as

Prayer for the dead in *ASB 1980* funerals

The prayers here are the product of considerable agreement in the Church of England. Section 13 has the exact form of words agreed by the Doctrine Commission as a petition for a happy resurrection, not implying any hypothetical intermediate state:

'May God in his infinite love and mercy bring the whole Church, living and departed in the Lord Jesus, to a joyful resurrection and the fulfilment of his eternal kingdom.'

Section 44 is interpreted in the same way, and the collect in the holy communion provision (49) concentrates on the living rather than on the dead. Among the optional additional prayers, section 53 prays for the dead person to continue to enjoy refreshment, light and peace, sections 56 and 59 for God's will to be fulfilled, and section 60 that the dead man may know 'the fullness of life which you have promised to those who love you'.

are purposely framed for the stirring up of men's minds unto a careful consideration of their estate both here and hereafter'. Take away the words which 'show at burials the peculiar hope of the Church of God concerning the dead, and in the manner of those dumb funerals what one thing is there whereby the world may perceive we are Christian men?'

So we would expect the *ASB 1980* Funeral Service to stir us up to consider where we stand before God, to demonstrate the (still peculiar!) hope we have as Christians, and to show the world that this is a Christian funeral. The Liturgical Commission put it like this in their 1973 Introduction to the service:

a to secure the reverent disposal of the corpse
b to commend the deceased to the care of our heavenly Father
c to proclaim the glory of our risen life in Christ here and hereafter
d to remind us of the certainty of our own coming death and judgement
e to make plain the eternal unity of Christian people, living and departed, in the risen and ascended Christ
f to offer some consolation to the mourners.

When you go to a funeral service, it is a good thing to pray that God will use it to do these things. Pray for the clergyman taking the service, for instance, that the glory of our risen life in Christ might be proclaimed.

Whom is the Funeral Service for?

There are two answers to this question. The 1973 Introduction says the service is designed to be used for all baptised persons, including suicides (who were exempted from the 1662 Funeral Service). The only exception is that a separate service (sections 20-32) is provided as The Funeral of a Child. This sensitive service majors on God's love, seen in the opening sections as that of a shepherd, in the verse from Revelation about God wiping away our tears, and in the 23rd Psalm. The readings (either or both may be read) are the one from Mark 10 about children being brought to Jesus and blessed, and the one from Ephesians 3 which is Paul's prayer that we might have the power to grasp the love of Christ, and to know it. This thought is taken up in the prayer (section 24) that God will give us both faith and also some understanding of what he is doing.

So one answer to 'For whom?' is that here we have provision for all baptised Christians. The other answer is that the service is not just for the dead, but for the living, and for the Christian dead and living. There are no parts of the service addressed to the dead, such as 'Go forth upon thy journey from this world, O Christian soul ...'. This was in place in the medieval funeral which was simply a continuation of the ministry to the dying man, but has no place here where it is recognised that body and soul have parted company. We are no longer ministering to a soul, but as the Commission says, securing 'the reverent disposal of the corpse'. But the service rings with the

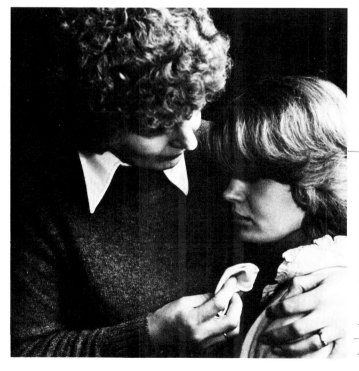

assurance that Christians, dead or alive, are united in Christ and share the future resurrection. The opening prayer said by all together (section 3) can only be said by people who have a true faith and a sure hope, and really want to live in the communion of saints, experiencing forgiveness and resurrection as they do so. The totally Christian context of the service is underlined by sections 12 and 13. It is all about people who have been given *new life in Christ Jesus*, who have faith that Jesus *died and rose again to save us and is now alive and reigns*. The service will only really make sense when both the corpse and the mourners are unashamedly Christian. Only then will the clear note of that assurance of unity in Christ's resurrection ring triumphantly through the service.

But what if either mourners or corpse are not clearly Christian? Should the service still be used? Perhaps not. Perhaps there is a case for a return to funerals in silence where there is nothing much that can be said with any Christian assurance. But the traditional Church of England position has always been to take a charitable and not a judging position, assuming the best about someone if there is the slightest outward evidence that it might be right to do so. And for those who come to the funeral service in any way open to meeting God, there is much here to challenge them. Do I have that new life in Christ? Am I really doing this in the faith of Jesus Christ who died and rose again to save me? Would my life be different if I were living and believing in the communion of saints, the forgiveness of sins and the resurrection to eternal life? There are psalms to remind me of the shortness of life and the shallow nature of earthly possessions. There are readings to explain the resurrection and the way to get to heaven. There is even a prayer (section 10) that I might make the best use of the time I've got left before I die, to turn away from sin and to follow Jesus. Perhaps one way in which the service might well be used is in personal ministry both to mourners and to the

dying. Read it and meditate on it as you go through it . . . .

When and where is the funeral service to take place?

There are a number of things to decide about the service, and the number of options provided for in the Alternative Service Book service reflects the variety of modern practice when compared with the Prayer Book custom of a service in church followed immediately by interment in the churchyard outside. Here are some of the decisions which need to be taken:

Burial or cremation?

Burial is traditional, but expensive. Cremation is comparatively new (the first crematoria were opened in the 1880s), and cheaper. Burial is sometimes a more painful experience for the mourners, especially in miserable weather. Cremation is comparatively painless for the mourners, but some find it psychologically unsatisfying as the coffin slides away on rollers while the words of committal are said: it disappears, but there is no true committal to the fire, as there is to the earth in burial when the earth is cast on the coffin. The Funeral Service provides for both burial and cremation. For

'Grant us, Lord the wisdom and the grace to use aright the time that is left to us here on earth . . .'.

ASB 1980,
Funeral Service

219

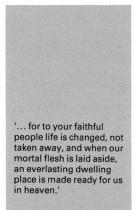

'... for to your faithful people life is changed, not taken away, and when our mortal flesh is laid aside, an everlasting dwelling place is made ready for us in heaven.'

cremation, the words 'earth to earth, ashes to ashes, dust to dust' in the committal (section 17) are left out, and sections 13-16 (the ending of the Service in Church and the words to be read while the body is prepared for the grave) are also omitted. Incidentally, these words (sections 14-16) are optional in any case because, as the Liturgical Commission noted as late as 1964, the hearse may go very close to the grave and 'when the weather is bad, the priest and mourners may well wait in their carriages ...'. For cremation, a Form that may be used at the Interment of Ashes is provided, with a variation designed to allow for the commital of ashes at sea. The very short service for burying the ashes cannot of course take place until some time after the cremation. Some think it may be distressing to have another service, maybe weeks later, but the ashes should be

buried, rather than scattered in some favourite place to be trodden under foot, or kept on the mantelpiece as a reminder. The burial of ashes can sometimes be in a special garden near the church or in the side of a family grave.

Service in church first, or committal first?
The Funeral Service is laid out with the Service in Church happening first, followed by the committal in churchyard, cemetery or crematorium. But the Notes to the service allow for the Committal to take place first, followed by the Service in Church, which then takes on something of the character of a memorial service. Indeed, it is designed so that it can be used as a memorial service, perhaps the same evening or at some later date. There is certainly something to be said for worship without the coffin present.

With or without Holy Communion?
Instructions are provided for combining Holy Communion with the Funeral Service, whether or not the Service in Church is split off from the Committal, and also for Holy Communion not combined with the Funeral Service itself. Now that there is no thought in the service of the medieval idea of saying mass for people to do them good in the after-life, there are clear advantages to making the funeral a eucharistic occasion when the dead person belongs to the local Church. It emphasises that the funeral is not a private, but a church community occasion, that everyone has suffered a loss, and everyone has something to give thanks for, in this death. It focusses our attention both on Christ's sacrifice on the cross and on our assurance of the future resurrection, reminding us forcibly of the communion of saints. And the presence and support of other Christians is a real help to the family. Sections 47-49 provide suitable material, instructions and suggestions such as the use of the seasonal material for Easter and two possible prefaces to insert into the eucharistic thanksgiving.

SOME DOS AND DON'TS FOR FUNERAL VISITORS

When you go to visit someone who is bereaved ...

DO relax, be patient, talk naturally about death.

DON'T avoid the subject if your friends want to talk about it.

DO help them to face the fact of death, maybe by going over again what happened, or talking about the funeral. God has some purpose for their lives even without their loved one.

DON'T pity, patronise or talk in platitudes.

DO be aware of the genuine fears your friends may have, for example of going into their empty house.

DON'T gloss over the problem your friends may have about where the dead person is now – and don't give false comfort.

DO pray, both with and for your friends. Thank God for the life of the person who has died. God promises, 'I will never leave you or forsake you.' Pray together that that might be true now.

DON'T be afraid of children. They are very resilient and speak about death in a very matter of fact way (which sometimes hurts!) Let them come to the funeral, and not be excluded from what the family is doing.

A service before the funeral day?

A further enrichment of the funeral provision in the Alternative Service Book is the brief order (section 46) for a service which can be used either if the body is brought to church the day before the funeral, or in the home. This might be something to ask for: it might, for instance, give shape and form to the pastoral visit of the minister before the funeral – using additional prayers and the general permission to preach at any point in the services!

With or without music?

Music is generally available, both in churches and crematoria, so long as it is requested. Carefully used, the right music can help set the atmosphere and be a help in the movement at the beginning and end of the service. To go out of church singing a hymn, for instance, may for some people fix their attention on Christ rather than on the mechanics of removing the coffin. Music can also hinder, for example by obscuring the words being said, or by producing a totally unreal atmosphere in syrupy music at the committal in a crematorium.

WHAT TO EXPECT AT A FUNERAL SERVICE

Let us assume that the service is going to be in the order laid out in the service book, with the Service in Church followed by the Committal in a crematorium, with music but without Holy Communion. What is going to happen? It is a help, if you are going to a funeral yourself, or if you are trying to help a friend who has been bereaved, to spend a few minutes going through the service beforehand. Apart from ministers and undertakers, not many people go to so many funerals that they are really familiar with what is to happen – a point the clergy sometimes forget!

Traditionally, the minister meets the coffin at the church door or graveyard gate, and walks in front of the procession into church, saying the opening sentences (or some of them) in sections 1 and 2 as he does so. One alternative to this is for the mourners all to be seated in church first, which avoids processing behind the coffin which some find distressing, and also gives a few moments to pray quietly before the coffin is brought in.

be the name of the Lord'. Then in the next three verses the voice of God reassuring us of his love for the dead person and for us: 'underneath are the everlasting arms'. Next the voice of the preacher, setting out why Jesus came and how we might have eternal life: 'God so loved the world that he gave . . .'. Perhaps a reply to this might be the voice of the mourners, sure of God's loving purpose: 'I am sure that neither death, nor life . . . will be able to separate us from the love of God in Christ Jesus our Lord'. And the last two sentences are the voice of the prophet, sure of the future in God's hands: 'Eye has not seen, nor ear heard, nor the heart of man conceived, what God has prepared for those who love him'.

After the sentences, the congregation will probably remain standing for the opening prayer (section 3, a prayer of assurance based on the creed) and for the psalms. Psalm singing has been part of the funeral service since the earliest days of the church, and the four printed here (and the four alternative psalms as well) all have different things to teach us as they direct our thoughts to God. They may be sung or said, and are in the translation originally prepared specially for this service.

The congregation then sits for one *or more* of the readings. Three, from John 14, 1 Corinthians 15 and 1 Thessalonians 4, are printed in full in *ASB 1980* as the first choice of those who compiled the service, but there are also ten alternative passages. These would be used if one of them particularly fitted the circumstances of this funeral, or when there is a need for variety if a minister is on duty all day at a crematorium.

If one of the printed bits is being used, it is a good idea to follow it in the service book as an aid to concentration at a time when this is difficult. The sermon follows. In their 1964 introduction the Liturgical Commission make the point that 'it should be a true preaching of the word, the temptation simply to eulogise

'Jesus said, I am the resurrection, and I am the life; he who believes in me, though he die, yet shall he live, and whoever lives and believes in me shall never die.'

John 11.25-26

Another alternative is for the coffin to be in church before the service begins, perhaps brought in with a short service (section 46) the night before. Whichever way it begins, the minister is bound to use the first sentence, which comes from the story of the raising of Lazarus in John 11. So the resurrection – and our way into it – are proclaimed right at the start of the service.

Think of these sentences perhaps as the voices of different people. The voice of Jesus, asserting that he is the resurrection and the life for those who believe in him: 'He who believes in me, though he die, yet shall he live'. Then the voice of the mourners, expressing their willingness to agree with God's will: 'The Lord gives, and the Lord takes away: blessed the dead being resisted'. Hence its place in the service, straight after the reading of the word.

The response to the word of God read and preached comes in section 7, the Te Deum which might be said or sung. This doesn't say, 'Yes, we believe the dead man was a good man', but, 'Yes, we believe Christ who came to set us free, to draw the sting of death, to open the kingdom of heaven to us'. This is followed by the responses, 'Lord have mercy upon us' and the Lord's Prayer.

More prayers may follow here. Some of them may come from the Selection of Additional Prayers in sections 50-60. Section 50 is a new prayer, giving an opportunity to thank God for the ordinary human things about the life of the dead person: 'we thank you for the life of your *son N*, for the love and mercy he received from you and showed among us.' If you are a close relative and want to give thanks for particular things about the dead man, the minister might be willing to mention them in prayer at this point. It is important to praise God even when we may not feel much in the mood to do so.

Section 51, 52 and 54 came in this form through the Convocation debates on Series 2 Burial in 1968. Section 53 is from the 1928 Prayer Book. Section 55 is the same as section 24 in the Funeral of a Child. Section 56 is a new composition, with the well-known phrase, 'those whom we love, but see no longer'. Sections 57 and 58 come from the 1928 Prayer Book, and section 59 is from the

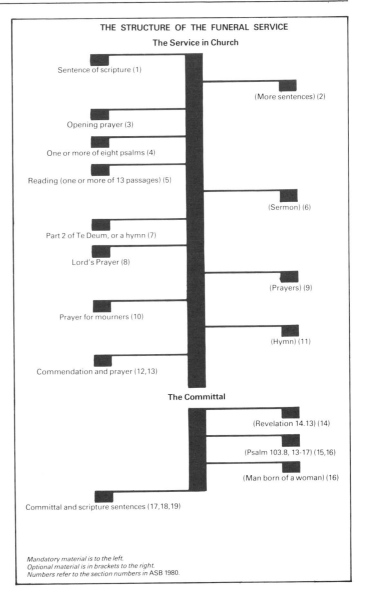

THE STRUCTURE OF THE FUNERAL SERVICE
The Service in Church

Sentence of scripture (1)

(More sentences) (2)

Opening prayer (3)

One or more of eight psalms (4)

Reading (one or more of 13 passages) (5)

(Sermon) (6)

Part 2 of Te Deum, or a hymn (7)

Lord's Prayer (8)

(Prayers) (9)

Prayer for mourners (10)

(Hymn) (11)

Commendation and prayer (12,13)

The Committal

(Revelation 14.13) (14)

(Psalm 103.8, 13-17) (15,16)

(Man born of a woman) (16)

Committal and scripture sentences (17,18,19)

Mandatory material is to the left.
Optional material is in brackets to the right.
Numbers refer to the section numbers in ASB 1980.

SOME SUITABLE HYMNS FOR A FUNERAL SERVICE

Brief life is here our portion: Bernard of Cluny
Give me the wings of faith: Isaac Watts
For all the saints: William Walsham How
For all who watch tonight: Constance Coote
He wants not friends: Richard Baxter
I know that my Redeemer: Icelandic burial hymn
I know that my Redeemer lives: Samuel Medley
In heavenly love abiding: Anna L. Waring
Jesus lives! your terrors now: Christian Gellert
Let saints on earth in concert sing: Charles Wesley
Praise, my soul, the king of heaven: Henry Francis Lyte
There's a light upon the mountains: Henry Burton

SOME PSALMS USED AT FUNERAL SERVICES

Psalm 23   The Lord is my shepherd
● God is our shepherd, he looks after us
● He is strong enough to help us (with rod and staff)
● He will bring us to feast with him in heaven
● So we need not fear the valley of the shadow of death
Jesus said, 'I am the good shepherd. I know my sheep and they know me. I am willing to die for my sheep' (John 10.11-15).

Psalm 90   Lord, you have been our refuge
● the eternal nature of God
● the shortness of man's life, by contrast
● a prayer (v. 12-16) for three things with three results

Psalm 121   I lift up my eyes to the hills
For those desperately wanting to know where they can go for help.
● the psalmist is sure the creator God helps him
● God doesn't sleep (if we're awake at night, he is too)
● He knows about our going out and our coming back home (and he will be there even if no one else is).

Psalm 130   Out of the depths have I called to you, O Lord
The assurance that
● God hears us
● God forgives and redeems us.

A carving from the church at Old Warden, Bedfordshire

intercessions in the old Series 3 Holy Communion Service. Section 60 is a new litany, with the response, *Hear our prayer*.

The prayers end (section 10) with a new prayer which reminds us of the shortness of life and of our need to repent and follow Jesus. There may then be a hymn before the commendation in section 12 when we express our faith in God by entrusting the dead person to him by name. The first part of the service ends with section 13, taken from the Doctrine Commission's report, *Prayer and the Departed*, which fixes our eyes clearly on the future resurrection.

There will probably be some music at this point as the undertaker and his men come forward to remove the coffin. The chief mourners usually follow on in pro-cession behind the coffin out of the church, and then get into cars as the coffin is put into the hearse. There is no need to be silent all the way to the crematorium, though if there is silence you may want to pray. But it is quite in order to talk about ordinary things, about the minister's sermon, about something else about the dead person of which the service has perhaps reminded you, that you want to praise God for. It might too be a time to 'comfort one another with these words' as the reading from 1 Thessalonians says.

On arrival at the crematorium the minister will again lead the way in front of the coffin, though the mourners can be seated first if they want to be. The sentence from Revelation 14 fixes our minds on heaven, where Christ is, and

may be followed by part of Psalm 103 (contrasting the shortness of life with God's enduring love for us) or by the ancient anthem 'Man born of a woman'. This was put together by Archbishop Cranmer in 1549 from Job 14.1,2 (the first paragraph) and Miles Coverdale's metrical translation (in his *Goostly Psalmes*) of Martin Luther's paraphrase of a Latin anthem. It is a very solemn reminder of the shortness of life, the holiness of God, and our need for forgiveness.

At section 17 the words of committal will be said by the minister and the coffin usually removed from view. If we were at the graveside this might be the moment at which the coffin was actually lowered into the grave, or if not at least some earth thrown onto the coffin.

The service ends with two sentences which again keep us looking forward rather than backward, as we contemplate the fullness of joy in God's presence to which he is able to lead us.

SOME SCRIPTURE READINGS USED AT FUNERAL SERVICES

The readings in the service tell us quite a lot about the bible's attitude to death and resurrection. Here are some questions which may assist meditation on them.

John 14.1-6

Do we identify with the bewildered Thomas, warned of his friend's death?

Do we believe in God and in Jesus? (v.1)

Have we found the way? (v.6)

1 Corinthians 15.20-26, 35-38, 42-44, 53-end

How did death and resurrection enter the world? (v.20, 21)

How does Paul argue for the connection between this life and the next? (v. 35-38)

Why can we be sure of victory? (v.53-end)

Does this have anything to say about the way we live now?

1 Thessalonians 4.13-18

What sort of grief is ours? Is it because we have no hope? (v.13)

Do we believe Jesus died and rose again? (v.14)

How much are we looking forward to that time when we too will be with the Lord? (v.17)

How can we use these words to comfort one another? (v.18)

The Ordinal

WHAT DOES ORDINATION MEAN?

The word ordination comes from a Latin word meaning to arrange or regulate; the Greek equivalent means to appoint or put in charge. So we may say that to ordain is to do no more than to appoint a person to do a particular job, but it has come to be used in a more restricted sense to refer to those who are appointed to the tasks of deacons, priests and bishops. More than that, their appointment takes place in a manner that is used for no one else. All of this suggests that they are special people doing special jobs, whereas in fact they are simply people who have been called to exercise their gifts in the fulfilling of certain responsibilities and ministries for the benefit of the whole Church. There are a few tasks that only clergy are allowed to carry out, but they are very few. A lay person, for example, may conduct a funeral, or indeed a baptism. There is virtually nothing that a deacon can do that he could not as a layman. He is not, according to Canon Law, permitted to preside at a communion service, nor is he supposed to pronounce absolution: those functions are reserved for priests. Similarly, an ordination cannot take place unless a bishop is present to lay hands on the candidate and a bishop alone is allowed to lay on hands in confirmation.

It would be wrong, however, to think of the tasks of the clergy as limited to those things that they alone are permitted to do. If we look at the opening paragraph of the Declaration in each of the services we shall see that the special tasks that are reserved for clergy are seen in the wider context of their pastoral oversight and care. A bishop, priest or deacon does not cease to be a layman, in the sense that he is a member of the people (the *laos*) of God. Nor does a bishop or priest cease to be a deacon. The word deacon, derived as it is from *diakonia*, reminds us that he is, as much as any, called to be a servant. A priest does not cease to be a servant, nor does a bishop. Essentially then, ordination is concerned with an appointment to service in the shape of pastoral oversight, but oversight may take several forms.

Who is ordained?

There are four services: The Ordination of Deacons, The Ordination of Priests (also called Presbyters), The Ordination of Deacons and Priests and The Ordination or Consecration of a Bishop.

The third is not a separate service but is provided so that it is not necessary to keep turning pages when deacons and priests are being ordained during the same service, as often happens.

We can see, then, that there are three orders: *deacon*, *priest* or presbyter, and *bishop*. It is normal in the Church of England for a man to be ordained deacon at the end of his training and the beginning of his parish ministry and to be ordained priest after a further year. The first year may then be regarded as a kind of probationary period.

A deacon cannot be an incumbent (vicar or rector of a parish), nor may he preside at a communion service or pronounce the blessing or absolution in a public service. Usually he must be at least 23 years old, a priest 24 and a bishop 30.

The progression from deacon to priest

to bishop is now well established, but according to early custom in the Church it was not necessary for a bishop to have been a priest or even a deacon, nor was it normal for a priest to have been a deacon, so that election and ordination as a deacon did not carry with it any expectation of promotion.

The service for the ordination of deacons may also be used in order to admit women to the order of deaconess, an order which has much in common with that of deacon, but which has some important differences, due not least to the fact that the Church of England has not as yet agreed that women should be ordained to the priesthood, nor that a deaconess is in 'holy orders' as a deacon is.

How is a bishop chosen?

The appointment is made by the crown, on the advice of the Prime Minister. He (or she) in turn has received (and is supposed to have taken) the advice of the General Synod's Crown Appointments Commission – a largely elected body of the Church, which sits with representatives of the vacant diocese and nominates to the Prime Minister. The reason for the involvement of the crown and government has always been that the Church of England is an established Church, enjoying certain rights and privileges as well as having certain legal obligations, with the monarch as its temporal head.

WHAT YOU WILL SEE AT AN ORDINATION

Where does an ordination take place?

Practice varies from diocese to diocese. In some it always takes place in the cathedral. In others some ordinations are held in the cathedral, some in one or other of the parish churches. The decision rests with the bishop and it is easy to see that there are advantages in both arrangements.

An ordination is a special occasion in the life of the Church, so it may be good to have a special place for it. Most people

The institution of a new vicar by the bishop is another reminder of the work he is called to by God

do not visit their own cathedral very often unless they live near it; perhaps they do not often visit churches other than their own. So when they gather in the cathedral with people from other parishes they may be reminded, and powerfully reminded, that to be a Christian is more than to belong simply to St Martin's Church. It can be enormously encouraging to be present at a huge gathering of Christians; so to hold an ordination in the cathedral is at the same time to remind the congregation that they belong to a body that is much bigger than any individual parish and also to remind us all that those who are being ordained are being ordained to the ministry of the whole Church and not simply of St Martin's, St Mary's or Holy Trinity.

On the other hand, there are advantages in holding an ordination in a parish church. If there are several candidates, it may be an opportunity to draw together the congregations of a particular deanery in a way that is not often possible. It may even be possible for the candidates to be ordained in the church of the parish in which they are to serve. In this way an ordination becomes a more domestic occasion and so may be of help and encouragement both to candidate and congregation.

When does an ordination take place?
Most take place either at Petertide (on or about the feast of St Peter, 29 June) or Michaelmas (on or about the feast of St Michael and All Angels, 29 September). A few take place during the season of Advent, but there is no reason why they should not take place at any other time of the year.

In the lectionary, certain days are labelled 'Ember Day'. The origin of the name is uncertain: possibly it means 'four seasons' (from the Latin *quattuor tempora*). These times (the Wednesday, Friday and Saturday of the weeks before Advent 3, Lent 2 and nearest to St Peter's Day and St Michael and All Angels) which were observed by Christians possibly as early as the third century, were originally associated with agriculture, but came to be the occasion

of ordinations. The changes to the present times have been made largely for practical reasons, but the Ember days remain as special times when Christians are reminded to pray for the ministry of the Church (and that, of course, does not simply mean for vicars and curates!).

The connection of Ember days with ordinations will suggest that ordinations do not, and have not, always taken place on a Sunday. It is, indeed, very common for the consecration of a bishop to take place on a weekday (although it must be a holy day). But the earliest account we have of an ordination, contained in the *Apostolic Tradition* of Hippolytus, prescribes that it should take place on the Lord's Day, that is, when Christians would normally meet for worship.

Who takes part in the service?
If the ordination takes place in a cathedral you may well see a large number of clergy dressed in a confusing variety of garments. Among them will be one who will stand out because he is dressed in a quite different manner: he will be wearing a wig and gown. He is the diocesan registrar, a barrister or solicitor who performs legal functions for and acts in an advisory capacity to the diocese. The reason for his presence at the ordination is that he supervises certain legal procedures (e.g. the swearing of the oaths of allegiance and of obedience, normally performed before the service begins) and legal documents.

The canons of the cathedral (ordinary clergy who are members of the cathedral staff) may well be dressed in colourful robes, the outermost being a cope, a rather splendid kind of cloak. The senior member of the cathedral clergy is the dean or, in some places, the provost. These clergy will take part in the service, perhaps by assisting with the administration at the communion, because they are the cathedral clergy. You will not expect to see them at an ordination in a parish church.

A bishop must preside at an ordination of a priest or deacon. He may be the

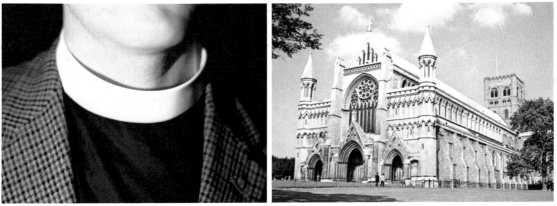

St Albans Cathedral

STEPS TO ORDINATION

God calls men into the ordained ministry in different ways. If you know your local vicar or curate well enough, why not ask him how God called him? Here's what happened to Tony: it's the sort of pattern you might expect if God was calling you into the ministry.

1 Tony became gradually conscious that God might want him to be ordained, and decided to explore.
2 He talked to his vicar, who lent him a book and suggested he discuss it with other leaders in the Church.
3 The vicar asked the church council how they felt, and also put Tony in touch with the bishop's director of ordinands.
4 The director of ordinands interviewed Tony. He then met the bishop, who decided to send him to a selection conference.
5 Tony went to the conference (a panel of clergy and laymen), which recommended him for training.
6 He visited two or three residential theological colleges, one of which accepted him for training. (He could have gone on a non-residential course and continued with his job.)
7 During his time of training both Tony and the college staff became more certain that God was calling him into the ordained ministry.
8 In his final year Tony went to look at a number of parishes suggested by his bishop and the college principal, to see if God was calling him to serve his first curacy (or 'title') there. He might have gone to another diocese if he hadn't found the right place in his own diocese. He would only have gone back to his own parish if he had been a candidate for the non-stipendiary ministry.
9 So Tony ended up, after much prayer, talking, training, and with a large number of people as well as himself convinced of his calling, kneeling before the bishop to be ordained deacon. Next year, almost certainly, he will be ordained priest (or 'priested').

ELIZABETH THE SECOND
BY THE GRACE OF GOD of the United Kingdom of
Great Britain and Northern Ireland and of Our other Realms and
Territories Queen Head of the Commonwealth Defender of the Faith

By Warrant under The Queen's Sign Manual

The Principal Registrar of the Province of Canterbury with the Queen's Letters Patent directing the Royal Commission to confirm the election of the new Archbishop of Canterbury

cassock and surplice. The remaining clergy present are likely to be connected in some way or other with the candidates, representing the parishes in which they are serving or will serve, or perhaps representing the colleges or courses attended by the candidates.

What do the candidates wear?

The candidates for ordination will all be wearing cassock and surplice or an alb. Those who are to be ordained deacon may carry a white stole. If they do, the stole will be put on them, worn over the left shoulder and tied under the right arm, during the service. This should take place at the end of the Declaration, but may be delayed until after the laying-on (or imposition) of hands. The stole is worn this way both at the ordination and at other services in order to distinguish a deacon from other ministers; it is rather like a badge of office. Similarly, the candidates for priesting at the ordination, who are already deacons, will probably wear the stole this way at the beginning of the service, but they may, if they prefer, wear a scarf or nothing apart from cassock and surplice. If they are wearing the stole, it will be untied and rearranged to hang around their necks.

If the same service is used for the admission of lay workers and deaconesses, those candidates are likely to be seated with the rest of the candidates, as may also any lay readers. A deaconess will in all probability, be dressed in a dark blue cassock and may at some point have a cross hung around her neck. A lady lay worker may wear a maroon gown and a medallion.

THE SERVICE

Look at the diagram on the facing page. Notice first that following the custom of the Church since the time of Hippolytus (and probably for some time before him) an ordination takes place in the course of a communion service. Indeed, the pattern of the modern communion service can be clearly seen from the beginning of

diocesan bishop, but he could, equally, be either a suffragan or an assistant bishop. Indeed there may be more than one bishop present and, at the consecration of a new bishop, canon law requires at least three. The bishop, of course, will be readily recognisable by his pastoral staff (sometimes called a crozier, or even a crook, because of its shape) even if he is not wearing cope and mitre.

The candidates will normally be presented to the bishop by an archdeacon, another senior office bearer in the diocese, but he will probably be dressed as most of the parish clergy present, in a

priests afterwards. Added to the end of the Presentation in each case will be the paragraph from the beginning of the Declaration in which are set out the responsibilities of each order as a kind of 'job description'.

The Declaration (sections 13,14)
Following this 'job description' is a series of eight questions in which the candidates are asked to state publicly their

the ordination service: the first part of the communion service is, as it were, adapted to incorporate the material of the ordination and the second part is taken up at the Peace. So the service opens with a specially appointed collect, a reading from the Old Testament, followed by an Epistle, Gospel and sermon. (Section numbers in the following paragraphs refer to the services for the ordination of deacons or of priests on their own. See diagram for section numbers for the ordination of deacons and priests together, or for bishops.)

The Presentation (sections 11, 12)
Instead of the intercessions, which would normally follow the creed, we come to the Presentation, when the archdeacon or his representative presents the candidates to the bishop, announcing both their names and the parishes where they will be serving. The bishop in turn presents the candidates to the congregation, asking about their approval of the candidates and their willingness to uphold them in their ministry.

If deacons and priests are to be ordained during the same service the deacons will be presented first and the

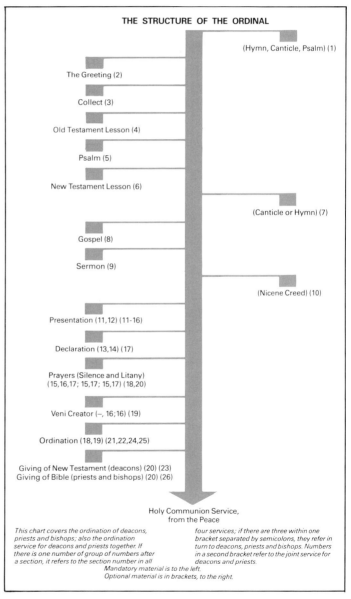

THE STRUCTURE OF THE ORDINAL

(Hymn, Canticle, Psalm) (1)

The Greeting (2)

Collect (3)

Old Testament Lesson (4)

Psalm (5)

New Testament Lesson (6)

(Canticle or Hymn) (7)

Gospel (8)

Sermon (9)

(Nicene Creed) (10)

Presentation (11,12) (11-16)

Declaration (13,14) (17)

Prayers (Silence and Litany) (15,16,17; 15,17; 15,17) (18,20)

Veni Creator (–, 16;16) (19)

Ordination (18,19) (21,22,24,25)

Giving of New Testament (deacons) (20) (23)
Giving of Bible (priests and bishops) (20) (26)

Holy Communion Service, from the Peace

This chart covers the ordination of deacons, priests and bishops; also the ordination service for deacons and priests together. If there is one number of group of numbers after a section, it refers to the section number in all four services; if there are three within one bracket separated by semicolons, they refer in turn to deacons, priests and bishops. Numbers in a second bracket refer to the joint service for deacons and priests.
Mandatory material is to the left.
Optional material is in brackets, to the right.

233

conviction of their calling to the ministry to which they are to be ordained and to affirm their acceptance of the responsibilities of that ministry. Like the paragraph preceding them, the questions repay careful reading. Unlike the 1662 services these services contain the same questions for both priests and deacons.

The Prayers (sections 15, 16)

After this serious and solemn part of the service it is right that we should all be called to prayer, in silence, in the form of the Litany (a responsive form of prayer) and in the ancient hymn *Veni Creator*, 'Come Holy Ghost, our souls inspire . . .'. Traditionally this hymn is sung only where there are priests or bishops to be ordained, but there seems to be no very good reason why it should not be sung also at services where deacons only are to be ordained.

The Ordination (sections 17, 18)

In the ordination prayer, said by the bishop, we give praise and thanks to God and ask for the gift of the Holy Spirit for the new tasks to which the candidates have been called. The prayer is different

for each of the three orders and, again, repays careful reading, for it is as much a prayer for the whole Church as for the candidates. During the first part, the bishop may stretch out his hands towards all the candidates, but the second part is repeated over each individual as hands are laid on him or her. The final part is said when hands have been laid on all.

It could be argued that the whole prayer should be said over each, but the service would be likely to become somewhat tedious if there were many candidates. It is for the sake of brevity that only the central section is repeated.

Ideally the bishop should move from candidate to candidate to repeat over each the central section, but it may be that each will come to him, following long standing practice in the 1662 services. If the bishop comes to the candidates the service will not only be briefer but it may perhaps express better our sense of the partnership of the ministry of the Gospel and avoid a possibly unfortunate sense of hierarchical power.

When hands have been laid on all, the bishop says the final part of the prayer.

The Giving of the bible (section 20)

After the ordination prayer the deacons are given a New Testament, and the priests a bible as a sign of the authority given them to carry out their ministry and especially to preach the good news of Jesus Christ.

You may be puzzled by the distinction made by the giving of a New Testament or a bible. It may appear to suggest that a deacon should only preach from the New Testament, but no such idea is intended, though it may serve to remind us that all our preaching and all our living for God takes its origin from and finds its power in God's revelation of himself in Jesus who gave himself for our salvation.

For a large part of the history of the Church it has been customary that a deacon should read the Gospel at the communion service. Indeed, in the Prayer Book services of ordination, as in the Latin rites preceding them, deacons are ordained before the reading of the Gospel in order that one of them should then carry out this deacon's task. In the Roman rites the deacon would be handed a book containing the Gospels alone. In the English services, he is handed a New Testament.

If the bible or New Testament is given as a sign of the task of preaching the Gospel, it has to be remembered that there are many more ways of making the good news known than standing in a pulpit or even at a street corner. So it may be argued that the candidates ought to be offered other symbols of their ministry in addition. After the giving of the bible, then, the priest who has just been ordained may also be handed a chalice and paten as a sign of his authorisation to preside at the holy communion, while a bishop may be handed his pastoral staff as a reminder of his responsibility for those who are committed to his care, as a shepherd cares for his flock.

This ceremony is sometimes known by

12th century Latin bible

QUESTIONS ASKED OF CANDIDATES FOR ORDINATION

Do you believe, so far as you know your own heart, that God has called you to the office and work of a priest in his Church?

Do you accept the holy scriptures as revealing all things necessary for eternal salvation through faith in Jesus Christ?

Do you believe the doctrine of the Christian faith as the Church of England has received it, and in your ministry will you expound and teach it?

Will you accept the discipline of this Church, and give due respect to those in authority?

Will you be diligent in prayer, in reading holy scriptures, and in all studies that will deepen your faith and fit you to uphold the truth of the Gospel against error?

Will you strive to fashion your own life and that of your household according to the way of Christ?

Will you promote unity, peace, and love among all Christian people, and especially among those whom you serve?

Will you then, in the strength of the Holy Spirit, continually stir up the gift of God that is in you to make Christ known to all men?

the Latin name *porrectio instrumentorum* which we might translate as 'the handing over of equipment', a little as though a doctor were handed a stethoscope or a mechanic a spanner.

Ordination of a Bishop

The service for the ordination of a bishop follows the same pattern as those for the deacons and priests, but there are some differences in detail that are worth our attention. The Presentation, for example, includes the reading of the royal mandate (the official document giving royal authority for the consecration to take place), a feature which owes its presence to the fact that episcopal appointments are made by the crown. Later in the Presentation, the bishop-elect reads the Declaration of Assent whereas deacons and priests normally read it in the presence of the bishop alone before the ordination service takes place. It is the same Declaration that a deacon has to read during a public service on the first Sunday on which he officiates.

Careful reading will show that there are some differences in the questions put to the bishop-elect in the Declaration from those put in the other services, while appropriate changes are to be found both in the preface to the Declaration, in the ordination prayer and in the words accompanying the Giving of the bible.

The remainder of the Service

We rejoin the communion service at the Peace, leading to the thanksgiving. According to the *Apostolic Tradition* a newly ordained bishop himself presides at the communion, but it is unlikely that this practice will be followed at an Anglican ordination, although those who have been newly ordained priest or bishop may perhaps stand with the presiding bishop or archbishop at the thanksgiving, while the new deacons may assist at the preparation of the bread and the wine and at the communion.

WHERE DO THE ORDINATION SERVICES COME FROM?

Ordination and the New Testament

We shall search in vain for an ordination service in the New Testament. But we will find occasions when Christians met together to elect or appoint someone for a particular task, and we shall find them at prayer in so doing. More than that, we may well find that hands are laid on the persons appointed. So, for example the seven men chosen by the Church in Jerusalem to look after the Greek speaking widows were presented to the apostles who prayed and laid hands on them (Acts 6.1-6). We notice here what have been regarded as the classical features of an ordination: election, prayer and the laying on of hands. Later in Acts we read of the appointment of Barnabas and Saul (i.e. Paul) as missionaries. Prompted by the Holy Spirit, the Church at Antioch laid hands on them after prayer and fasting (Acts 13.1-3). Later still we are told that Paul and Barnabas appointed elders (the Greek word is *presbyteros*, from which both presbyter and priest are derived) for the congregations at Lystra, Iconium and elsewhere, with prayer and fasting (Acts 14.23).

If we turn on in the New Testament to 1 Timothy, a letter which speaks of the qualifications needed for the holders of the offices of bishop and deacon, we find that Timothy is urged not to neglect the spiritual endowment given to him under the guidance of prophecy and through the laying on of hands (1 Timothy 4.14). What, precisely, is meant here is not clear, but it may refer to Timothy's ordination to a particular, though unspecified, ministry. We do know, however, that it was customary for rabbis to be ordained with the laying on of hands, so Christians may well have copied Jewish custom.

The Ministry in the New Testament

We are accustomed to talk about 'going into the ministry', 'going into the

Church', 'being ordained', or to using other phrases all of which refer to the same thing, to becoming a clergyman, and therefore being ordained deacon and subsequently priest. Such talk would have sounded very strange to the Christians of the New Testament. Indeed, in recent years we have been rediscovering the fact that 'the ministry' is not the exclusive business of the vicar or the curate. Rather there are many ministries, or kinds of service to which anyone may be called by appointment or by the possession of a particular gift. So in the Church at the time of St Paul there appear to have been many Christians with special gifts of use to the Church, such gifts being acknowledged by the members of the congregation and exercised among them. We find lists of various gifts and the ministries they lead to in Romans 12. 6-8,1 Corinthians 12.4-10 and Ephesians 4.11-12. At the same time there were many jobs needing to be done, as for example, the care of widows to which we have already referred. For these tasks suitable members of the congregation might be nominated and appointed.

As new churches were established they needed leaders. Perhaps we may find in the New Testament the very beginnings of a pattern of leadership; for example, the letters to Timothy and to Titus speak of bishops, elders and deacons. But we must be careful not to jump to any conclusion that we find here the blueprint of the threefold order we find in the Church of England. It would appear that 'bishop' and 'elder' are both used to refer to the same office, (cf Titus 1.3,7; Acts 20.17,28) and there is no evidence whatever to suggest that a deacon might expect to become an elder, or that an elder should first be a deacon. In addition there is sufficient evidence to show that even if a regular pattern was beginning to emerge in the later part of the first century, there continued to be such other ministries as those exercised, for example, by prophets and evangelists.

WHO LAYS HANDS ON THE CANDIDATES?

It is a rule of the Church of England, following long tradition and with the intention of expressing the involvement of the whole Church in the act, that at least three bishops (including, normally, the archbishop of the province) should join in laying on hands at the consecration of a bishop. Also, following customs dating back at least to Hippolytus, other priests join with the bishop in laying hands on candidates for the priesthood while the bishop alone (possibly accompanied by his suffragans) lays hands on those being ordained deacon. Hippolytus says that the reason for this is that the deacon is being ordained to the service of the bishop, while other priests (or presbyters) lay hands on those being ordained to their own order, not to ordain them but, as it were, as a mark of recognition and welcome. These reasons, however, are not very convincing and we should not necessarily take them as a basis for our own practice.

Bishops, presbyters and deacons

We do not know why both the words bishop and elder were used to describe the same office. The practice of appointing elders was well known in Jewish circles (cf Luke 7.3) and so taken over by Christians. Perhaps they used the term bishop (which is derived from the Greek *episkopos*, as are our words episcopate and episcopacy), in order to distinguish elders of the Christian congregation from those of the Jewish congregations. Perhaps it was a way of describing their job more exactly: a bishop is one who has oversight or is a guardian. The Greek word is a perfectly ordinary one that could be used to refer, for example, to an inspector of drains. Just as an inspector

> 'If your gift is prophecy, then use it as your faith suggests; if administration, then use it for administration; if teaching, then use it for teaching. Let the preachers deliver sermons, the almsgiver give freely, the officials be diligent, and those who do works of mercy do them cheerfully.'
>
> *Romans 12.7-8*

> 'It is not permissible apart from the bishop either to baptise or to hold an agape.'
>
> Ignatius, *Letter to the Church at Smyrna*

of drains had to ensure that drains were kept clean and were repaired when necessary so that they worked properly, so the elders or bishops had as their task to see that things ran smoothly in the congregations for which they were responsible, including making sure that orphans and the sick were cared for. Others might be appointed to look after the orphans and sick, but the elders were there to ensure that the job was done.

It used to be normal to speak of the

seven, appointed in Acts 6 to care for the widows, as deacons, but although they were appointed for that task or service, and the Greek word for service is the same word from which we derive our word 'deacon', Acts 6 does not call them deacons. Indeed if they were deacons, then so also were the apostles, since they are described as devoted to the ministry or *service* of the word (i.e. to preaching – Acts 6.4). Again, even though 1 Timothy 3 speaks of the qualifications of a deacon it tells us nothing about his job, so we can only assume that a deacon might exercise any of a number of responsibilities of service to the Church. The point that we must understand here is that there are many forms of service (*diakonia*) in the Church but the exercising of service does not entail also holding the office of deacon (*diakonos*). Just as we know little about a deacon's job, so we know little of how the jobs of bishop and presbyter came to be separated. Perhaps it came about as the Church expanded and developed several congregations in the same area, so that it became necessary to appoint chief superintendents or coordinators. Eventually his general oversight came to mean that certain tasks were reserved for him (such as, for example, the laying on of hands that was from the third century part of baptism but was later separated off into the rite known as confirmation). Perhaps there were other reasons, but we know that the process of development took a long time: Ignatius, bishop of Antioch in Syria, who was martyred about 115 AD, argued strongly for the authority of a single bishop which suggests that there were still places where a group exercised authority. Pope Innocent I, in 416, argued just as strongly for the right of the bishop alone to lay hands on those who had been baptised, which suggests that there were still places where the idea was new.

By the time of Hippolytus, however, there were three major orders of ministry (bishops, presbyters and deacons) with other minor orders (e.g. readers and subdeacons) in addition. We find ourselves conscious, as we read his *Apostolic Tradition*, of the growing importance of the particular part played in the worshipping life of the Church as a major distinguishing feature of the various ranks of the ministry.

Having said all this, however, we remember that even if the names bishop, presbyter and deacon are well established by the year 215 as the names of three orders of ministry they are not the exact equivalent of the three orders of the Church of England.

THE DEVELOPMENT OF ORDINATION SERVICES
Hippolytus: a simple service

The service that Hippolytus gives us is very simple. When a bishop is ordained, having first been chosen and approved by all, the people gather together on the Lord's Day with the elders and as many bishops as can be present. The bishops lay hands on the man who has been chosen and everyone prays silently. Then one bishop lays his hand on the candidate and prays aloud for him. Hippolytus gives us an example of a suitable prayer, as he also does for a presbyter and a deacon. After the ordination the Peace is exchanged and the communion service continues with what we would now call the thanksgiving, with the new bishop presiding.

Developments and elaborations in western Europe

As ideas changed, so ordination rites tended to become more complicated and to develop in different ways in different parts of the Church. Most important for the history of our own ordination services are two streams of tradition, that of Rome and that of a group of services known collectively as the Gallican rites (from Gaul, much of which was constituted by what we now call France). The Gallican rites, originating in Spain, Ireland, England and Northern Italy as well as Gaul itself differ among themselves

but they introduce a number of new ideas, whereas the Roman practice was much slower to develop.

It is in one of the Gallican rites that we first find mention made of a stole being hung around the neck of a presbyter (who is then further dressed in a chasuble) and over the left shoulder of a deacon. That same rite also mentions that the presbyter is given a manual or handbook (a book which included the 'occasional offices' such as baptism and marriage) while the deacon is given a book containing the Gospels. If we then look at the services in the 1662 Prayer Book we find that the deacon is ordained before the reading of the Gospel, so that he may exercise that diaconal function. Another book introduces us to the practice of anointing the hands of the presbyter with oil, a practice still preserved in the Roman Catholic rite. (The original intention was, apparently, the sanctifying of the hands of one who was to offer the sacrifice of the mass.) Early in Gallican practice the congregation is called on to register their approval of the candidates with a great shout of *Dignus est* ('He is worthy') but later the practice was abandoned. It is that practice, however, which lies behind the question put to the congregation in our modern service 'Is it ... your will that they should be ordained?' and it is a practice that has long been a feature of the ordination services of the eastern Orthodox churches. Strangely, however, in spite of all their innovation it is the Gallican rites that tend to think of the ministry of the Church along the lines of the New Testament understanding. Roman practice, by contrast, was to interpret the three orders in Old Testament terms of high priest, priest and levite, rather than in New Testament terms.

We can trace in the services of *ASB 1980* the three elements that are found both in Hippolytus and in New Testament practice: the election and approval of the candidates, the prayer of the Church for them and the laying on of hands.

'God and Father of our Lord Jesus Christ, Father of mercies and God of comfort ... you appointed princes and priests, and did not leave your sanctuary without a ministry ... now pour forth that power which is from you, of the princely Spirit ... You who know the hearts of all, bestow upon this your servant, whom you have chosen for the episcopate, to feed your holy flock and to exercise the high-priesthood before you blamelessly ...'

Hippolytus, *Apostolic Tradition*, 3

Episkopos – an inspector of drains

239

words *Accipe Spiritum Sanctum* ('Receive the Holy Spirit').

Cranmer: simplifying the services

Cranmer produced two sets of services, in 1550 and 1552, which differed little from each other, but enormously from the medieval rites he inherited. The minor orders were dispensed with, leaving simply the three orders of bishop, priest and deacon which, it was believed, could be traced to the New Testament. There was to be no vesting with stoles, chasuble or dalmatics and, in 1552, no *porrectio instrumentorum* either. Another practice, still current in the modern Roman Catholic rites, underwent a change in the 1552 service: instead of a bible being laid on the neck or head of a bishop, as a symbol of his submission to the yoke of the Gospel, it was put into his hands, as also happens in our present services.

However, although Cranmer dispensed with the double laying on of hands he kept the medieval practice in which the laying on of hands on priests was accompanied by the words 'Receive the Holy Ghost: whose sins thou dost forgive, they are forgiven: and whose sins thou dost retain they are retained', with a similar formula for bishops. He even composed words to fill the silence that had accompanied the laying on of hands on deacons.

An era of disputes

Cranmer's services, with very few changes were carried over into the 1662 Prayer Book and have remained in use until the present day, but they were the subject of endless debates between Anglican and Roman Catholic scholars about the validity of Church of England ordinations. One area of the debate was whether Anglican ordinations *intended* to ordain priests to celebrate the mass as the Catholic Church has understood it: the answer to that involves an examination of the eucharistic rite as much as of the ordination service. The other area of debate, whether the ordination service

Bishops and canons, from Richard II's Book of Hours

The Middle Ages: further elaborations

In the middle ages these two traditions were brought together, producing a thoroughly muddled and repetitious kind of service. It was during this time that the hymn *Veni Creator* became a regular feature. Similarly the practice of *porrectio instrumentorum*, originally copied from civil practice for the appointment of minor orders (an acolyte received a linen bag used to carry the consecrated hosts, and a subdeacon received an empty chalice), was introduced into the ordination of priests and bishops, the priest being given a chalice and paten, a bishop his ring and pastoral staff. The business of vesting (or clothing) became more elaborate still, but in some respects the most important change was that the ordination prayer became separated from the laying on of hands. As a result the laying on of hands took place in silence. A second laying on of hands was added in the case of priests and bishops with a form of contained all that was necessary, has become clearer as scholars have found that the early Church did not use the formula 'Receive the Holy Spirit'; that it had no *porrectio instrumentorum* for the orders of bishop, priest and deacon; that the Gospel book or bible was not laid on the head or neck of a bishop. Apparently the early Church had accepted ordinations which consisted of little more than the laying on of hands and prayer as perfectly valid.

Twentieth century developments

The most important revisions for the Alternative Service Book services are those of the Church of South India of 1958 and the proposed Anglican-Methodist Ordinal of 1968. The preface to the CSI services affirms that the three essential elements of an ordination are election, prayer, and the laying on of hands, a pattern which it traces back to Acts 6. These same features are to be found in *ASB 1980* services and, indeed, some care has been taken to ensure that the services are not unduly cluttered with unnecessary additions. If we were to compare the services of *ASB 1980* with those of CSI we should find that the debt owed is considerable, not least in the way in which (unlike the 1662 services) there is an order of events common to all.

Why is a special service used?

We have inherited a particular way of conducting our business. We do not know whether the early Church formally appointed all who exercised ministries; certainly some were appointed with prayer and the laying on of hands; others may simply have exercised their ministry without formal recognition. But we may perhaps say that for certain tasks in the Church, and in particular those that involved pastoral oversight of the congregation and the leading of worship, it became necessary or advisable to have some form of appointment which included a public ceremony, however brief. In this way the Church acknowledged both the candidates' calling by

God and their authority to carry out their ministry, and at the same time committed itself to pray that those who had been called would also be equipped for the task before them.

All of this is not to say that a long and elaborate service is necessary. Indeed, we may be glad that our services are now so much more simple and straightforward than those of the middle ages. Nor is it to say that those whom God calls to other forms of service in the Church ought not to have their call and their authority acknowledged. On the whole, however, the reason for there being a fuller service for the ordination of bishops, priests and deacons, is that their ministry is one that is exercised both within, but also beyond, the boundaries of a single parish.

Furthermore, an essential feature of the pastoral oversight which they exercise is the ministry of the word and of the sacrament, a ministry without which the

After an ordination: bishop, candidate and archdeacon

Church cannot exist. It is the proclaiming of the redeeming work of God in word and in sacrament that calls the Church into being, draws new members in and feeds the faithful. It is appropriate then, that those who are called to that ministry should be publicly appointed and publicly prayed over.

Is there any special reason for three orders?

We have already seen that although the three names of our orders can be found in the New Testament, they are not used there in the same way as today. Even today there is a lot of debate about them. For example, there have been many discussions during the last hundred years concerning the diaconate, whether it should be abolished, or whether, as already happens in the Roman Catholic Church, there should be permanent deacons, not expecting or expected to proceed to the priesthood.

Most of the Free Churches do not have bishops, but most have some form of pastoral oversight involving the appointment of a virtual equivalent even though he is not given a permanent status (a bishop may retain his title, a Moderator does not). What is important in the end is not so much that the Church of England has bishops, priests and deacons, but that pastoral oversight is exercised properly.

It is not essential, therefore, that there should be three orders, but present practice should not lightly be abandoned, unless it is quite certain that there is something better with which to replace it.

Once a priest, always a priest?

A bishop retains his title, even when he ceases to hold diocesan responsibility; that is a fact, although a strange fact, because it could very well be argued that the pastoral oversight of a bishop is of a very special kind and that to be a bishop one must exercise that oversight, and so when a bishop retires he should surrender his title. Similarly a priest remains a

priest even if he retires from parochial responsibility or if he returns to a secular job. For practical reasons it is convenient that this should be so: his assistance is still available in the leading of worship and especially at eucharistic worship, if the vicar is away on holiday or sick, if there is no vicar or if he needs assistance which is not otherwise available. But it might be argued that, as in the case of the bishop, a priest who ceases to exercise pastoral oversight ceases to be a priest. Logically, then, he ought to be ordained again if he returns to a position of oversight. Some Christians, however, would want to argue that ordination is not simply, or even primarily a matter of pastoral oversight, but of a status which, even if he wishes to lay aside pastoral duties, a priest does not lay down. Moreover, present practice is sanctioned by long-standing custom which is not lightly laid aside.

What is the difference between a 'priest' and a 'presbyter'?

The services of *ASB 1980* make it clear that there is no difference whatever, but both words have chequered histories, even though they come from the same word in Greek. Christianity was a most unusual religion in the first and second centuries of its existence when it was difficult to imagine a religion that had neither priests nor sacrifices. Because they lacked both sacrifices and priests to offer them Christians could easily be made to feel inferior. Their sacrifice was a sacrifice of praise and thanksgiving not of bulls, goats or even incense, but increasingly they came to speak of the eucharist as a sacrifice in a way that could sound like the offering of pagan sacrifices. The use of imagery from the Old Testament (priest and high priest) encouraged Christians to think of their clergy in sacrificial terms. If at first it was usually the bishop who was spoken of in this way (e.g. by Tertullian and Hippolytus) the practice was extended (for example by Cyprian) to presbyters. Eventually bishops and presbyters came to be seen

as priests offering sacrifices. No wonder, then, that those who rejected the sacrificial views of the priesthood wanted to do away with the term priest because of its connection with pagan sacrificial cults and to replace it with presbyter, indicating both a different view of the ministry and one more closely in line with the New Testament. The Church of England in its services has never intended to ordain a sacrificing priesthood, but it has retained the term priest partly because it is derived from *presbyteros* and partly because it was difficult in any case to use the term presbyter in the 16th and 17th centuries, since those who wanted it to be used also, for the most part, wanted to do away with bishops and to change the structure of Church government.

However, in the present century it has been possible both to admit the common derivation of priest and presbyter from the same Greek word and through ecumenical contacts and through the creation of the Church of South India to recognise that both terms can be used. Doubtless some will continue to prefer the one, some the other, but the services of *ASB 1980* wish to see no distinction – and rightly.

The Liturgical Psalter

THE CHURCH OF ENGLAND AND THE PSALTER

The Psalter which is printed in the 1662 Prayer Book – and set out in many a parish psalm book, like *The Parish Psalter* – is one of the earliest bits of English translation in the Prayer Book. It comes from seventy years *before* the Authorised Version of the bible, and is usually attributed to Miles Coverdale in the 1530s. Although at many periods in the life of the Church of England since Coverdale's time there has been a preference for metrical psalms (such as those of Sternhold and Hopkins in 1560, or of Tate and Brady in 1696), yet the non-metrical version has remained in the Prayer Book, and has been used for the *saying* of psalms even when not used for singing. And in the last hundred years there has been a great growth of the singing of these non-metrical psalms in parish worship.

The fashion of using the psalms this way led to the Church of England looking for a revision of the more obscure parts of the Coverdale translation, and in 1958 a Commission was established under the chairmanship of Dr Donald Coggan (and including C.S. Lewis and T.S. Eliot) to do this. *The Revised Psalter* was published in 1963, and was authorised in the Church of England under the Versions of the Bible Measure. It was a conservative revision – and, in particular, it still called God 'thou'.

When it became clear that the Liturgical Commission would be using 'you' as the form of address to God in the Series 3 services, Dr David Frost, then an English don at Cambridge and a member of the Commission, set himself the task of producing a more truly modern non-metrical psalter, and combined with two Hebrew specialists – first Dr Andrew Macintosh and then also Professor John Emerton – to ensure a high degree of accuracy. The first psalms to be so translated were published by them as *Twenty-Five Psalms from a Modern Liturgical Psalter* in 1973. At the same time the Commission started to include such psalms in its proposals – in Funeral Services in 1973, Morning and Evening Prayer in 1974, Marriage in 1975, and Ordination Services in 1977. Synod accepted these forms, and thus gave some expectation that this psalter would find its place in *ASB 1980*.

The full psalter first saw the light of day when published in the draft Australian Prayer Book in June 1977 – an interesting accompaniment to David Frost's own emigration to Australia! It was accepted by the Australian General Synod in August 1977, and the psalter on its own was published as *The Psalms – A New Translation for Worship* in September 1977.

In 1978 the General Synod gave the new psalter authorisation for its public use in worship. But when, in July 1978, the Synod was asked to vote for its inclusion in *ASB 1980*, the motion was defeated. There was a fluttering in the dovecots. A year went by – the minimum time Synod allows itself to change its own mind. Then in July 1979 Synod voted that *ASB 1980* should be published in two editions – one with a psalter, one without. Time ran out before it was decided which psalter should be used. Finally, in November 1979, it was agreed

A model of Jerusalem at the time of the Second Temple.

that the version to be used should be the Frost-Macintosh-Emerton translation. The versions which print it say so on the outside cover – *ASB 1980* is reckoned complete without it, but some editions are labelled on the outside 'Alternative Service Book 1980 with the Liturgical Psalter'. And the title 'The Liturgical Psalter', which did not actually appear in the separate edition of the psalter in 1977, is now firmly established as *the* title, and is being confirmed by use.

WHAT ARE THE PSALMS?

The Book of Psalms was the hymn book of the Second Temple – the temple that the Jews rebuilt when they came back from exile in Babylon around BC 520. Later, the psalms were collected into the Hebrew bible, and from there were taken into our Christian bible as part of the Old Testament.

We do not know exactly when the individual hymns were gathered

כג
: מזמור לדוד יהוה רעי לא אחסר
בנאות דשא ירביצני על־מי
מנוחת ינהלני : נפשי ישובב ינחני
: במעגלי־צדק למען שמו

The opening verses of Psalm 23 (only the consonants written down at first)

כג
: מִזְמוֹר לְדָוִד יְהוָה רֹעִי לֹא אֶחְסָר
בִּנְאוֹת דֶּשֶׁא יַרְבִּיצֵנִי עַל־מֵי
מְנוּחֹת יְנַהֲלֵנִי : נַפְשִׁי יְשׁוֹבֵב יַנְחֵנִי
: בְמַעְגְּלֵי־צֶדֶק לְמַעַן שְׁמוֹ

The same verses (with the vowels written in, many hundreds of years later)

together, but the book was certainly the *Hymns Ancient and Modern* of its day. It contained poems that were very old indeed, and some of them may well go back to the time of David – there was a persistent tradition that he had composed many of them. On the other hand, the book contained some modern compositions, and even poems which refer to the destruction of the First Temple and the Jews' enslavement in Babylon (Psalms 74 and 137, for example).

Some ancient notes on these hymns (they appear at the start of many psalms in our modern bibles) tell us who was believed to have written them, and sometimes record the tunes and instruments they should be sung to. Seventy-three are given to David, but others are put down to another individual, 'Asaph', or to a group of people, 'the sons of Korah' (who were probably a group of temple musicians). We must imagine that the Book of Psalms (like any other hymn book) contains some old hymns whose words have been changed a little from when they were first written, perhaps because later Jews thought the ideas or words could be improved, and sometimes because a word had become old-fashioned or difficult to understand. And a little detective-work will show that (like modern hymn books) the Book of Psalms was built up by taking hymns from other books: in our Psalms the same hymn sometimes appears twice, and has clearly come in slightly different versions from two different collections. If you compare Psalm 14 with Psalm 53, for instance, you can see the basic similarity and the slight differences.

David may have composed a number of psalms, but there are many he could not have written: a lot of them refer to the temple, which was not built in his day. However, most of the psalms were written for temple worship, and many of the oldest are for a temple worship in which an important part was played by a king of David's line. Some seem to come from his coronation service (Psalms 2 and 110), and there is even one for his wed-

ding celebrations (Psalm 45). The king in ancient Israel was thought of as in a special sense 'the Son of God' and he combined the job of king and priest. In other words, he had not only to enforce God's law and keep his nation faithful to God, but he was expected to pray to God on behalf of his people. It was believed that the king had a special agreement with God, so that (if Israel stayed faithful) God would favour him and his subjects. Some psalms tell of God's promise to David and his successors (e.g. Psalm 110), and even ask God to remember his agreement (e.g. Psalm 89), while in others the king recollects what he himself must do (Psalm 101).

Psalms often speak of the king as if he were a model of goodness and fidelity to God. With bad kings on the throne, and later with *no* kings (because the monarchy collapsed with the fall of Jerusalem and the destruction of the First Temple), the Jews came more and more to see the psalms as being about some *future* king of David's line, some Messiah who would save Israel from ruin. Jesus and the first disciples saw the psalms as being about Jesus himself, and for many centuries Christians have treated them as a prophecy of Christ.

If you ask 'Were they *really* about Jesus?', the answer is somewhat complicated. Almost certainly, the writers of the psalms were thinking of the king who was on the throne at the time – or of the king they would like him to be. It has never been easy to see a prophecy of Jesus – even Jesus in judgement – in the bloodthirsty monarch who will break the nations 'with a rod of iron and shatter them in pieces like a potter's vessel' (Psalm 2.8), or in the priest-king, born on the 'holy hill' of Jerusalem, who will 'shatter heads over a wide land' (Psalm 110.5). But poets write by inspiration, and they often tell greater truths than they realise. Writing about the king they knew, or about what they hoped that king would be, the psalmists were inspired to write about an ideal priest-king, one who would fully live up to the dreams and longings of mankind for a wise, just and holy ruler. Through inspiration, the writers grasped an ideal in the mind of God, an ideal which waited to be made known in Jesus Christ, who would be the perfect king that the psalmists dreamed about.

WHY DO WE USE THE PSALMS IN CHURCH?

One reason we use the psalms in worship is that Christians have always done so, from the earliest days of the Church. Jesus and his disciples were good Jews, who used the Psalms in their prayers and praises: the hymn which the Gospels tell us he and his followers sang after the last supper was almost certainly a psalm (see Matthew 26.30 and Mark 14.26). When we use the psalms, we are linked not only with other present-day Christians but with an army of believers through the ages and from earliest times. The psalms take us back to the worship of God's ancient people the Jews, and sometimes we may even be using the words of King David himself, words he composed approximately three thousand years ago.

But we don't just use the psalms for old time's sake. Martin Luther once said that the Book of Psalms was 'the bible in miniature': anything said or felt about God, about man and about God's world elsewhere in scripture is briefly summed up in the psalms. Furthermore, the psalms are a fine expression of the variety of feelings, moods and attitudes you will have to go through as a servant of God. If you feel thankful, full of praise, entranced by God's power, his love, his righteousness, or by the beauty of his world, or if (another time) you feel anxious, angry, hurt, betrayed, abandoned by God, depressed, lonely or despairing – in all these states you will find a psalm that will express your feelings in prayer to God.

One last reason for using the psalms is that in studying them we meet something that mattered to Jesus. He knew them well, and would quote from them

Before the mountains were born, or the earth and the world were brought to be: from eternity to eternity you are God. Psalm 90.2

(Matthew 22.44, Mark 12.36, Luke 20.42-4). It is likely that some of his ideas of what he must do were formed by reading the psalms. When he was crucified, it was lines from the psalms which came into his mind (Psalm 22, verse 1, according to Matthew 27.46 and Mark 15.34; Psalm 31, verse 5, according to Luke 23.46). One way of understanding

PSALM 23
*Written in Hebrew (about
BC 1000?)*

מִזְמוֹר לְדָוִד יְהוָה רֹעִי לֹא אֶחְסָר :
בִּנְאוֹת דֶּשֶׁא יַרְבִּיצֵנִי עַל־מֵי
מְנֻחוֹת יְנַהֲלֵנִי : נַפְשִׁי יְשׁוֹבֵב יַנְחֵנִי
בְמַעְגְּלֵי־צֶדֶק לְמַעַן שְׁמוֹ : גַּם כִּי־
אֵלֵךְ בְּגֵיא צַלְמָוֶת לֹא־אִירָא רָע כִּי־
אַתָּה עִמָּדִי שִׁבְטְךָ וּמִשְׁעַנְתֶּךָ הֵמָּה
יְנַחֲמֻנִי : תַּעֲרֹךְ לְפָנַי שֻׁלְחָן נֶגֶד
צֹרְרָי דִּשַּׁנְתָּ בַשֶּׁמֶן רֹאשִׁי כּוֹסִי רְוָיָה :
אַךְ טוֹב וָחֶסֶד יִרְדְּפוּנִי כָּל־יְמֵי חַיָּי
וְשַׁבְתִּי בְּבֵית־יְהוָה לְאֹרֶךְ יָמִים :

*Translated into Greek (the
Septuagint, around BC
250?)*

ΚΓ.
Ψαλμὸς τῷ Δαυίδ.

ΚΥΡΙΟΣ ποιμαίνει με, καὶ οὐδέν με
ὑστερήσει. ² Εἰς τόπον χλόης ἐκεῖ με
κατεσκήνωσεν· ἐπὶ ὕδατος ἀναπαύσεως
ἐξέθρεψέ με. ³ Τὴν ψυχήν μου ἐπέ-
στρεψεν· ὡδήγησέ με ἐπὶ τρίβους δι-
καιοσύνης, ἕνεκεν τοῦ ὀνόματος αὐτοῦ.
⁴ Ἐὰν γὰρ καὶ πορευθῶ ἐν μέσῳ σκιᾶς
θανάτου, οὐ φοβηθήσομαι κακά, ὅτι σὺ
μετ' ἐμοῦ εἶ· ἡ ῥάβδος σου καὶ ἡ βακτη-
ρία σου, αὐταί με παρεκάλεσαν. ⁵ Ἡτοί-
μασας ἐνώπιόν μου τράπεζαν, ἐξεναντίας
τῶν θλιβόντων με· ἐλίπανας ἐν ἐλαίῳ
τὴν κεφαλήν μου, καὶ τὸ ποτήριόν σου
μεθύσκον ὡς κράτιστον. ⁶ Καὶ τὸ ἔλεός
σου καταδιώξεταί με πάσας τὰς ἡμέρας
τῆς ζωῆς μου, καὶ τὸ κατοικεῖν με ἐν οἴκῳ
Κυρίου εἰς μακρότητα ἡμερῶν.

*Jerome's Latin version
('According to the
Hebrews', 390-405 AD)*

XXIII.
Canticum David.

DOMINUS pascit me, nihil
mihi deerit. ² In pascuis herba-
rum accubavit me : super aquas
refectionis enutrivit me : ³ Ani-
mam meam refecit. Duxit me per
semitas justitiæ, propter nomen
suum. ⁴ Sed, et si ambulavero
in valle umbræ mortis, non time-
bo malum : quoniam tu mecum.
Virga tua, et baculus tuus, ipsa
consolabuntur me. ⁵ Pones co-
ram me mensam, ex adverso
hostium meorum. Impinguasti in
oleo caput meum : calix meus
inebrians. ⁶ Sed et benignitas
et misericordia subsequentur me,
omnibus diebus vitæ meæ : et
habitabo in domo Domini, in lon-
gitudine dierum.

*Coverdale's version (1539:
used in the Book of
Common Prayer)*

XXIII.
* * *

THE Lord is my shepherd : therefore can I lack nothing. ² He shall
feed me in a green pasture : and lead
me forth beside the waters of comfort.
³ He shall convert my soul : and bring
me forth in the paths of righteousness,
for his Name's sake. ⁴ Yea, though
I walk through the valley of the shadow of death, I will fear no evil : for
thou art with me ; thy rod and thy
staff comfort me. ⁵ Thou shalt prepare a table before me against them
that trouble me : thou hast anointed
my head with oil, and my cup shall be
full. ⁶ But thy loving-kindness and
mercy shall follow me all the days of
my life : and I will dwell in the house
of the Lord for ever.

a man well is to know those books he
values: especially the books which he
remembers when he is in a crisis.

Aren't some of the psalms un-Christian?

All the psalms were written before God's
full revelation of his nature and purpose
for man in Jesus Christ. They are a stage
along the road. It is no accident that they
come early in Church services – anything
not quite right in their attitudes can be
corrected in the light of the Gospel.

The psalmists sometimes curse their
enemies, ask God to avenge wrongs, and
assert how righteous their own conduct
has been. They grouse at God, and on
occasion they fall into despair. But before
we decide that Christians ought to throw
the psalms out – don't *we* behave just like
that at times? The psalms are the one
part of a church service where we don't
have to pretend or be on our best
behaviour. A Sunday-best suit isn't

required. We are easily tempted in worship to hide what we really are from
ourselves and from others. The psalms
enable us to give voice to our hates, our
aggression, our self-righteousness, our
despair. These feelings come out into the
open, where we can admit them and
where Christ can deal with them. If you
like, the psalms are the sinner's prayer
book. The psalms enable us to express
ourselves, to keep talking to God, in
whatever state we are.

Because we probably will not want to
say the most vengeful and curse-filled
parts of the psalms, the worst verses are
bracketed in *ASB 1980*, as an indication
that they can be left out. And we can't
expect that an occasional worshipper or a
newcomer to Christianity will always
understand why we use even the 'un-
Christian' Psalms. So the lectionary in
The Alternative Service Book selects 'a
hundred best psalms' (as it were) for use
at Sunday worship.

Bury St Edmunds Psalter, in use in the abbey 1348-1415

HOW ARE THE PSALMS USED IN CHURCH?

The use of a psalm between the lessons at communion is a very old custom: Tertullian (c. 155-220 AD) tells us it happened in his church. At Morning and Evening Prayer (which developed from the daily services of monks), the Church of England uses all the psalms in their biblical order. This recitation *'in course'* (from 1 to 150) happens on all weekdays. *The Book of Common Prayer* expected all the psalms to be got through in a month; in the lectionary for *The Alternative Service Book* the psalms are spread over a ten-week period, so that each one can be thoroughly thought about. The exception to the 'course' is Sunday, where (for reasons mentioned above) a selection of psalms has been made, and the psalms are chosen to fit the theme of the day.

The week-day psalms do not fit any theme (except on holy days). They roll on from Psalm 1 to Psalm 150, taking no account of the season or of the mood of the worshippers. You may find yourself using miserable psalms after Easter, or despairing psalms when you feel particularly joyful. There is a reason for this. We can none of us remain fixed in attitudes and feelings. The psalms remind us of what we may shortly feel, of what we may soon have to face. In joy we are reminded of grief, in sorrow we remember the possibility of joy. Every phase of the religious weather is there in the psalms, and by reciting them we prepare ourselves for change.

The psalm or portion of a psalm set f[or] the communion service has been chosen to fit the lessons and the theme or subject of the day. Usually the connection will be obvious. Psalms which the Jews came to associate with the Messiah are used on special festivals of Christ, such as Christmas Day: we must remember that they were originally written about a human king, so not all the verses will necessarily fit Jesus – but by inspiration the psalmist imagines the ideal King.

On Easter Day, we use Psalm 114,

He rescues the poor from their affliction and makes their family increase like flocks. Psalm 107.41

which tells of Israel's escape from bondage in Egypt. This psalm is chosen for the *typology*. Typology is the art of seeing similarities between people and events in the Old and the New Testaments. As God rescued the chosen people from bondage in Egypt by sending them Moses, so God gives another Moses, Jesus Christ, to lead his new chosen people out of enslavement to sin and death. The connection between the two events is the unchanging nature of God, who regularly rescues his servants when all seems lost, by raising up one just man to deliver them from evil and to lead them to his promised land.

How can my church use the psalms?

The psalms may be used in various ways. You may listen to the choir singing, or sing them yourselves to Anglican chant, or even to plainsong (which is probably closest to how they sounded in the Jewish Temple). You may sing or read them, with each half of the congregation taking alternate verses. The minister may read one verse, and the congregation the next. Or a cantor may sing or say the whole

The Old Bailey,
symbol of justice

psalm, and the congregation may reply with a line from the psalm, used as a chorus (this seems to be how it was done in the early Church). A reader may read a verse, and the people sing it over again to trumpets and drums – or to guitars.

Whatever way you perform the psalms, notice how the verses are put together as poetry, because that will help you to enjoy them. Jewish poetry had a special structure. The first line will say something, the next will say it in different words; or the second line will carry the idea forward a little by adding to it; or the second line will give you an opposite notion. Here are example of all three possibilities:

> The Lord frustrates the counsels of
> the nations:
> he brings to nothing the devices of the
> peoples.
>
> Psalm 34.10

> In peace I will lie down and sleep:
> for you alone, Lord, make me dwell
> in safety.
>
> Psalm 4.8

> For the Lord cares for the way of the
> righteous:
> but the way of the ungodly shall
> perish.
>
> Psalm 1.7

Because there is a slight pause at the colon (:) some churches are tempted to divide each half of the verse between different singers or speakers. That makes the psalm sound like ping-pong, especially if there is a longish pause in the middle. It breaks up the structure of the poetry and often makes the sense difficult to follow. If you want to alternate, it is much better to alternate *verses*.

One last use of psalms in a service is for private devotions: before the service, while waiting for communion, after communion. When the sermon is bad, or you can't follow it, it is often a help to turn to the psalms in the prayer book and read them quietly to yourself.

Why does the translation in *ASB 1980* seem different to others?

The translation of the psalms in *The Alternative Service Book* was specially made for the new book by a team of Hebrew scholars from different churches (Church of England, Roman Catholic, Methodist and United Reformed) and by a writer of English. It aims to be good for public reading and easy to sing to the old chants. The translation is already in *An Australian Prayer Book*, and parts of it are being used in service books in South Africa and India.

However, you may be worried to find that it sometimes gives a different translation to that in the old Prayer Book psalms, in the King James Bible, or even in some modern versions. The reason is that some of the Hebrew in which the psalms were first written is extremely difficult: not enough of the Hebrew language has come down to us for us to know what all the words and expressions mean. But scholars are increasing our understanding all the time, and this new translation is perhaps the most accurate so far produced. Trying to find out what difficult passages in the Hebrew meant, translators in the past looked at translations into other languages, Greek, Syriac, Aramaic, Latin (some made well before the birth of Jesus), and they also studied the tradition of the Jewish rabbis. Scholars still do this, but they have developed additional methods. The authors of the psalms only wrote down the consonants, and the reader read the psalms by filling in vowels *between* the consonants, according to a tradition which was handed down from teacher to pupil over hundreds of years. Sometimes when a verse doesn't make sense, scholars can put *different* vowels with the same consonants (guessing that somewhere along the line some reader remembered wrongly) – and then the meaning becomes clear. In this century, a third method has been added. When scholars meet a word or expression in Hebrew which isn't found anywhere else, they look at what that word means in other Middle Eastern languages which are related to Hebrew. In the same way, if we couldn't understand an English word, we might look at a word in French or German which

looked the same, and which we *did*
understand, so as to be able to make a
sensible guess at the English word. All
these methods make the meaning of the
psalms increasingly clear – but they also
show that the old translators often gues-
sed wrong.

The Hebrew psalms are in a special
poetical language, and the English version in *The Alternative Service Book* aims
to be poetical too. So as to say things
accurately, forcefully and with a good
rhythm, unusual words are sometimes
used. The translators also wanted to keep
to the Jewish way of saying things, and
tried to make a version which would not
sound *too* different from the great translations of the past. This means that the
flavour will sometimes be a little old-
fashioned – but the psalms *are* very old,
and the translators have tried to make
sure that it can be *understood* by speakers
of modern English. The great sixteenth
and seventeenth century translators of
the psalms quite shamelessly stole good
phrases from earlier translations, and this
one has done the same. Many of the most
famous psalms will not seem much
different, and if a new phrase does jar, it
is likely that it will not do so for long.

SOME DIFFICULT WORDS AND IDEAS IN THE PSALMS

The image of God Before people can get any clear idea of God at all they probably have to think of him as a human being – and God had to make himself known to us through the human nature of Jesus. But the psalmists sometimes seem to carry things too far. When they talk about God with smoke coming out of his nostrils, riding the cherubim, 'swooping upon the wings of the wind' (Psalm 18.9, 11), we must be clear that this is *picture-language* – their way of making vivid to their imagination God's anger at evil and the eagerness with which he will rescue his servants. Enjoy the pictures, but remember – 'God is Spirit'. He has no form that anyone can see.

Lord God of hosts The psalmists sometimes think of God as a warrior commanding the angelic armies (the hosts) of heaven. We may think of those hosts as being the multitudes of spirits who serve God, including the millions of Christians past and present.

God's righteousness The Hebrew word translated in English 'righteous' has something to do with 'being right' – but it means more than that. God was not only good: the Jews thought of him as a God passionately concerned to protect the innocent and vulnerable, as a God who would *intervene* in history to deliver those oppressed by wrong, to give just judgement, and to condemn the guilty. In particular, he would show his right-eousness by honouring his agreement with the Jewish nation.

The righteous man The 'righteous man' in the psalms honours his side of the bargain with God by keeping God's laws. Like his righteous God, he too must be passionately concerned with jus-tice, he must intervene to protect 'the widow and the fatherless'. But we may find off-putting the way in which the psalmists see themselves as part of a holy set, as opposed to the 'wicked' or the 'ungodly': it sounds hypocritical when they ask God to recognise their righteousness and reward them. However, we must remember that Christians *are* to think of themselves as righteous, but only as *made* righteous by the sacrifice of Jesus Christ. We may make these psalms our own, but only if we remember that we are distinguished from other people not by having been better than them, but by faith that Christ has died for us.

The nations   By the 'nations', the psalmists means the heathen nations who surrounded Israel, despised Israel's God and frequently made war on the Jews. It is best for Christians to think of 'the nations' as being the hostile forces of evil, inside and outside, which surround the Christian and attempt to overcome him or her.

Jerusalem or Zion   Jerusalem was and is the capital city of Israel. It was the capital of the priest-king, and God was believed to be present in the city in a special way. Psalm 132 celebrates the bringing of the ark, the symbol of the presence of God, into its resting-place in Jerusalem. Christians have only one real home, one 'special place': the kingdom of heaven where faithful souls enjoy the knowledge of God. When the psalms speak lovingly of Jerusalem, it is helpful to think of the heavenly Jerusalem, where we shall see God as he is.

Sacrifice   The Jews sacrificed animals, grain and other produce to God, thinking to show praise, gratitude and penitence towards him, and hoping by sacrifice to get into contact with him. The sacrifice of Christ on the cross restores our contact with God, and other sacrifices are not needed for this purpose. When the psalmists speak of making sacrifice, we may think of an offering which is always pleasing to God: our praise and thanksgiving, and our service to him and to our fellow-men.

Law   The psalmists talk of the 'sweetness' of the law, and we may find that odd, since we tend to find laws restricting and frightening. The Jews rejoiced at God's law because they saw it as making clear what was right for man in a world which might otherwise be bewildering. The Jewish law has been made perfect and replaced by Jesus Christ's law of love – love for God and for one's fellow-men. This law Christians keep, not by sticking to a book of rules, but by asking Christ to inhabit our personalities as our director. When the psalmists speak of law, it is helpful to think of the presence of Jesus in our minds and hearts.

The poor, meek, humble, afflicted   The psalmists often use these words to refer to a class of people who are specially in need of God's protection, who are dependent on him, and who are contrasted with the proud, the arrogant, the scornful and the oppressors. There is still debate over what exactly the psalmists meant. We may regard the 'poor' as those who are 'poor in spirit' – in other words, Christians who 'know their need of God', and rely on him (rather than on worldly power and riches) to save them.

Subject index

Index of people

(Page numbers in italics indicate pictures)

Index of bible references

(References are given only to passages of the bible quoted in full, or discussed in the text.)

Acknowledgements

We are grateful to the following who have helped with the text in one way or another:
Mr and Mrs Ian Bensted, Rt Revd Cyril Bowles, Rev Capt T. Henderson CA, Rev Tom Jamieson, Dr Ronald Jasper, Miss Anne Jenkins, Mrs Jean Mayland, Rev Christian Merivale, Rev Richard More, Miss Pat Morris, Mr Dennis Nutter, Rev Geoffrey Riley, Rev David Runcorn, Miss Anne Salisbury, Rev C. Michael Wilson.

The estate of Siegfried Sassoon, for permission to quote the poem on p.9.

Translations of accounts of the eucharist in Justin and Hippolytus are taken from *Prayers of the Eucharist: Early and Reformed* (ed. R.C.D. Jasper and G.J. Cuming), Collins, 1975, and are used with permission.

Extracts from *Alternative Service Book 1980* are reproduced by persmission of the Central Board of Finance of the Church of England.

The Book of Common Prayer of 1662 is Crown Copyright and extracts are used with permission.

For the cartoons: Rev Taffy Davies.

For permission to reproduce pictures:
Barnaby's Picture Library: 11, 22, 43, 56, 64, 89, 110, 139, 146, 147, 151, 162, 169, 184, 188, 190, 194, 198, 201, 204, 208, 209, 215, 222, 223, 225, 245, 249;
Courtesy of the Benedictine Nuns of Cockfosters: 59;
M.A. Foster: 96;
Richard Bewes: 97, 142, 145, 231;
Sandy Boyle: 5, 206, 247;
British and Foreign Bible Society: 13, 83, 88, 99, 114, 116, 235 (bible);
British Tourist Authority: 28, 76, 97 (choir), 102, 161, 178, 248;
Paul Buckley: 14;
Courtesy of *Buzz* Magazine: 60, 69, 150;

Camera Press: 9, 41, 191, 196, 230;
J. Allan Cash: 10, 15, 47, 164, 167, 218, 250;
David Chalmers: 136;
Central Office of Information: 205 (family), 241;
Church Information Office: 52 (choir), 70, 74, 85, 207, 220, 228;
Church Missionary Society: 39, 56, 138, 163, 167, 174;
Church Pastoral Aid Society: 84 (lady), 112, 121, 125, 142, 159, 183, 195, 202, 235, 237;
Courtesy of *Crusade* magazine: 35, 61 (congregation);
David Frost: 245 (texts);
Michael Holford: 117, 140;
Alan Hutchison Library 243;
Keystone Press: 6, 29, 200, 217;
Trevor Lloyd: 157, 226 (both);
Mansell Collection: 25 (except Cranmer), 26, 45, 78 (all), 80 (all), 90, 128 (Laud), 153, 210 211, 212, 213;
Mary Evans Picture Library: 111;
Adrian Neilson: 89 (sun), 182, 247 (mountains), 251 (both);
National Portrait Gallery: 25;
Christopher Phillips: 54 (courtesy of the Cedar Dance Theatre), 62, 205;
Tricia Porter: 75, 214;
Press Association: 232;
Radio Times Hulton Picture Library: 51, 52, 123, 186, 187;
Adrian Reith: 105;
Rex Features: 219, 252;
Courtesy of Ridley Hall, Cambridge: 91 (book), 119;
Michael Sadler: 53;
Clifford Shirley: 7, 16-17, 19, 48, 57, 60 (communion), 61 (communion), 72, 73, 84, 86, 93, 94, 100, 103, 108, 131, 172, 176, 181, 227, 238;
The Revd. Andrew Talbot Ponsonby: 130;
Topham Picture Library: 67, 153, 171, 229;
United Society for the Propagation of the Gospel: 20, 21, 36;
Kenneth White: 30, 31, 33, 34, 42, 91, 106, 120, 125 (altar), 126, 129, 141, 156, 180, 231 (cathedral), 234, 240.